THE DIVE SITES OF
THE GREAT
BARRIER REEF
AND THE CORAL SEA

NEVILLE COLEMAN
with Nigel Marsh

Series Consultant: Nick Hanna

PASSPORT BOOKS
NTC/Contemporary Publishing Group

This edition first published in 1997 by
Passport Books, a division of NTC/Contemporary Publishing Group, Inc.,
4255 West Touhy Avenue, Lincolnwood, IL, 60712-1975
U.S.A.

ISBN 0-8442-4860-6

Library of Congress Catalog Card Number: on file
Published in conjunction with
New Holland Publishers
London • Cape Town • Sydney • Auckland

Commissioning editor: Sally Bird
Editors: Gerda Pretorius, Jacquie Brown
Design concept: Philip Mann, ACE Ltd
Design and DTP by: Gerda Pretorius, Mark Seabrook
DTP Cartography: John Loubser

Reproduction by cmyk prepress
Printed and bound in Singapore by Tien Wah Press (Pte) Ltd

Photographic acknowledgements
All photographs by Neville Coleman with the exception of the following:
Nigel Marsh: 4, 30, 43, 59, 67, 70, 73, 74, 75, 95, 99, 116, 125, 130, 131, 133, 134,
135, 137, 138, 144, 153; Anthony Johnson: Front cover inset, 10, 16, 28/9, 87;
Shaen Adey: 12; Bruce Elder: 22; Kevin Deacon: Front cover.

Although the author and publisher have made every effort to ensure that the information
in this book was correct at the time of going to press, they accept no responsibility for
any loss, injury or inconvenience sustained by any person using this book.

Photography
Most of the photographs in this book were taken on Kodak film, using Nikonos
cameras and strobes and Nikon cameras and lenses.

Dedication

The best is yet to come...

Author's Acknowledgments

The photographs in this book are from the files of the Australasian Marine Photographic Index (AMPI), which contains colour transparencies of animals and plants, cross-referenced against identified specimens housed in museums and scientific institutes. It also covers related marine activities. The project is housed at Sea Australia Resource Centre, under the network of educational services offered by Neville Coleman's Underwater Geographic Pty Ltd. Nigel Marsh's extensive photolibrary is also housed at the centre.
The authors would like to thank the following people for their assistance:

Australian Marine Conservation Society, Rick Miller (Haba Dive), **Pure Pleasure Cruises, André Thomsen** (Great Adventures), **Dianne Vella** (Great Barrier Reef Marine Park Authority), **Peter Grudnoff** (Lady Elliot Diving), **Jerry Comans** (Boomerang Cruises), **Denis Kemp, Mike Ball Dive Expeditions, Pacific Star Charters, Gittan and Wayne Inglis** (Rum Runner), **Quicksilver Diving Services, Passions of Paradise, Pro-dive Townsville, Undersea Explorer, Cairns Dive Centre, Tusa Dive, Salty's Dive Team, Lady Musgrave Cruises, Ocean Spirit Cruises, Pro-dive Cairns, Deep Sea Divers Den, Graham McCallum** (Auriga Bay), **Reef Explorer, Tony Fontes** (Great Barrier Reef Diving Services), **Department of Environment and Heritage, RACQ, Jenny Bartlett** (Orpheus Island Resort), **Kevin Burke** (Quick Cat Dive), **Dan Duyer** (Hayman Dive and Snorkel Centre), **Gay Bowden** (Whitsunday All Over Travel Service), **Jayrow Helicopters** and the myriad underwater people we met along the way.
A special thank you to **Karen Handley, Helen Rose** and our typist, **Anne Thomson**, for helping to put it all together.

Publishers' Acknowledgments

The publishers gratefully acknowledge the generous assistance during the compilation of this book of the following:

Nick Hanna for his involvement with developing the series and consulting throughout, and **Dr Elizabeth M Wood** for acting as Marine Consultant and contributing to The Marine Environment section.

CONTENTS

HOW TO USE THIS BOOK

THE REGIONS

The text has been loosely arranged according to the zoning of the Great Barrier Reef Marine Park Authority and modified slightly to encompass areas outside the park itself, beginning at the southernmost point of the Great Barrier Reef and following the reefs and islands to the tip of Cape York. The chapters are as follows: Capricorn and Bunker Groups, Keppel Islands, Swain Reefs and Pompey Reef Complex, Southern Coral Sea, Whitsunday Islands and Reefs, Townsville Wrecks and Reefs, Northern Islands, Cairns and Port Douglas Reefs and Islands, Northern Coral Sea, and Far Northern Reefs. Little diving is done on the mainland shore due to shallow, turbid waters, large river discharges and the general topography of low-lying swamplands and mangrove forests which fringe the coastal areas.

Only dive sites on reefs, islands, bommies, cays and pontoons that are serviced by professional diving resorts, charter and daytrip boats, and organisations well established in the tourism, travel, eco-tourism or diving industries have been selected. It is not practical or possible to evaluate every dive site on the Great Barrier Reef, as many reefs have never been surveyed or even named. Only sites that are regularly dived have been evaluated.

THE MAPS

A detailed map is included in each regional section for easy identification of the location of the dive sites described. The number of the dive site in the text corresponds to the one on the map. The map legend illustrated below pertains to all maps used in this book. Please note that the border around the map is not a scale bar.

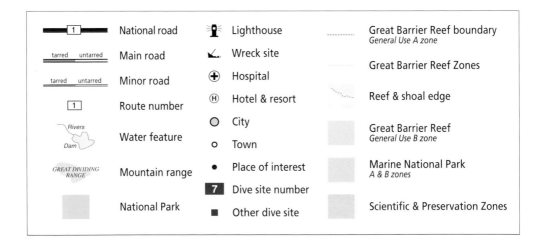

THE DIVE SITE DESCRIPTIONS

Each area's premier dive sites have been listed. Entries begin with a number corresponding to the relevant map, a star rating and symbols indicating key information (see below) pertaining to that site. Practical details such as location, access, conditions and average and maximum depths precede the description of the site, its marine life and points of interest.

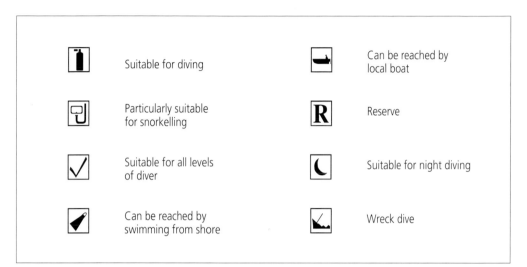

THE STAR-RATING SYSTEM

Each site has been awarded a rating, with a maximum of five and a minimum of one star.

    * pertains to scuba diving, and
    * to snorkelling, as follows:

***** first class
**** highly recommended
*** good
** average
* poor

THE REGIONAL DIRECTORIES

At the end of each region in the dive sites section is a regional directory with helpful telephone numbers and addresses. Here you will find practical information on how to get to an area, where to stay and eat, dive facilities, regional highlights and emergency measures.

OTHER FEATURES OF THIS BOOK

• Each section of the book is colour coded for ease of reference, according to the contents page.
• A general introduction to Queensland explains some of the history of Australia and tells you a bit about the people and the economy of the country. This is followed by travelling tips – how to get to the Great Barrier Reef and how to get around once you are there. There is a wealth of information on diving and snorkelling in each region.
• Boxes containing tips and information on various topics are given throughout the book.
• Feature spreads on special items of interest, such as the Crown-of-Thorns Starfish, appear in the dive site text, making this an informative book that no diver should be without.

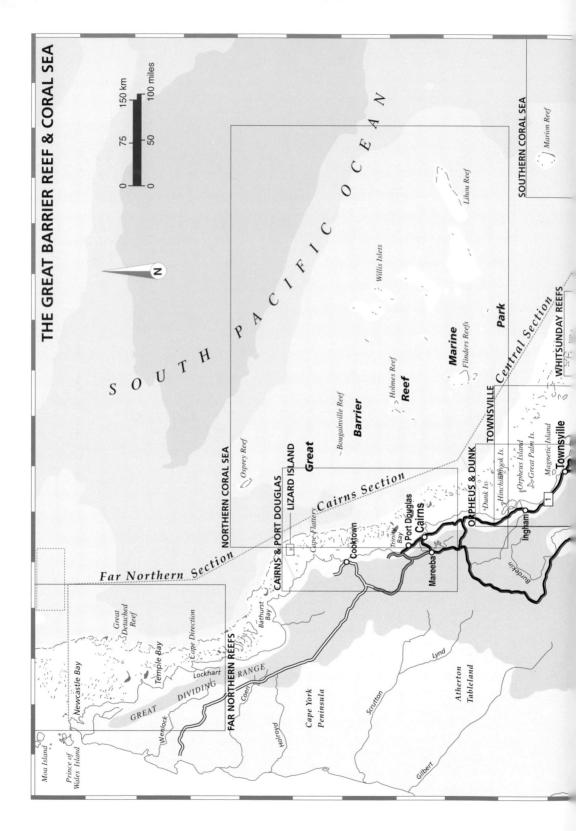

THE GREAT BARRIER REEF & CORAL SEA

150 km

75

0

100 miles

50

0

N

SOUTH PACIFIC OCEAN

SOUTHERN CORAL SEA

Marion Reef

Lihou Reef

NORTHERN CORAL SEA

Willis Islets

Marine

Flinders Reefs

Park

Osprey Reef

Great

Barrier

Reef

Holmes Reef

Bougainville Reef

Central Section

WHITSUNDAY REEFS

TOWNSVILLE

LIZARD ISLAND

CAIRNS & PORT DOUGLAS

Cairns Section

ORPHEUS & DUNK

Orpheus Island

Great Palm Is.

Magnetic Island

Townsville

Hinchinbrook Is.

Dunk Is.

Ingham

Burdekin

Cape Flattery

Port Douglas

Cairns

Cooktown

Trinity
Bay

Mareeba

1

Far Northern Section

FAR NORTHERN REEFS

Great
Detached
Reef

Bathurst
Bay

Cape Direction

Temple Bay

Lockhart

Coen

Lynd

Atherton
Tableland

Newcastle Bay

GREAT DIVIDING RANGE

Cape York
Peninsula

Scrutton

Moa Island

Prince of
Wales Island

Wenlock

Holroyd

Gilbert

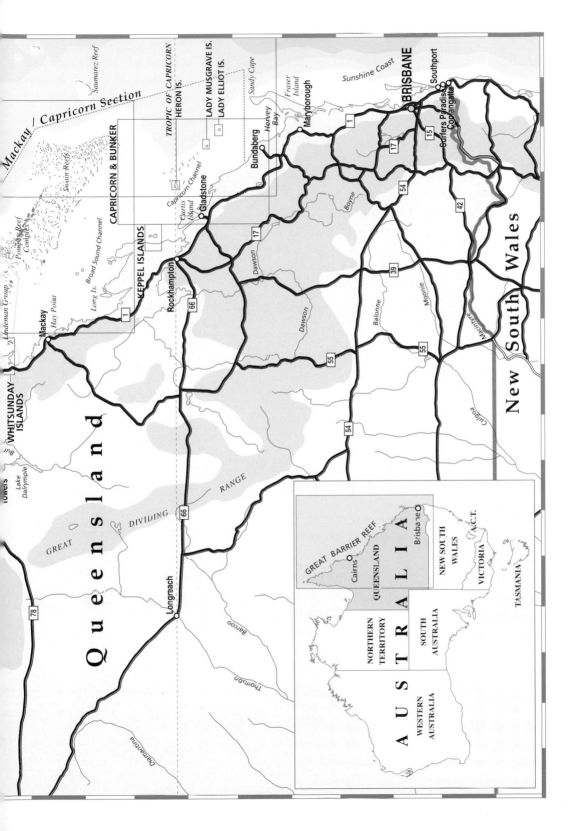

INTRODUCING QUEENSLAND

Queensland, the second largest state in Australia, is known as the 'Sunshine State' and rightfully lays claim to being Australia's premier holiday destination. Visitors flock here for the seemingly endless days of sunshine, the magnificent coastal scenery and the spectacular Great Barrier Reef. Diving here and in the neighbouring Coral Sea is truly memorable and no diver should miss it.

This mainly tropical state has an incredible variety of natural attractions ranging from mountains and gorges to grasslands, mangrove swamps to deserts, rainforests and rivers to giant sandhills and a thousand offshore islands. Japan or the British Isles could fit into Queensland five times over, which explains why one can drive for hundreds of kilometres without seeing another vehicle.

Queensland has an essentially outdoor way of life and is culturally vibrant. Aboriginal culture in particular has been actively promoted in recent years.

HISTORY

When Europeans first visited Queensland in the 1600s, it was populated by some 200 tribes of mostly nomadic hunter-gatherers now known as Aborigines, thought to have arrived by way of land bridges from Papua New Guinea over 40 000 years ago. Although appearing primitive and half-starved to European eyes, the Aborigines were very successful at surviving not only on the fertile coastal plain, but also in arid inland conditions.

In 1821 the Governor of New South Wales, Sir Thomas Brisbane, sent his Surveyor-General, John Oxley, north to find a site for a new penal settlement. Oxley chose Moreton Bay, but when the first troops arrived in 1824, the lack of fresh water coupled with the hostility of the Aborigines drove them up-river to the present site of Brisbane. The European settlers had a devastating effect on the Aborigines and islanders, who were oppressed and dispossessed of their tribal lands and culture.

Left: Hamilton Island, the Whitsundays.
Above: Townsville's Castle Rock at sunset, a landmark worthy of its name.

Snorkelling in the coral reefs of Lady Musgrave Island.

Queensland became a colony in 1859 and grew rapidly. The economy in the early pioneering days depended on farming, beef and wool production, guano mining and pearl shell harvesting. Gold fever hit the state in the 1860s and each new discovery brought huge numbers of miners to areas like the famous Palmer River goldfields west of Cooktown, stretching north from Gympie to the Atherton Tableland.

ECONOMIC DEVELOPMENT

Queensland's fertile coastal plains are ideal for sugarcane farming and today there are sugarcane farms from the New South Wales border almost to Cooktown in the north. Second only to Western Australia in seafood production, Queensland's fishing industry brings in over $6 billion per year and some success has been achieved with commercial hatcheries.

Above all, Queensland has immense mineral riches – copper, lead, zinc, gold and bauxite – which are processed at giant mining complexes and processing plants in industrial towns such as Mt Isa and Gladstone. The state also produces oil and gas and, although small by world standards, has 105 oil- and 126 gasfields.

THE LAND

The landmass of Queensland is 1 733 000km^2 (699 000 sq miles) and includes 1050 mainland islands and reefs. The coastal fringe stretches over 7400km (4600 miles) and, if the islands around the coast are included, the total coastline is 9800km (6100 miles).

Deep in the heart of Queensland's vast brown land, a network of sealed roads runs from Charleville in the south to Karumba in the Gulf of Carpentaria. This is outback country and life goes on in much the same way as it did in generations past. The pioneering spirit still burns in some of the loneliest, and at times, most barren terrain imaginable. There is new interest in the outback today and visitors travel there to experience the solitude, space, sights, sounds and people. The west is mostly flat, hot and parched, veined with a myriad dry rivers, creeks and washaways, with rugged, tortured terrain towards its edges.

The Great Dividing Range between east and west has been described as Queensland's backbone. The range starts about 200km (125 miles) south of Cape York and follows the eastern coastline in a series of low-lying ranges and tablelands. It is most spectacular near the coast, where the mountains rise quite sharply and numerous waterfalls tumble over the escarpment. The views of the range, its rainforests and gorges from the Skyrail cable car between Cairns and Kuranda are astounding. In the south, the Glasshouse Mountains, named by Captain Cook in 1770, are equally impressive.

The Queensland climate is as varied as its landscape. From south to north it is divided equally by the Tropic of Capricorn, the beginning of the true tropics. In the north, the state is subject to a northwest monsoon in summer and the southeast trade winds in winter, when a subtropical high pressure belt has a drying effect. Queensland has some of the wettest areas in Australia with most rain falling during the monsoon season (December to March). Tully, north of Townsville, known as Australia's wettest town, has an annual average rainfall of 4400mm (173in). The far western town of Birdsville, on the other hand, is the driest on the continent with less than 150mm (6in) per year. Temperatures soar to 40°C (105°F) in the outback in summer, but the average is 30–35°C (86–95°F). In winter, averages run from 22–26°C (72–80°F).

THE COASTLINE

Brisbane, capital of Queensland and the third largest city in Australia, straddles the winding Brisbane River. It retains its old-world charm despite being a modern, vibrant city with many beautiful parks and restored colonial buildings.

South of Brisbane, the Gold Coast and Surfers Paradise epitomise Queensland's wealth. This is a luxurious, popular holiday destination with 42km (26 miles) of golden, unpolluted beaches. Although the Gold Coast region experiences heavy rain during the monsoon season, in most years it can boast up to 300 days of sunshine.

Inland from the Gold Coast and rising 1000m (3278ft) the land is lush, with over a million hectares (2 470 000 acres) of national parks, mountain retreats, rainforest, walking trails, waterfalls, valleys and unique wildlife.

The Sunshine Coast, with its almost unbroken string of beaches, stretches from Caloundra to Noosa Heads. This area is famous for its holiday resorts and beaches, huge surf lines, national parks, extensive inland lake system, waterfalls, fishing, wildlife sanctuaries, tropical agriculture, and arts and crafts.

Bundaberg and Townsville, the Whitsunday Islands and Fraser Island – the largest sand island in the world – fall in Queensland's central coast area. Bundaberg, the southernmost entry point of the Great Barrier Reef, is known for its sugarcane farms and the famous Bundaberg (Bundy) rum. Visitors can witness the magical sight of Loggerhead, Green and Flatback turtles coming ashore to lay their eggs in the Mon Repos Environmental Park. Fraser Island to the north has spectacular pure-white beaches, cool inland rainforests and crystal-clear freshwater lakes.

The Whitsunday Islands are peaks of a coastal range that was flooded and became separated from the mainland during the ice age. Only seven of the 74 islands have resort facilities, the rest are uninhabited and collectively form the Whitsunday National Park.

Townsville, north of the Whitsunday Islands, is a leading centre of tropical research and home to the Australian Institute of Marine Science, the Great Barrier Reef Marine Park

Authority, a Tropical Agricultural Research Station and the north Queensland branch of the Queensland Museum. Here, too, is the Great Barrier Reef Wonderland Aquarium which has the only living coral reef in captivity. An important port, Townsville is a centre for sugar, copper, beef and mineral exports.

Far north Queensland – Cairns, Port Douglas and Cooktown – receives more visitors than any other area in the state. Cairns is the closest city to the Great Barrier Reef. Once a quiet port, it is now an international tourist centre. To the west of Cairns lie the beautiful rainforest village of Kuranda and the lush Atherton Tableland.

North of Cooktown, the gravel road to Cape York is rough, with over 28 creek and river crossings which can only be used during the dry season. Washaways are common and even four-wheel-drive vehicles get into trouble. However, it is spectacular country and in most areas it is best to go off-road with an experienced tour operator.

THE REEFS

Extending east from Australia and New Guinea, the Coral Sea is one of the most exciting diving locations in the world. Covering an area of around 4 791 000km^2 (1 886 000 sq miles), the Coral Sea contains scattered coral reefs and sand cays which are mostly inhabited by large populations of seabirds. Some of the better known islands are Cato, Chilcott, Bird Islet and Wreck Islet, part of Wreck Reef. The region was surveyed by Captain James Cook during his explorations in 1770 and guano was collected here in the late 1800s.

The Great Barrier Reef has the largest system of tropical and coral reefs, supporting the greatest number of marine life forms anywhere in the marine world. The Reef has some 600 continental or mainland islands (most with fringing reefs) and 300 reef islands or cays, 87 of which support per-manent vegetation. There are also approximately 2900 individual reefs in an area of 350 000km^2 (220 000 sq miles), most of which are submerged and range in size from 10m^2 (33 sq ft) to more than 100km^2 (62 sq miles).

The reef's vast marine system supports a huge and diverse fauna, including over 1500 species of fish, more than 4000 species of molluscs, some 350 species of reef-building corals and over 400 sponges. Many thousands of crustaceans, worms, echinoderms, bryozoans, soft corals, anemones and ascidians also occur. A large number of species still remain undiscovered and undescribed. New species are being found continually.

THE MARINE PARK ZONES

The **General Use A Zone** covers an area where you can do just about anything within reason, consistent with conservation of the reef. Spearfishing with scuba is prohibited, as are commercial drilling, mining and littering. The taking of estuary or greasy cod and giant gropers over 1200mm (48in) is also prohibited anywhere in the park without a permit. Commercial trawling, shipping and limited shell collecting are allowed. The **General Use B Zone** excludes trawling and commercial shipping

The **Marine National Park A Zone** is similar in concept to a national park on land in the sense that natural resources are protected. The difference is that some fishing activities such as trolling for pelagic fish and line-fishing (with one hand-held rod or line used with one hook or lure) is permitted. This is to protect significant areas from extensive extractive activities such as netting, collecting and spearfishing. The **Marine Park National Park B Zone** is a 'look but don't take' zone; fishing of any sort and collecting are prohibited. This zone protects areas of special value so that they may be appreciated and enjoyed in a relatively undisturbed state.

The general public may not enter **Scientific Research Zones** and **Preservation Zones**, and scientists need permits to do so. Noone may enter Preservation Zones except in an emergency. Prohibited zones are marked clearly and patrolled regularly by rangers.

Zoning plans are produced as area maps and are available free of charge from the Great Barrier Reef Marine Park Authority, PO Box 1379, Townsville, Queensland, 4810.

Learning to dive is a popular tourist activity on the Great Barrier Reef.

The Great Barrier Reef is the habitat and exclusive breeding grounds for many species of endangered wildlife, including the Dugong (*Dugong dugong*) and the largest Green Turtle (*Chelonia mydas*) and Loggerhead Turtle (*Caretta caretta*) rookeries in the world. Its sand cays are the only breeding grounds for millions of seabirds no longer able to breed on the mainland due to predators and human presence.

In 1975, the Federal Parliament passed the Great Barrier Reef Marine Park Act, one of the first pieces of legislation in the world devoted to the management of large natural areas through ecologically sustainable development. Unlike many terrestrial national parks, the Great Barrier Reef Marine Park is a multiple-use area. It has been divided into three broad zones, namely General Use where most human activities are allowed, National Park where living resources may not be removed, and Preservation or Scientific Research Zones where only research may take place. Visitors should refer to the zoning plans of permissible activities in the area when planning their trip (see panel).

TRAVELLING TO AND IN QUEENSLAND

The Great Barrier Reef can be reached from most major towns, and Queensland's three international airports (at Brisbane, Cairns and Townsville) provide easy access for overseas visitors. There are bus and rail services along the coast, and air, boat and helicopter services to many islands. Day cruises or extended live-aboard trips to the outer reef depart from various locations. There are holiday packages to suit every pocket, from five-star hotels, first-class resorts and self-contained apartments to backpacker and camping accommodation.

ENTRY REQUIREMENTS

Passports
A passport, valid for a longer period than your stay, is required. Two unused facing pages are needed for the Australian visa and entry stamps. Although not compulsory, try to ensure that your passport will be valid until three months after leaving Australia.

Visitor visas
All visitors (except Australians and New Zealanders) must obtain visas prior to arrival.

Vaccinations
You don't have to have vaccinations if you are travelling direct from the US, UK or Canada. Health certificates are not required unless you have come from an endemic zone or an area where diseases such as yellow fever, smallpox, cholera or typhoid are found.

TIME ZONE
Queensland's standard time is 10 hours ahead of Greenwich Mean Time. Visitors should check for daylight saving time when entering any other state from November and March.

Left: Whitehaven Beach, Whitsunday Islands.
Above: Emperor Angelfish.

Snorkellers enjoying one of the many outer Barrier Reef experiences.

HEALTH

Australia has no tropical diseases apart from small outbreaks of dengue fever and Ross River fever in the Townsville and Cairns regions. These mosquito-borne diseases are not widespread but precautions should be taken when out of doors, especially during the wet season. Most hotels and motels have insect screens and airconditioning, so unless you are camping or otherwise unprotected at night, general precautions are adequate.

Queensland has the highest incidence of skin cancer in the world, so look out for the sun. It is extremely potent and UV readings are high even on overcast days.

Locals always wear wide-brimmed hats, long-sleeved shirts and 15+ sunscreen. Snorkellers and divers are particularly prone to reflection from the water and should be careful when there is a breeze and water lapping over the body as it is easy not to feel the burning sensation until it is too late. Lycra suits give excellent protection from sunburn if it's too hot for wetsuits.

It is always a good practice to have hepatitis vaccinations before visiting foreign countries. HIV is present but not common; safe sex is recommended.

There is not a high incidence of crime in relation to tourism but it's wise to be cautious with valuables and hitch-hiking alone is not recommended. Normal commonsense safety precautions are all that are required. The Great Barrier Reef resorts are all trouble-free.

Medical services are on par with the rest of the world. However, there is only one public recompression chamber for all of Queensland and the Great Barrier Reef (located in Townsville) and, taking into account the enormous size of the region, this is not the place to take chances while diving.

October till May is the box jellyfish season on the northern coasts and around the inshore continental islands. These animals are extremely venomous and their sting can kill. They do not occur on the Great Barrier Reef proper. During summer, Portuguese man-of-war are also brought in from the Pacific Ocean by northerly winds. Take precautions and cover up.

MONEY
Australia has a decimal currency (dollars and cents). Most hotels, resorts, restaurants, car-hire firms, dive operators, boat charters and shops accept cash, all major credit cards and travellers' cheques. Banks are open from 09:00 to 16:00 from Monday to Friday and most have automatic teller machines.

COMMUNICATIONS
Post offices, some of which have stamp machines outside, are generally open from 09:00 to 17:00 from Monday to Friday. The telephone system is good, although some of the island resorts do not have telephones in the rooms. The mobile telephone systems are excellent.

POWER AND ELECTRICITY
Electricity is 240 volts AC 50Hz, and three-point flat-pin plugs are used throughout the country. Island resorts have their own generators, but camping areas have no electricity. Generators are not allowed on some national park islands. Some island resorts may only have one power outlet, so in the case of rechargeable strobes or underwater torches, it's best to carry a power pack and a converter. Batteries for cameras, strobes and torches are available at supermarkets, camera and film processing shops, but may not always be available at all Great Barrier Reef resort islands. Multi-voltage adaptors are generally available at airport duty-free stores and most hardware, luggage and department stores.

Liquid petroleum gas (LPG) is available at most service stations and small canisters for lights or stoves can be purchased at camping stores.

LANGUAGE AND CUSTOMS
Australia is an English-speaking country, though some slang terms may appear foreign until you get used to the lingo. Visitors may bring personal effects into Australia duty free, and if you are older than 18, you may carry 250 cigarettes or 250 grams of cigars or tobacco and one litre of alcohol. Dutiable goods to the value of $A400 included in personal baggage are exempt. Strict regulations apply to all narcotics and controlled substances.

GETTING AROUND BY AIR
There are air services along the entire coastline and airports at most major towns. Planes fly to Great Barrier Reef islands such as Lady Elliot, Hamilton and Lizard Island, and there are helicopter services to many islands and pontoons on the outer reef. Check with travel agents and/or resorts for up-to-date information and brochures.

GETTING AROUND BY RAIL
Queensland has a good rail system which extends along the coast from Brisbane to Cairns.

GETTING AROUND BY ROAD
With a good road system (though long distances take a bit of getting used to), coaches run regular services all along the Queensland coast from Brisbane to Cairns and are the major mode of transport for visiting backpackers. At most major towns, buses are met at the depot by representatives of backpacker hotels.

There are car rental agencies at all major airports and in most towns and cities. Unless you are used to driving long distances, you should plan time and distance effectively.

CAMPING ON THE GREAT BARRIER REEF

Under the jurisdiction of the Queensland Department of Environment and Heritage, camping is permitted on some of the Great Barrier Reef National Park islands. However, all areas are regularly checked by National Park rangers and a permit must be obtained and camp fees paid before the camp site is visited. As some islands are very popular with school groups, permits are restricted to protect the areas. Book at least six weeks in advance, especially during school holidays. It is possible to book up to 12 months in advance.

The maximum stay in any national park is three weeks and though some islands have tank water, most do not. When camping on isolated Great Barrier Reef islands, always carry communications equipment, a first-aid kit and be prepared for bad weather. Quite often charter boats can't get close enough to pick up campers, who may be stranded for up to a week while the sea is rough.

For more information, contact the Department of Environment and Heritage/Queensland National Parks and Wildlife Service, Ground Floor, 160 Ann Street, Brisbane 4000, or Albert Street, Queensland 4002 or phone: 07-3227 8186. Camping in this region is discussed more fully on page 100.

BACKPACKING IN QUEENSLAND

There is a huge and well-serviced backpacker organisation in Queensland, which offers competitive prices, especially in the Cairns/Townsville areas. Dive centres have an excellent range of brochures at all backpacker establishments and travel agents. Many dive operators have a pick-up service for their customers.

The Youth Hostel Association of Queensland (YHA) has hundreds of backpackers' resorts that offer low-cost accommodation in prime and remote locations. Overnight accommodation is well under $A20 for a shared room. Most have twin or double, single and family rooms. You can join the YHA either in your country or when you arrive in Queensland. For more details contact Backpackers Resorts of Australia, PO Box 1000, Byron Bay, NSW 2481, Tel: 066-858 888, Fax 066-847 100, or Youth Hostels Association of Queensland, 1st Floor, Westpac Building, Cnr George and Herschel Sts, Brisbane, Queensland 4000, Tel 07-3236 1680, Fax 07-3236 1702.

CALLING QUEENSLAND DIRECT

(A) Dial your country's international access code, then (B) Australia's country code, then (C) the Queensland area code, and finally (D) the telephone number of the Queensland holiday operator.

For example, to call 61-70-995 525:

A	B	C	D
Your country's international access code	61	70	995 525

SHOPPING HOURS

In Queensland, shopping hours are generally 08:00 to 17:00 Monday to Friday and 08:00 to 21:00 on Thursday; 08:00 to 17:00 on Saturday and trading on Sunday takes place in the major shopping centres of the Gold Coast, Brisbane city centre, the Sunshine Coast and Cairns.

Cairns is a popular yachting destination.

TIPPING
Tipping is not compulsory in Queensland nor is it a widespread practice. However, 10 per cent is usual.

METRIC CONVERSION
Celsius to Fahrenheit: multiply by 1.8 and add 32 (or double and add 30).
Fahrenheit to Celsius: subtract 32 and multiply by 0.50.

TELEPHONE NUMBER CHANGES
All telephone numbers in Australia are receiving extra digits.
In Queensland, the following changes will take place:

Brisbane (existing)	(07)	will be (07) 3	July 1995
Rockhampton (existing)	(079)	will be (07) 49	November 1997
Maryborough (existing)	(071)	will bc (07) 41	November 1997
Townsville (existing)	(077)	will be (07) 47	November 1997
Cairns (existing)	(070)	will bc (07) 40	November 1997

DIVING AND SNORKELLING ON THE GREAT BARRIER REEF AND THE CORAL SEA

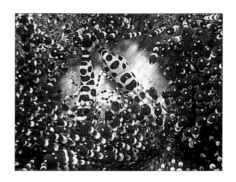

The diving industry in Queensland is healthy and vigorous. There are millions of hectares of ocean worth investigating, fantastic dive sites, thousands of unexplored reefs, and the sea life is unique. The Great Barrier Reef and Coral Sea region is a gigantic underwater playground where fantasy becomes reality. Around this island continent the diver can experience the full range of tropical and temperate water conditions. Unlike other parts of the world, diving in Australia is always an adventure as the wind almost never stops blowing, causing ocean swells and surface wave chop.

DIVING FACILITIES
As most of the reef lies from 16km (10 miles) to 300km (187 miles) off the coast, most diving and snorkelling is done from boats or pontoons. There are facilities in most major towns along the Queensland coast where dive trips to the Great Barrier Reef can be arranged.

The main training agencies are PADI Australia (Professional Association of Diving Instructors), SSI (Scuba Schools International), NAUI (National Association of Underwater Instructors), and NASDS (National Association of Scuba Diving Schools, Australia Inc).

WHEN TO VISIT AND DIVING CONDITIONS
The Great Barrier Reef resorts, charter boats and daytrip catamarans work all year. Most boats don't put to sea in winds exceeding 25 knots. As weather conditions can deteriorate overnight, there are few guarantees even in good seasons. Queensland has a tropical to subtropical climate with four seasons (not as distinct as in the northern hemisphere). Spring is from September to November, summer from December to February, autumn from March to May and winter from June to August. Diving conditions are best in late winter to early summer. The tropical monsoon season is from January to March and cyclones can occur then.

Left: Diving from a platform on the Whitsundays outer reef.
Above: Coleman's Shrimps are only found on Ijima's Sea Urchin.

In Queensland divers need a current certification card, diving medical certificate and a current log book before they may scuba dive. If these are not available, the diver must undergo a proof of competency dive or complete a resort or introductory course.

With hundreds of professional dive shops and dive boats operating in Queensland, the services available to divers are on par with any in the world. Besides providing sales and service, most dive centres offer training, from open-water to advanced diving, to specialised courses for underwater photographers, naturalists and diving instructors. A variety of eco-dive tours and underwater naturalist educational tours, generally presented by professional instructors, are also regularly offered.

An average open-water diving certificate course costs approximately $A300. Equipment can be hired, from mask and snorkel to full scuba gear, wet suits, Lycra suits and tanks.

Most daytrip diving includes at least two dives and costs vary from $A30 per dive to $A140 per day, depending on the site and the services. Boat trips can take from 15 minutes to 2½ hours to reach their destination.

Nowhere else can one find the incredible range of dive sites that occurs along the Great Barrier Reef and in the Coral Sea. The area is mostly unexplored, uncharted, undived and the possibilities are unlimited.

The Great Barrier Reef stretches over 2000km (1250 miles) from south to north, with great diving opportunities and a remarkable variety of weather conditions. For example, 40 knot winds may be blowing at Wreck or Osprey Reef in the Coral Sea while winds of only 10 knots prevail off Cairns.

As the temperature in the north of Australia can reach 35°C and slip down to 3°C in winter, one should be fully protected at all times. In general, a 5mm or ¼in wetsuit is adequate. There may be stiff winds and big swells between reefs, yet behind them in the lee of an island, the diving may be perfect, with sheltered water and relatively calm conditions. Water temperatures range from 18°–22°C (65°–72°F) in the south and 26°–29°C (80°–84°F) in the north, and visibility from 3m (10ft) at the inshore islands around Cairns to 40m (130ft) in the Coral Sea.

Weather is a major factor to consider when planning a trip. Diving and snorkelling take place throughout the year from daytrip catamarans which have enough power to sail in strong winds and choppy seas to the sheltered lagoons where their pontoons are moored, but this may not apply to monohulled dive boats.

From May to August (winter), the southeast trade winds blow, averaging between 15 and 30 knots. In September, the weather warms up and, except for localised weather patterns, is fairly stable. In January, the wet, monsoon, or cyclone season begins, with violent thunderstorms (generally late afternoons and at night) persisting until March. Quite often during late December and early January there is a period of doldrums (perfect diving conditions), but this is neither predictable nor stable.

RECOMMENDED EQUIPMENT

All dive facilities along the reef offer full equipment hire, but in general, divers seem to prefer to travel with their own regulators, masks, snorkels, fins, B.C. (Buoyancy Compensator) and wet suits. A personal dive computer is not mandatory, but is certainly recommended, especially when more than three dives a day are planned. Tanks and weight belts are available at all regular facilities, daytrip boats and live-aboards. An octopus (regulator) is mandatory in Queensland.

Due to the hot sun and heat build-up on the surface, snorkelling generally requires a Lycra suit for protection from factors such as sunburn, stings and abrasions. It is always a good practice to carry a safety sausage or extendible Divers' Alert Safety Flag or pick-me-up device suitable for location detection on the surface. This is particularly important during drift diving when there is wind chop and swell movement on the surface, making detection difficult over a wide area.

Nothing is more daunting than to surface 100km (62 miles) offshore in what seems to be the middle of the Pacific Ocean and to see an empty, 360° horizon. Remember, the nearest recompression chamber may be over 1000km (620 miles) away and it may take you a day or more to get there.

Eco-diving and Underwater Naturalist Courses

On a number of the daytrips that are offered on catamarans at Cairns, Port Douglas and Townsville, videos about the reef are shown on the outward and return trips. Guided snorkelling tours are presented at most centres, and general snorkelling, scuba diving and introductory dive packages are also available. Some dive operators present underwater naturalist courses, which are certificate courses presented as workshops over two days full-time, or part-time over a week. Marine biologists regularly present talks on various aspects of marine biology.

Wrecks and Salvage

All divable shipwrecks within the boundaries of the Great Barrier Reef Marine Park have been proclaimed under the Historic Shipwrecks Act and although diving is allowed, nothing may be removed from the vicinity of the wreck. Apart from bits and pieces such as anchors, ballast bricks and engine blocks encrusted with coral, there isn't much left of the hundreds of ships which have been pounded onto the ramparts of the reefs.

The wreck of the *Yongala* off Cape Bowling Green, Townsville, and that of the *Quetta* off the tip of Cape York, attract many divers. Take note, however, that diving on the *Yongala* is always subject to strong currents and that the *Quetta* can only be dived on the slack tide. The boats which take divers to these wrecks provide all necessary information and warnings and guides for short penetration dives.

Price Lists

To help you budget for your diving holiday in Queensland's incomparable Great Barrier Reef and Coral Sea, the following is a guide to average prices for dive courses, hire gear, charter boats and accommodation.

Dive Courses

Resort or introductory dive courses vary in price from $A40 to $A100, which sometimes includes your daytrip to the reef. Open-water dive courses cost approximately $A300, including hire gear, dives and certification. The Great Barrier Reef is an excellent place to learn to dive, and many operators include a weekend live-aboard trip to the reef, allowing you to do up to ten dives. Courses are run over four to five days, so make sure that you allocate enough time. Contact the dive shops in the area you wish to visit for more information.

Hire Gear

Gear can be rented from most dive shops and charter-boat operators, and discounts are generally available for extended periods. Contact individual operators to find out about special package deals.

Average prices per day
Regulator (including gauge and octopus) – $A10
B.C. – $A10
Dive computer – $A10
Nikonos camera – $A30
Strobe for camera – $A20
Snorkelling equipment – $A8
Wetsuit – $A10

Charter Boats
The price of a charter boat trip is generally based on the distance travelled, the size of the boat and the features of the boat. All boats provide tanks, weight belts, towels and unlimited dives. Daytrips vary in price from $A90 to $A150, but this price may include pick-ups from your accommodation, lunch and light snacks and sometimes all gear. Prices in bigger centres are competitive, but remember that the lower-priced boats will probably visit the inner reefs, and the higher-priced boats the outer edges of the reef. Live-aboard trips to the Great Barrier Reef vary in price from $A120 to $A250 per day, with an average of $A150 per day. Trips to the Ribbon and Swain reefs are more expensive. Live-aboard trips to the Coral Sea and Far Northern Reefs cost from $A250 to $A450 per day.

Accommodation
Accommodation prices are quoted per night, but package deals are available for extended stays. Prices for resorts may include meals and most activities, but not diving. High price-range resorts and hotels (four- to five-star ratings) vary from $A120 to $A1200, with an average of $A200 to $A300; medium price-range motels (two- to three-star ratings) average $A60 to $A80 and lower price-range backpacker accommodation and caravan parks (one- to two-star ratings) vary from $A15 to $A30.

THE CODE OF PRACTICE FOR RECREATIONAL DIVING AND RECREATIONAL SNORKELLING AT A WORKPLACE IN QUEENSLAND
For some years authorities have been working in conjunction with professional diving operators, the major diving instruction agencies and Dive Australia representatives to bring about greater control over diving practices throughout the Great Barrier Reef in an effort to reduce accidents.

Although in the early stages, the proposals were very stringent on scuba diving and for some years damaged the dive industry tourism from countries such as the United States (due to the restrictions on number of dives allowed each day). With the publication of the new Code of Practice, these restrictive practices have been relaxed and a system worked out in order to include the normal number of dives per day as allowed elsewhere in the world.

The Code of Practice has been implemented for safety reasons and is there for the benefit of all divers. However, there are a number of requirements which may seem somewhat overreactive and unnecessary compared with other countries' practices – these are mandatory under Queensland law and may not be contravened. Professional operators will, of course, instruct divers in the necessary requirements. See page 169 for more details.

While shooting underwater, underwater photographers should stay clear of the coral.

REGIONAL TOURIST ASSOCIATIONS

Brisbane Visitors & Convention Bureau
Ground Floor, City Hall
King George Square, Brisbane Qld 4000
tel 07-3221 8411
fax 07-3229 5126

**Bundaberg District Tourism &
Development Board Ltd**
Cnr Mulgrave & Bourbong Streets,
Bundaberg Qld 4670
tel 071-522 333
fax 071-531 444

Capricorn Tourism &Development Organisation Inc
Capricorn Information Centre, 'The Spire'
Gladstone Road, Rockhampton Qld 4700
tel 079-272 055
fax 079-222 2605

Far North Qld Promotion Bureau Ltd
Cnr Grafton & Hartley Streets,
Cairns Qld 4870
tel 070-513 588
fax 070-510 127

Fraser Coast South Burnett
Regional Tourism Board Ltd
1st Floor, 224 Bazaar Street,
Maryborough Qld 4650
tel 071-223 444
fax 071-223 426

Gold Coast Tourism Bureau Ltd
2nd Floor, 64 Ferny Avenue,
Surfers Paradise Qld 4217
tel 075-922 699
fax 075-703 144

Tourism Mackay Inc
Tourist Information Centre
The Mill, 320 Nebo Road,
Mackay Qld 4740
tel 079-522 677
fax 079-522 034

Townsville Enterprise Ltd
Enterprise House, 6 The Strand,
Townsville Qld 4810
tel 077-713 061
fax 077-714 361

Whitsunday Visitors Bureau
Beach Plaza, The Esplanade,
Airlie Beach Qld 4802
tel 079-466 673
fax 079-467 387

QUEENSLAND TRAVEL CENTRES

Brisbane
Cnr Adelaide & Edward Streets
tel 07-3221 6111
fax 07-3221 5320

Sydney
75 Castlereagh Street
tel 02-9232 1788
fax 02-9231 5153

Canberra
25 Garema Place
tel 06-248 8411
fax 06-257 4160

Melbourne
257 Collins Street
tel 03-9654 3866
fax 03-9650 1847

Adelaide
10 Grenfell Street
tel 08-8212 2399
fax 08-8211 8841

Perth
Shop 6, 777 Hay Street
tel 09-322 1777
fax 09-322 1800
or tel 131 801

The coastline north of Port Douglas, Queensland.

DAYTRIPS FOR DIVERS AND SNORKELLERS

Bundaberg Seaplane Tours
PO Box 1986, Bundaberg Qld 4670
tel 071-552 068
fax 071-552 068

Capricorn Cruises
PO Box 571, Yeppoon Qld 4703
tel 079-336 744
fax 079-336 429

Dolphin Reef Charters
Gladstone Qld 4680
tel 079-736 730
Mobile 018 458 750

Fantasea Cruises
PO Box 616, Airlie Beach Qld 4802
tel 079-465 111
fax 079-645 520

Great Adventures
PO Box 898, Cairns Qld 4870
tel 070-515 644
fax 070-313 753

Lady Elliot Island Resort
PO Box 206, Torquay Qld 4655
tel 071-516 077
fax 071-531 285

Lady Musgrave Barrier Reef Cruises
1 Quay Street, Bundaberg Qld 4670
tel 071-529 011
fax 071-524 948

Ocean Spirit Cruises
PO Box 2140, Cairns Qld 4870
tel 070-312 920
fax 070-314 344

Pure Pleasure Cruises
Great Barrier Reef Wonderland
PO Box 898, Townsville Qld 4810
tel 077-213 555
fax 077-213 590

Quicksilver Connections Ltd
PO Box 171, Port Douglas Qld 4871
tel 070-995 500
fax 070-995 525

1770 Barrier Reef Day Cruises
7 Tyron Court, Gladstone Qld 4680
tel 079-749 188
fax 079-749 254

Sunlover Cruises
PO Box 835, Cairns Qld 4870
tel 070-311 055
fax 070-313 886

Whitsunday Connections
PO Box 821, Airlie Beach Qld 4802
tel 079-469 577
fax 079-469 702

Yellowfin Charters
PO Box 7005, North Bundaberg Qld 4670
tel 071-516 448
fax 071-531 215

THE CAPRICORN AND BUNKER GROUP

Located at the southern end of the Great Barrier Reef, the Capricorn and Bunker Groups of islands and reefs offer some of the most interesting and varied diving on the whole reef. Surrounding these islands and reefs are dense coral gardens, pinnacles and drop-offs which are home to a wealth of fish, turtles, reef sharks, sea snakes, Manta Rays and Humpback Whales in winter. Nearly all the dive sites are under 30m (100ft) deep, with an average depth of 15m (50ft), allowing plenty of time to explore, photograph and encounter some astounding marine life forms.

The Capricorn and Bunker Groups are located in the Capricornia Marine Park. The area has a multipurpose zoning, which includes general use, replenishment, preservation, seasonal closure and scientific areas. There are two marine research stations in the Capricorn Group, one on Heron Island which can be visited and the other on One Tree Island which is closed to recreational divers. The scientists at these research stations are involved in vital research on the dynamics and protection of the reef, reef ecology, the effects of pollution and other necessary and valuable topics. Watch out for scientists conducting strange experiments in the shallows.

Visitors to the Capricorn and Bunker Groups start out from Urangan, Bundaberg or Gladstone by boat, plane or helicopter. One visit to the Capricorn and Bunker Groups is never enough; many divers return year after year to this coral wonderland.

While Heron and Lady Elliot islands are easily the most popular locations in the Capricorn and Bunker Groups, dive charter trips are also popular with divers wanting to visit reefs and islands from the luxury of a boat. All the islands and reefs in the region except One Tree Island and Wreck Island may be visited.

Charter boats, which also run fishing trips, leave from the ports of Urangan and Gladstone. They generally take group bookings from dive shops and clubs, but can usually take a few other passengers. Trips to this area normally last five days to a week.

Left: Friendly Leopard Sharks appear at Lady Elliot Island in summer.
Above: Snorkelling at the Heron Island bommie is an exhilarating experience.

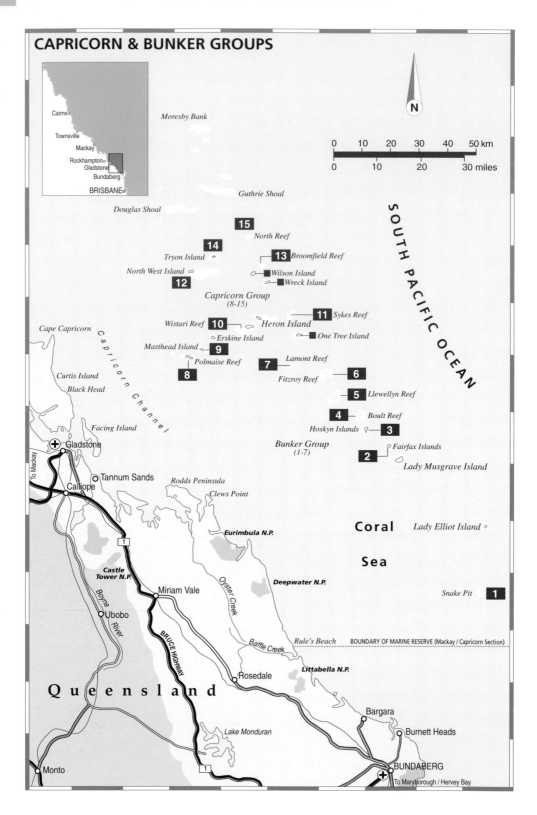

CAPRICORN & BUNKER GROUPS

Cairns
Townsville
Mackay
Rockhampton
Gladstone
Bundaberg
BRISBANE

N

0 10 20 30 40 50 km
0 10 20 30 miles

Moresby Bank

SOUTH PACIFIC OCEAN

Guthrie Shoal

Douglas Shoal

15

North Reef

14

Tryon Island

13 Broomfield Reef

North West Island

Wilson Island

12

Wreck Island

Capricorn Group
(8-15)

11 Sykes Reef

Wistari Reef **10**

Heron Island

Cape Capricorn

Erskine Island

One Tree Island

Masthead Island **9**

Polmaise Reef

Lamont Reef

7

6

8

Fitzroy Reef

Curtis Island

5 Llewellyn Reef

Black Head

4

Boult Reef

Facing Island

Hoskyn Islands

3

Gladstone

Bunker Group
(1-7)

Fairfax Islands

2

Tannum Sands

Lady Musgrave Island

Rodds Peninsula

Calliope

Clews Point

Coral

Lady Elliot Island

Eurimbula N.P.

Sea

Castle
Tower N.P.

Miriam Vale

Snake Pit **1**

Ubobo

Deepwater N.P.

Baffle Creek

Rule's Beach

BOUNDARY OF MARINE RESERVE (Mackay / Capricorn Section)

Rosedale

Littabella N.P.

Queensland

Bargara

Lake Monduran

Burnett Heads

Monto

BUNDABERG

To Maryborough / Hervey Bay

To Mackay

Capricorn Channel

Boyne River

Oyster Creek

BRUCE HIGHWAY

1 SNAKE PIT

★★★★★

Location: South of the Bunker Group, 80km (50 miles) from Urangan.
Access: By boat, 4hr from Urangan.
Conditions: Strong currents. Can only be dived in calm seas. Average visibility 20m (65ft).
Minimum depth: 20m (65ft)
Maximum depth: 45m (150ft)
The Snake Pit is a pinnacle that rises from 45m (150ft) to within 20m (65ft) of the surface. The coral on top of the pinnacle isn't spectacular, but the marine life is amazing. Fish species include trevally, sweetlips, batfish, hussars, snapper, Maori Wrasse, coral trout, Estuary Cod, coral cod, fusiliers, surgeonfish, squirrelfish and barracuda. Eagle Rays and reef sharks cruise the top of the pinnacle in the constant current. The most impressive feature is the sea snakes – there are dozens of Olive and Banded sea snakes in mid-water, in the coral, among the fish and around the divers. Though quite docile and easy to handle, it is still unnerving when several sea snakes peer into your mask or become intertwined with your gauge hoses. This unforgettable dive site is rarely dived, due to its location and unpredictable weather conditions. One of the few charter boats that visits the Snake Pit is *Boomerang*, based in Urangan Harbour.

2 FAIRFAX ISLANDS

★★★★★★★

Location: Northern end of Bunker Group, 110km (70 miles) from Gladstone.
Access: Over 6hr sailing time from Gladstone.
Conditions: Protected by reef, mostly calm, slight currents. Average visibility 20m (65ft).
Minimum depth: 6m (20ft)
Maximum depth: 16m (52ft)
Numerous pinnacles dot the sandy bottom on the northern side of Fairfax Islands. Around the smaller pinnacles divers are likely to see turtles, pufferfish, coral trout, stingrays, reef sharks and sometimes leopard sharks and Manta Rays. There is a massive pinnacle taller than a two-storey house, standing 10m (33ft) high in 16m (52ft) water. It is riddled with caves and has one big swim-through packed with baitfish. If you can part the baitfish, you will also find lionfish, coral trout, angelfish, sweetlips, squirrelfish and moray eels. Beware of Tasselled Wobbegong sharks which seem to be everywhere – you could quite easily kneel on one without knowing it until it bites you. Turtles, stingrays, Maori Wrasse, Estuary Cod, and parrotfish are also sometimes seen. At night,

this pinnacle becomes a kaleidoscope of colours by torchlight. The cave walls are lined with *Tubastrea* coral, their beautiful golden polyps pulsating under the light beam. Soft corals, feather stars, anemones, sponges, ascidians and hydroid coral also offer splashes of colour. Banded Coral Shrimps, sleeping fish and coral crabs can also be seen in the area.

3 HOSKYN ISLANDS

★★★★★★

Location: Northern end of Bunker Group, 110km (70 miles) from Gladstone.
Access: Over 6hr sailing time from Gladstone.
Conditions: Protected by reef, mostly calm. Average visibility 20m (65ft).
Minimum depth: 3m (10ft)
Maximum depth: 15m (50ft)
There is wonderful diving in the healthy coral gardens in shallow water on the northern side of Hoskyn Islands. In this coral wonderland you can meet Manta Rays, turtles, Blue-spotted Stingrays, Painted Crays, sweetlips, reef sharks, Rainbow Runners and all sorts of reef fish. This reef is even more beautiful at night and under torchlight divers will see shrimps, crabs, molluscs, brittle stars, sea stars and perhaps large Spanish Dancers – the biggest of the nudibranchs. A close look at the coral will reveal sleeping damsels, Moorish Idols, butterflyfish, fusiliers, boxfish and delicate little pufferfish.

4 BOULT REEF

★★★★★★

Location: Northern end of Bunker Group, 110km (70 miles) from Gladstone.
Access: Over 6hr sailing time from Gladstone.
Conditions: Protected by reef so mostly calm. Average visibility 20m (65ft).
Minimum depth: 3m (10ft)
Maximum depth: 15m (50ft)
There are extensive coral gardens on the northern side of Boult Reef. These are cut with gutters and ledges, and there is a number of small coral heads to explore. Small reef fish such as angelfish, Fairy Basslets, gobies, hawkfish, filefish, blennies, boxfish and wrasse are prolific. Pelagic fish constantly sweep over the reef, and divers will see lone barracuda and mackerel, and massive schools of trevally and Rainbow Runners. Turtles seem to be particularly common, sleeping under ledges or slowly swimming over the reef. Manta Rays are also found here; they 'fly' in, buzz divers and disappear. If one looks up to the surface, one can see them feeding on plankton, their

huge mouths open wide to filter out the tiny organisms. After dark, molluscs, shrimps, crabs and squirrelfish depart from their daytime haunts. Sleeping in the coral are parrotfish, butterflyfish, damsels and wrasse. Painted Crays come out of hiding and walk the reef in search of

food or a mate, and Leopard Morays patrol the reef. To see a 2m- (6ft) long moray eel hunting is quite a spectacle – it searches every hole, tastes the water and when it locates its prey, usually a sleeping fusilier, it launches at it, almost biting the fish in two, and gulps down the remains. A close search will reveal flatworms, nudibranchs, hermit crabs, coral crabs and many other small, colourful invertebrates.

TURTLE BREEDING

All species of turtle are protected in Australian waters as they are all on the endangered species list. Unfortunately, even though the law protects them, numbers are still declining due to shark nets, trawler nets, plastic waste and disease. The three main species on the Great Barrier Reef are the Green, the Loggerhead and the Hawksbill turtle. Leatherbacks are rarely observed at sea and there are few records of them breeding in Australian waters. The main breeding months are October to May. Turtles mate in the shallow waters surrounding the islands and cays of the Great Barrier Reef. Females come ashore at night on the high tide and dig a body pit and an egg pit into which they lay around 50 to 100 ping-pong ball-shaped eggs. These are covered up with sand before the females make their way back to the water. The juvenile turtles hatch out at night six to eight weeks later and scramble down to the water's edge to begin life in the sea. Islands such as Heron and Lady Elliot have regularly hosted turtle-breeding walks for visitors during the season.

5 LLEWELLYN REEF

✷✷✷✷✷✷✷

Location: Northern end of Bunker Group, 100km (62 miles) from Gladstone.
Access: Over 6hr sailing time from Gladstone.
Conditions: Protected by reef, mostly calm. Average visibility 20m (65ft).
Minimum depth: 6m (20ft)
Maximum depth: 18m (60ft)
Llewellyn Reef's structure is similar to many of the reefs around, with a steep drop-off on the southern side and shallow coral gardens on the northern side. Llewellyn Reef is protected and as such it has some of the richest coral gardens in the area. A large variety of fish species can be found throughout, including lionfish, parrotfish, tuskfish, Maori Wrasse, filefish, Fairy Basslets, scorpionfish, hogfish, goatfish, flutemouth, sweetlips, rock cod, anemonefish, triggerfish and angelfish. Divers are also likely to encounter turtles, reef sharks, sea snakes, stingrays and the odd school of pelagic fish.

Loggerhead Turtles are commonly seen swimming around at this group of islands and reefs.

6 FITZROY REEF

★★★★★★★

Location: Northern end of Bunker Group, 110km (62 miles) from Gladstone.
Access: Over 6hr sailing time from Gladstone.
Conditions: Protected by reef, mostly calm. Average visibility 20m (65ft).
Minimum depth: 6m (20ft)
Maximum depth: 18m (60ft)

Fitzroy Reef has large pinnacles and gutters on the northern side. These pinnacles are dotted with small caves and covered in healthy hard and soft corals and sea whips, anemones, gorgonians and sponges. Maori Wrasse, barramundi, cod, angelfish, bannerfish, unicornfish, flutemouth, coral trout, mackerel, jobfish, batfish and parrotfish are just some of the fish encountered here. Green Turtles can be found resting under ledges and Whitetip Reef Sharks are commonly seen patrolling the gutters. Night diving is interesting at Fitzroy Reef, which has a large, sheltered lagoon offering safe anchorage for boats. The lagoon floor is peppered with coral heads of all sizes, and is home to a wealth of small marine life such as coral and decorator crabs, lionfish, molluscs, sea stars, flatworms, colourful shrimps, boxfish, pufferfish, squid and hermit crabs.

7 LAMONT REEF

★★★★★★★★

Location: Northern end of Bunker Group, 95km (60 miles) from Gladstone.
Access: Over 5hr sailing time from Gladstone.
Conditions: Protected by reef, mostly calm, slight currents. Average visibility 20m (65ft).
Minimum depth: 6m (20ft)
Maximum depth: 30m (100ft)

The southern side of Lamont Reef is dominated by a sheer coral wall which is washed by gentle currents, thus allowing for drift diving. This wall is undercut with many deep ledges and caves which hide sleeping turtles, Tasselled Wobbegong sharks, Tawny Nurse Sharks, lionfish, stingrays, moray eels and sometimes masses of baitfish. The wall itself is decorated with sea whips, small soft corals and gorgonians, hard corals, sponges, ascidians and golden *Tubastrea* corals. Numerous fish patrol it: trevally, barracuda, mackerel, turrum, fusiliers and surgeonfish. Shy Whitetip Reef Sharks cruise the wall, while Olive Sea Snakes search every hole in the coral for food. On the northern side there is a pretty reef, cut with gutters and riddled with pinnacles. Fish life is prolific and includes jobfish, trevally, surgeonfish, turrum, barracuda,

Huge schools of hussars are often encountered.

tusk fish, coral trout, lionfish, boxfish, batfish, parrotfish and a variety of wrasse. Exploring the gutters you are likely to find Green Turtles, stingrays, Painted Crays, moray eels and Tasselled Wobbegong sharks. This is also a brilliant spot for macro photography as divers will find sea stars, nudibranchs, shrimps, flatworms, clams, anemonefish and brittle stars.

8 POLMAISE REEF

★★★★

Location: Western side of Capricorn Group, 60km (38 miles) from Gladstone.
Access: Over 4hr sailing time from Gladstone.
Conditions: Reef offers little protection, slight currents. Average visibility 15m (50ft).
Minimum depth: 6m (20ft)
Maximum depth: 10m (33ft)

A collection of small pinnacles on the northwest corner of Polmaise Reef is constantly swept by currents and attracts masses of fish life. Schools of barracuda, trevally and batfish sweep over and around the pinnacles, while coral trout, hussars, sweetlips, Estuary Cod and angelfish stay close to the reef. When exploring the pinnacles you are also very likely to find Tasselled Wobbegong sharks lazing on the coral, Olive Sea Snakes searching the bottom for food, butterflyfish picking at coral polyps and Green Turtles drifting in the slight current. The pinnacles are colourful, with a good range of corals but it is the outstanding and abundant fish life that makes this such a special dive site.

Sunshine corals can be seen on night dives.

AUSTRALIAN SLANG

A **bommie** is a pinnacle or coral head. A **wobby** is short for a wobbegong shark. **Cod** means groper. Fish known as **trevally** are known elsewhere as jacks. A **cobia** is commonly known as a Black Kingfish. **Leopard Sharks** are also known as Zebra Sharks and Napoleon Wrasse as **Maori Wrasse**.

⑨ MASTHEAD ISLAND

★★★★★★

Location: Western side of Capricorn Group, 65km (40 miles) from Gladstone.
Access: Over 4hr sailing time from Gladstone.
Conditions: Protected by reef, mostly calm. Average visibility 15m (65ft).
Minimum depth: 3m (10ft)
Maximum depth: 15m (50ft)
Masthead Island is a popular camping island that is occasionally visited by charter boats. A maximum of 60 people are allowed to stay on the island at any one time and as compressors are not permitted, most campers are snorkellers. Around the island, numerous coral gardens and small pinnacles are home to a variety of fish and invertebrate life. Angelfish, parrotfish, butterflyfish, sweetlips, bat-fish, wrasse, filefish, surgeonfish and tuskfish are commonly seen, but it is also possible to see stingrays, reef sharks, turtles and the odd sea snake.

⑩ WISTARI REEF

★★★★★★★★

Location: Centre of Capricorn Group, southwest of Heron Island, 75km (45 miles) from Gladstone.
Access: Over 5hr sailing time from Gladstone.
Conditions: Protected by reef, mostly calm, slight currents. Average visibility 20m (65ft).
Minimum depth: 6m (20ft)
Maximum depth: 35m (115ft)
On the northern side of Wistari Reef is a continuous reef wall that drops into the channel between it and Heron Island. This drop-off is decorated with a wealth of lush coral growth. In the shallows are forests of staghorn coral, while on deeper parts of the wall are gorgonians, sea whips, encrusting sponges, soft corals and ascidians. There are plenty of reef fish, including hawkfish, angelfish, butterflyfish, flutemouth, soapfish, gobies, scorpionfish, filefish and pufferfish. Large reef fish such as coral trout, sweetlips, Estuary Cod, tuskfish, parrotfish and triggerfish are also found and pelagic fish sometimes cruise the wall. Divers will see trevally, fusiliers, surgeonfish, Rainbow Runners and occasionally barracuda. Reef sharks, turtles, Painted Crays, Tasselled Wobbegong sharks, stingrays and Epaulette Sharks also feature in the area. Drift diving is popular along this wall, and snorkellers will have fun exploring the rich coral gardens on top of the drop-off.

⑪ SYKES REEF

★★★★★★★★

Location: Eastern side of Capricorn Group, 80km (50 miles) from Gladstone.
Access: Over 5hr sailing time from Gladstone.
Conditions: Protected by reef, mostly calm. Average visibility 20m (65ft).
Minimum depth: 3m (10ft)
Maximum depth: 18m (60ft)
A series of gutters on the north and east sides of Sykes Reef offer action-packed diving. At certain times of the year these gutters are overflowing with baitfish, which attract a lot of bigger fish such as Estuary Cod, coral trout, sweetlips, trevally, turrum and Rainbow Runners, among others. Divers are also likely to encounter surgeonfish, parrotfish, batfish, turtles, stingrays, moray eels and occasionally Bottlenose Dolphins. Sharks are plentiful, from bottom-dwelling Tawny Nurse Sharks, Tasselled Wobbegongs and Ornate Wobbegongs, to the faster reef sharks, Whitetip, Blacktip and Grey. These gutters offer exciting snorkelling or scuba diving.

12 NORTH WEST ISLAND

* * * * * * * *

Location: Northern end of Capricorn Group, 80km (50 miles) from Gladstone.
Access: Over 5hr sailing time from Gladstone.
Conditions: Protected by reef, mostly calm. Average visibility 15m (50ft).
Minimum depth: 3m (10ft)
Maximum depth: 15m (50ft)

North West Island is the busiest camping location in the Capricorn Group. Diving and snorkelling are excellent all around the island, with extensive coral gardens, pinnacles, and numerous gutters and caves to explore. The southern side of the reef has a small drop-off to 15m (50ft) where pelagic fish sometimes gather. Divers will see barracuda, trevally, Rainbow Runners, mackerel and reef fish like lionfish, squirrelfish, angelfish, butterflyfish, parrotfish and surgeonfish. Turtles, stingrays and reef sharks are common, as are nudibranchs, flatworms, sea stars, anemones, crabs, shrimps and molluscs. Snorkelling is popular all round the island, from the reef flat to the reef edge. The reef flat is worth a visit at high tide as Epaulette Sharks, small moray eels, Blue-spotted Stingrays, Shovelnose Rays, schools of feeding parrotfish, clams, sea stars, sea cucumbers and small reef sharks can be seen.

13 BROOMFIELD REEF

* * * * * * *

Location: Northern end of Capricorn Group, 80km (50 miles) from Gladstone.
Access: Over 5hr sailing time from Gladstone.
Conditions: Protected by reef, mostly calm. Average visibility 20m (65ft).
Minimum depth: 6m (20ft)
Maximum depth: 15m (50ft)

There are many pinnacles at Broomfield Reef. These large coral heads attract a wealth of marine life, from pelagic to resident reef fish. Common are barracuda, batfish, coral trout, mackerel, moray eels, lionfish, trevally, baitfish, Tasselled Wobbegong sharks, turtles, stingrays and reef sharks. The fringing reef is worth looking at as there are many gutters and small caves to explore. Reef fish are particularly abundant and divers will see parrotfish, surgeonfish, tuskfish, rock cod, pufferfish, rabbitfish, Moorish Idols, damsels, anemonefish and sweetlips.

Divers wade out to the landing barge dive boat at Lady Elliot Island.

Staghorn corals come in a wide variety of shapes and colours.

14 TRYON ISLAND

★★★★★★★

Location: Northern end of Capricorn Group, 85km (53 miles) from Gladstone.
Access: Over 5hr sailing time from Gladstone.
Conditions: Protected by reef, mostly calm. Average visibility 20m (65ft).
Minimum depth: 6m (20ft)
Maximum depth: 20m (65ft)

Tryon Island is probably the most remote and unspoilt of the camping islands in the Capricorn and Bunker Groups. The southern side of Tryon Island has extensive coral gardens, cut with gutters, and is home to many reef fish; the eastern side has a short drop-off, regularly visited by pelagic fish. The most popular dive sites are the numerous pinnacles on the northern and western sides. Some of these coral heads are 10m (33ft) high and are riddled with small caves and ledges. Lionfish, scorpionfish, squirrelfish, moray eels, angelfish, pufferfish, Fairy Basslets, coral trout and flutemouth are all common. These pinnacles also attract passing pelagic fish, reef sharks, stingrays, Eagle Rays, turtles and Manta Rays that come for cleaning by the Cleaner Wrasse population. Snorkellers will, therefore, find lots to explore and will have close encounters with most of the local marine life.

15 NORTH REEF

★★★★★★★

Location: Northern end of Capricorn Group, 95km (60 miles) from Gladstone.
Access: Over 5hr sailing time from Gladstone.
Conditions: Protected by reef, mostly calm. Average visibility 20m (65ft).
Minimum depth: 6m (20ft)
Maximum depth: 20m (65ft)

On the northern side of North Reef is a nice drop-off with many ledges. A great many schooling fish gather here to feed on the baitfish, coral trout, sweetlips, trevally and fusiliers. It is also home to moray eels, Tasselled Wobbegong sharks, Estuary Cod, Maori Wrasse, lionfish, rock cod, barramundi cod and squirrelfish. The drop-off leads to a small coral bay dotted with coral heads where divers will see smaller reef fish, blue spotted stingrays, batfish, parrotfish, angelfish and Green and Loggerhead turtles. Manta Rays are common in this area, so watch the surface for the amazing sight of these magnificent creatures feeding in formation. On the southern side of the reef lies the wreck of the *Cooma*, which broke up after hitting the reef in 1926. All that remains is a twisted collection of steel in the shallows – a boiler can even be seen on top of the reef.

Lady Elliot Island

Lady Elliot Island is the southernmost island of the Great Barrier Reef and many unique animals live on its reefs due to its location near the continental shelf. For many years it was the well-kept secret of a handful of Australian divers, but word spread and now divers from around the world visit this outstanding destination. The main reason people visit Lady Elliot Island is its famous Manta Rays, but there are many other marine creatures to be seen in the area. Sea snakes and Leopard Sharks can be seen during summer; turtles, stingrays, reef sharks and schooling fish are common throughout the year, and whales and dolphins are sometimes seen in the winter. Lady Elliot offers great diving all year round.

The island was discovered and named in 1816 by Captain Thomas Stewart after the ship *Lady Elliot*. Over the years the island was mined for guano and the waters fished for bêche-de-mer (sea cucumbers). The guano miners stripped Lady Elliot of trees and removed 2m (6ft) of topsoil from the entire island. In this time a number of ships were lost on the reef. Today wreckage is scattered around the perimeter, but not enough to make wreck diving popular. A lighthouse was built in 1866 to prevent any more ships from foundering on the reef.

In 1969 the island was opened to tourism. An airstrip was built and trees were planted. It is a low-key resort with a range of accommodation, a souvenir shop, a marine education centre, library, bar, pool and dive shop which conducts dive courses and offers daily dives from boat or shore to various sites. There are regular night dives, depending on conditions. Lady Elliot diving is quite easy, whether drift diving from the boat or exploring pinnacles from the shore. Strong currents sometimes affect the dive sites.

Snorkellers will have a great time as there is plenty to explore. Even nondivers will soon find themselves spending most of the day in the water. Other daytime activities include reef walks, whale-watching in winter, and birdwatching as there is a large sanctuary where thousands of birds nest each year.

To reach Lady Elliot Island, fly from Bundaberg airport. The flight is only 40 minutes and that first view of the island from the air, with Manta Rays swimming in the clear, blue waters is absolutely spectacular.

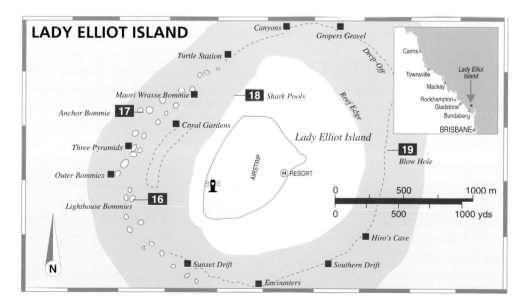

Lady Elliot Island from the air.

16 LIGHTHOUSE BOMMIES

****

Location: Western side of Lady Elliot Island, 100m (330ft) from shore.
Access: By boat or shore only minutes from resort.
Conditions: Protected by reef, mostly calm, slight currents. Average visibility 25m (80ft).
Minimum depth: 3m (10ft)
Maximum depth: 16m (52ft)

The Lighthouse Bommies are small coral outcrops packed with marine life. After snorkelling across a sandy patch, you descend past a coral ledge where schools of surgeonfish and sweetlips mingle. From the ledge you can drift onto the bommies, where you are likely to see Manta Rays waiting to be cleaned by Cleaner Wrasse. Manta Rays almost always hover around the bommies and sometimes swim in circles around divers. The Lighthouse Bommies are home to batfish, stingrays, White-spotted Shovelnose Rays, Green and Loggerhead turtles, sea snakes, moray eels, coral trout, Eagle Rays, lionfish, Tasselled Wobbegong sharks, reef sharks, trevally, barracuda and many others. Leopard Sharks are seen during summer and divers may be lucky enough to photograph them. This is an incredible location, with good coral and an interesting variety of marine life.

17 ANCHOR BOMMIE

★★★★★

Location: Western side of Lady Elliot Island, 100m (330ft) from shore.
Access: By boat or shore, only minutes from resort.
Conditions: Protected by reef, mostly calm, slight currents. Average visibility 25m (80ft).
Minimum depth: 10m (40ft)
Maximum depth: 20m (65ft)

Beyond the Coral Gardens a rope trail leads divers past numerous coral heads. The last one, Anchor Bommie, is as tall as a two-storey house. Lying at its base are two large anchors that were lost by guano ships. The bommie itself is cut with numerous caves and ledges which are home to baitfish and cardinalfish. Schools of small reef fish cover the bommie, along with lionfish, Fairy Basslets, damsels, butterflyfish, triggerfish, hawkfish and blennies. Schooling trevally and barracuda sometimes swoop across the area, and divers are also likely to see mackerel, coral trout, the rare Leaf Scorpionfish, Estuary Cod, Potato Cod, surgeonfish and Maori Wrasse. Manta Rays are common and if undisturbed will stay around the bommie for the entire dive. On the sand colonies of garden eels, stingrays, Leopard Sharks, Shovelnose Rays and sometimes Olive Sea Snakes can be seen, curiously inspecting every hole. Green, Loggerhead and Hawksbill turtles are also to be found, sleeping under ledges, drifting with the current or feeding.

18 SHARK POOLS

★ ★ ★ ★ ★ ★ ★ ★ ★ ★ ★

Location: Western side of Lady Elliot Island, 100m (330ft) from shore.
Access: By boat, or shore, only minutes from resort.
Conditions: Protected by reef, mostly calm, slight currents. Average visibility 15m (50ft).
Minimum depth: 1m (40in)
Maximum depth: 10m (33ft)

The Shark Pools are a series of gutters where reef sharks show interesting, specialised behaviour. They gather at the pools at low tide and wait there for the tide to turn, then race across the reef to feed on the fish which have been trapped in the tidal pools. Blacktip Reef Sharks, Grey Reef Sharks, Bronze Whalers and Whitetip Reef Sharks can all be seen cruising up and down these gutters – there are dozens at any given time, which can be unnerving for the inexperienced diver. Most of the sharks are frightened of scuba bubbles, so for really close encounters snorkelling is recommended. The sharks will then come right up you, especially the Grey Reef Sharks which will zoom in to inspect you thoroughly. The pools, too, are quite interesting to explore. There are many caves and swim-throughs, and with luck you will find resting Whitetip Reef Sharks, Tasselled Wobbegong sharks, schooling fish and turtles. This is a high-adrenalin dive where you are bound to see plenty of sharks up close.

19 BLOW HOLE

★ ★ ★ ★ ★

Location: Eastern side of Lady Elliot Island, 200m (660ft) from shore.
Access: By boat, only minutes from resort.
Conditions: More exposed part of reef so generally rough, slight currents (can be very strong on occasions). Average visibility 25m (80ft).
Minimum depth: 15m (50ft)
Maximum depth: 26m (83ft)

The Blow Hole is one of Lady Elliot Island's most popular dive sites, and for good reason. There is a large dark hole 6m (20ft) in diameter in the top of reef at 15m (50ft).. Entering the hole, you drop 6m (20ft) to the cave floor from where you will see another exit 20m (65ft) away in the reef wall. The walls of this giant swim-through are lined with black coral trees, *Tubastrea* coral and small soft corals. Feather stars cling to the wall and, if you look closely, you may also find Banded Coral Shrimps, cowries and decorator crabs. In summer the cave usually overflows with cardinalfish, making it difficult to see anything else. The cardinalfish attract sweetlips, coral trout, trevally and other predators. Divers are likely to find Tasselled Wobbegong sharks, Black-blotched Rays, Potato Cod, rock cod, lionfish, bannerfish and schools of colourful Fairy Basslets. The reef wall offers fascinating diving with its many caves and ledges crowded with Painted Crays, angelfish, hawkfish, octopus, giant murex, giant thorny oysters, squirrelfish, moray eels and Blue Tangs. Off the wall you may see Spotted Eagle Rays, Manta Rays, reef sharks, turtles and large pelagic fish. Take a torch on this exciting dive, and a camera if you have one.

At close range, the colours of hard corals are even more vivid.

Lady Musgrave Island

Lady Musgrave Island is an 18ha- (44 acre) coral cay which sits on the edge of a huge reef and lagoon almost 1200ha (2960 acres) in area. Like Lady Elliot Island, Lady Musgrave was stripped of its topsoil by guano miners, and later ravaged by goats. The island has recovered a lot better than Lady Elliot Island, and now has a thick cover of Pisonia trees, She Oaks and Pandanus Palms.

There are no facilities on the island except for a toilet block for campers and daytrippers. The catamaran MV *Lady Musgrave* moors almost daily at a permanent pontoon located in the lagoon. Charter boats and yachts shelter overnight in this large, safe anchorage. From this base boats can explore the Bunker Group or the reefs around the island. Camping is popular, especially during school holidays.

The diving around Lady Musgrave Island is exciting and varied, from the lagoon to the coral gardens to the extensive drop-off on the southern side of the reef. Manta Rays, turtles, schooling fish, reef sharks, colourful reef fish, stingrays and even sea snakes can all be seen. There are many shallow spots for snorkellers to discover.

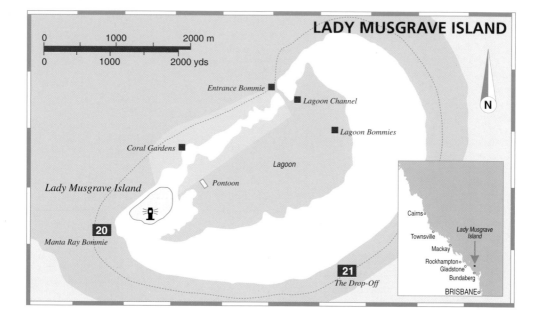

⑳ MANTA RAY BOMMIE

★★★★★✩✩

Location: Western side of Lady Musgrave Island, 110km (70 miles) from Bundaberg.
Access: By boat, 3hr from Bundaberg, 15min from Musgrave Lagoon.
Conditions: Protected by reef, mostly calm, slight currents. Average visibility 20m (65ft).

Minimum depth: 6m (20ft)
Maximum depth: 12m (40ft)
Manta Ray Bommie is one of a number of pinnacles that dominate the reef on the western side of Lady Musgrave Island. The reef is patchy, but pufferfish, anemonefish, shrimps, clown triggerfish, filefish, flutemouth, goatfish and lizardfish abound, and the pinnacles attract a wealth of marine life, including turtles, coral trout, reef sharks, sweetlips, unicornfish, and Manta Rays. Gliding in from the blue like fighter planes, Manta Rays cruise effortlessly over the heads of divers. These rays are definitely the highlight when diving here.

Manta Rays can be seen most of the year.

21 THE DROP-OFF

* * * * *

Location: Southern side of Lady Musgrave Island, 110km (70 miles) from Bundaberg.
Access: By boat, 3hr from Bundaberg, 20min from Musgrave lagoon.
Conditions: Rough in strong winds or large seas, slight currents. Average visibility 20m (65ft).
Minimum depth: 10m (33ft)
Maximum depth: 26m (83ft)
On the southern side of Lady Musgrave Island is a steep reef wall that provides exciting diving anywhere along its length. The reef wall is undercut with numerous ledges and caves packed with baitfish. Parting the baitfish you will find Tasselled Wobbegongs, resting turtles, Painted Crays, stingrays and lionfish. The reef wall and most of the caves are highly decorated with sea whips, black coral trees, gorgonians, sponges, soft corals and *Tubastrea* coral. There is a number of pinnacles off the wall where divers will encounter Olive Sea Snakes, sweet-

lips, coral trout, Estuary Cod, batfish and Maori Wrasse. The wall is patrolled by reef sharks, mackerel, tuna, barracuda and schools of trevally and Rainbow Runners. With a slight current running, this makes for incredible drift diving.

ENCOUNTERS WITH MANTA RAYS

Manta Rays must be the most majestic of all the creatures on the Great Barrier Reef. If you want to be certain of encountering them, Lady Elliot Island is the place to visit. These huge rays are found near the island all year round, either feeding on the surface plankton or hovering over pinnacles waiting to be serviced by a colony of Cleaner Wrasse. Close encounters with Manta Rays are possible when scuba diving or snorkelling, and if you don't chase them or try to ride these gentle giants, they will stay in the vicinity for the entire dive. Divers have been able to play tag with these gentle giants, who peek over the shoulders of underwater photographers or wait to have their bellies scratched.

Heron Island

Heron Island is situated 72km (46 miles) out to sea from the town of Gladstone, 620km (39 miles) north of Brisbane. The largest established dive resort on the Great Barrier Reef, Heron Island Resort was constructed from the remains of the old turtle-processing factory built in the 1940s to exploit the huge numbers of turtles in the surrounding waters. The resort offers a wide range of accommodation, and facilities include a dining room, bar and entertainment complex, pool, dive shop and souvenir shop.

The island is owned and serviced by P&O, which runs regular cruises to and from the island in the giant ocean-going catamaran, *Reef Adventurer*. The boat trip takes approximately 2½ hours. Helicopters also provide an excellent service from Gladstone airport.

Heron Island houses a marine research station and guests are free to visit the research facilities, talk to scientists and maybe learn a little more about the Great Barrier Reef.

The island is an important hatching ground for Green Turtles. From October till March is the turtle-breeding season and visitors can observe this amazing event. Quite often up to 20 turtles at a time come ashore to lay their eggs on any single night.

Although shore snorkelling can be undertaken without supervision, all offshore snorkelling and scuba diving is done from boats. Heron Island Dive Shop has specially constructed dive boats with boat-to-shore communications and all necessary safety equipment. Every dive is accompanied by at least one divemaster and special assistance is provided for inexperienced divers or beginners. There are dozens of dive locations within 15 minutes of the harbour and the divemaster of the day decides, according to prevailing conditions, which is the best location for the day. All dive sites are buoyed and although most dives are stationary, drift diving at some locations is necessary due to strong currents.

MORAY EELS

Moray eels may be shy and retiring normally, but when food is produced, they will usually snap at any object waved near them, be it bait or fingers. At one time hand-feeding of moray eels was popular, but it is now frowned at as they are very aggressive when there is food in the water and too many divers have been bitten. Dozens of species of moray eels are found on the Great Barrier Reef, from the beautiful Blue Ribbon Eel to the giant Leopard Moray which can grow up to 3m (10ft) long. Leopard Morays are the star attraction at many dive sites, but the most famous ones live at The Bommie of Heron Island. These two, named Harry and Fang, may not always be seen, but if in residence will swim right out of their holes to inspect the divers. Some 100 species are found in tropical and subtropical seas around the world. Little is known about their breeding behaviour, but a few species have been observed intertwining and releasing eggs and sperm into the water. The larvae eels drift with the plankton and are clear-bodied and greatly compressed. When they finally settle on a reef, they become rounded.

② HARRY'S BOMMIE

****

Location: Western side of the Heron Island reef, 2km (1 mile) from the boat harbour.

Access: Approximately 10min from the boat harbour at Heron Island.

Conditions: Stationary boat dive, subject to some current, especially on spring tides. Buoyed dive site. Average visibility 10m (33ft).

Minimum depth: 3m (10ft)

Maximum depth: 25m (80ft)

This is a large coral head consisting of several individual structures, with excellent caves and a swim-through which requires care to negotiate as it is narrow and not advised for beginners. Large fish such as coral trout, coral cod, sweetlips, flutemouths and emperors are resident and several angelfish are also present in the area. The surrounding coral growths along the inshore area are luxuriant with reef patches and smaller coral heads are present in the deeper waters as the sand-packed slope meanders down into the channel proper. Often rays and turtles are also seen.

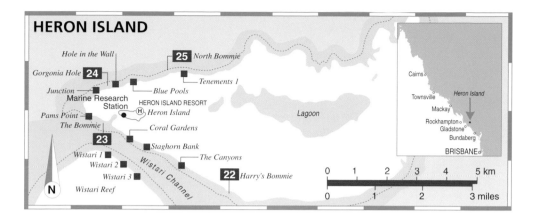

HERON ISLAND

Hole in the Wall
25 *North Bommie*
Gorgonia Hole **24**
Tenements 1
Junction — *Blue Pools*
Marine Research Station
HERON ISLAND RESORT
Pams Point —
The Bommie
(H) *Heron Island*
Coral Gardens
23
Staghorn Bank
Wistari 1
The Canyons
Wistari 2
Wistari 3
22 *Harry's Bommie*
Wistari Channel
Wistari Reef
N

Lagoon

Cairns
Townsville
Heron Island
Mackay
Rockhampton
Gladstone
Bundaberg
BRISBANE

0 1 2 3 4 5 km
0 1 2 3 miles

23 THE BOMMIE

* * * * * * * *

Location: North-western side of the Heron Island reef, 300m (990ft) from the boat harbour.
Access: Approximately 5min from the boat harbour at Heron Island.
Conditions: Stationary boat dive, likely to be a drift dive if the current is too strong during spring tides. Buoyed dive site. Average visibility 10m (33ft).
Minimum depth: 2m (6ft)
Maximum depth: 25m (80ft)
This bommie consists of five coral heads ranging in depth from 3m (10ft) to 25m (80ft). A huge fish-cleaning station, it supports many resident daytime fish, including big schools of hussars, Spangled Emperors, Reticulated Emperors, fusiliers and batfish. Coral cod, pufferfish, firefish, sweetlips, snappers, parrotfish, wrasse, butterflyfish and angelfish abound. Excellent examples of *Tubastrea* corals grow beneath the ledges. Flatworms, nudibranchs, sponges and ascidians occur, and turtles, Eagle Rays and Mantas cruise overhead. There are two 2m- (6ft) long resident Leopard morays and several Tasselled Wobbegong sharks live in the lower caves.

24 GORGONIA HOLE

* * * * * * * *

Location: Northern side of the Heron Island reef opposite the resort, 1km (⅔ mile) from the boat harbour.
Access: Approximately 10min from the boat harbour at Heron Island.
Conditions: Stationary boat dive, drift dive on occasions of big tidal range. Buoyed dive site. Average visibility 10m (33ft).

Minimum depth: 2m (6ft)
Maximum depth: 20m (65ft)
This is one of the nicest dive venues at Heron Island. The buoy is situated among several bommies and reef edge formations, with sea fans and soft corals and lots of feather stars and coral crests. Below are caves and ledges bedecked with marine life in every hue imaginable. Schools of Fairy Basslets flash past like living jewels, and large coral cod and bright orange and red squirrelfish inhabit the labyrinths. Towards the east, orange and red sea fans are quite common, and turtles and rays are regularly observed. There are also serpent stars and a black coral tree.

25 NORTH BOMMIE

* * * * * * * *

Location: Northern side of the Heron Island reef, 2km (1 mile) from the boat harbour.
Access: Approximately 15min from the boat harbour at Heron Island.
Conditions: Stationary boat dive, subject to drift dive when currents are running. Buoyed dive site. Average visibility 10m (33ft).
Minimum depth: 2m (6ft).
Maximum depth: 25m (80ft)
Quite a large complex of free-standing coral heads, the North Bommie is an outstanding dive with prolific marine life, and big schools of fish including goatfish, sweetlips, fusiliers and damsels. There are excellent caves and swim-throughs and the entire area is rather awe-inspiring. Various coloured feather stars can be seen, and under the ledges coral cod, firefish, coral trout, squirrelfish and Barramundi Cod and a multitude of butterflyfish swim in and out of the reef. On the outside the sea floor angles down into deeper water where large rays dig for food in the sandy bottom.

How to Get There

The coast adjacent to the Capricorn and Bunker Groups is commonly known as the Capricorn Coast. The first point of departure is Urangan Harbour at Hervey Bay, a popular holiday destination located 290km (180 miles) north of Brisbane. Just up the coast in the heart of sugarcane country is the town of Bundaberg, 368km (230 miles) north of Brisbane. Gladstone is the final access point to the Capricorn and Bunker Groups. This industrial town and fishing port is 534km (332 miles) north of Brisbane. After arriving in Brisbane you can transfer to Flight West or Sunstate Airlines, which operate flights to these destinations. Coach and train travel are probably more economical if you have time, or you could hire a car and drive up the Bruce Highway. Lock-up facilities are available in all the towns, just ask the dive operators who they use.

Where to Stay

Accommodation on **Lady Elliot Island Resort** ranges from safari tents, bunkhouses which are roomy and comfortable with communal toilets and showers, to self-contained units and deluxe suites sleeping up to six people. Package deals including accommodation, meals, transfers and diving are available. For bookings, contact 167b Bourbong St, Bundaberg, tel 071-516 077, fax 071-531 285.

To camp on **Lady Musgrave Island**, obtain a permit from the State Government Department of Environment & Heritage, 160 Ann Street, Brisbane, tel 07-3227 8186. Campers can travel to Lady Musgrave Island on their own, by charter boat, or on MV *Lady Musgrave*.

Heron Island Resort offers comfortable lodge cabins with communal toilets and showers; reef units are fully self-contained and sleep up to four people, and the Heron and Point units (the most luxurious), sleep two to three. Package deals are available for diving, meals, transfers and accommodation. For bookings contact P&O Resorts, tel 132 469.

There is a good range of accommodation on the Capricorn Coast, from motels to cabins.

Medium price range
Hervey Bay Motel, 518 Esplanade, Urangan, tel 071-289 277, fax 071-253 675, close to Urangan Harbour. Rooms have TV, video player, cooking facilities, and pool.

Bert Hinkler Motor Inn, Takalvan St, Bundaberg, tel 071-526 400, fax 071-513 980, has a pool, spa, half-court tennis, sauna and restaurant.

Country Plaza International, 100 Goondoon St, Gladstone, tel 079-724 499, fax 079-724 921, is a four-star, four-storey complex. Reasonable prices.

Lower price range
Colonial Log Cabin Resort, Pulgul St, Urangan, tel 071-251 844, budget cabins or bunkhouse with a pool, tennis court and barbecue.

Midtown Caravan Park, 61 Takalvan St, Bundaberg, tel 071-522 768, fax 071-512 075, self-contained cabins and units with cooking facilities. Pool and barbecue area.

Clinton Van Park Holiday Village, Dawson Hwy, Gladstone, tel 079-782 718, fax 079-782 718, units, vans or tents at quite good prices. This is a large caravan park complex with a pool, tennis court, laundry and other facilities.

Where to Eat

While Hervey Bay and Bundaberg are holiday towns and have a varied selection of take-away food places and restaurants, the choice in Gladstone is more limited. At Hervey Bay and Bundaberg, Chinese, seafood, Italian, Greek, Indian, and Mexican food are on offer, or cheap meals can be found at pubs. In Gladstone you can choose from French, pub meals, Italian, and Chinese restaurants; a number of the motels have good restaurants.

Dive Facilities

Lady Elliot Island Resort, Booking Office 167b Bourbong St, Bundaberg, tel 071-516 077, fax 071-531 285. The dive shop on the island conducts resort, open-water and specialty courses. They have an extensive range of hire gear, a small retail section and can do limited repairs to dive gear. They offer shore and boat dives, two to three times per day, and several night dives each week.

Heron Island Tourist Resort, P&O Resorts, Via Gladstone tel 079-781 488 fax 079-781 457. Heron Island has a fully-equipped dive store and offers dive courses, boat dives, night dives and adventure dives. They operate four dive boats to local dives sites and nearby reefs. The staff at Heron Island are very professional and well-organised. Holidays on both Lady Elliot and Heron island can be booked through most travel agents.

Lady Musgrave Barrier Reef Cruises, 1 Quay St, Bundaberg, tel 071-529 011, fax 071-524 948, operate daytrips to Lady Musgrave Island every Tuesday, Thursday, Saturday and Sunday and every day during school holidays. Semi-submersible and glass-bottomed boat coral viewing, island walks, lunch and snorkelling, and diving in conjunction with Salty's Dive Team, 22 Quay St, Bundaberg, tel 071-534 747, fax 071-526 707. Book if planning to visit during school holidays.

Charter boats operating to the Capricorn and Bunker Groups include;

Boomerang Cruises, 22 Byron St, Scarness, Hervey Bay, tel 071-242 393.

Spirit of Bundaberg, 39 Baldwin Crs, Bundaberg, tel 071-522 780, offers daytrips.

Sewah Charters, Gayndah Rd, Oakhurst, tel 071-213 155.

Reef Knot Charters, 19 The Esplanade, Gladstone, tel 079-724129.

Booby Bird, Marine Drv, Gladstone, tel 079-726 990, fax 079-726 990.

Australiana, 45 Hickey Ave, Gladstone, tel 079-783 956.

Max Allen Cruises, 7 Illawong Crt, Gladstone, tel 079-791 377.

Diver's Mecca, 472 Esplanade, Hervey Bay, tel 071-251 626.

Bernie's Dive Connection, 382 Esplanade, Hervey Bay, tel 071-241 133.

Bundaberg Scuba Centre, 200 Bourbong St, Bundaberg, tel 071-516 422.

Harris Undersea Services, 44 Higgins St, Gladstone, tel 079-722 784.

Last Wave Watersports, 16 Goondoon St, Gladstone, tel 079-729 185.

Gladstone Reef Charters, Marine Dve, Gladstone, tel 079-725 166 provide island drop-offs for groups wishing to camping on North West, Tryon and Masthead islands.

FILM PROCESSING

E6 processing may be restricted.

HOSPITALS

Bundaberg Health Services, Bourbong St, Bundaberg, tel 071-521 222.

Hervey Bay Hospital, Long St, Point Vernon, tel 071-281 444.

Maryborough General Hospital, 185 Walker Rd, Maryborough, tel 071-238 222.

Gladstone Hospital, Kent St, Gladstone, tel 079-763 200.

For any emergency, fire, police or ambulance tel 000.

For any diving accident anywhere in Australia contact DES (Diving Emergency Service) on 1800 088 200. For more information see Diving Accidents, page 169.

LOCAL HIGHLIGHTS

Hervey Bay is the centre of Australia's whale-watching industry from August to October, when thousands of tourists come to see the Humpback Whales. Sight-ings are guaranteed and on some days the whales come right up to the boats. There are strict guidelines for whale-watching in Australia.

Hervey Bay is the gateway to **Fraser Island**, the largest sand island in the world. Fraser Island is a popular location for camping and four-wheel-drive holidays. The entire island is a national park and home to wildlife such as kangaroos, wallabies, goanna, dingoes and many species of bird. There are magnificent freshwater lakes, huge sand dunes, rainforest, endless beaches and clear fresh-

water streams. Daytrips to Fraser Island can be made from Urangan, or one can hire a 4WD to explore the island.

Bundaberg is the home of Bundaberg Rum, the birthplace of famous Austra-lian aviator Bert Hinkler, and is surroun-ded by sugarcane plantations. In winter there are a number of worthwhile local shore-diving sites, including **Hoffman Rocks**. Visibility isn't always good, but there are plenty of small fish, nudibranchs, sea fans, sea snakes and other creatures. There is a number of boat dives on small reefs and the wreck of a World War II bomber.

The beaches of Bundaberg are inundated with tourists each summer who come to watch the Green and Loggerhead turtles lay their eggs. The nesting sites, especially **Mon Repos**, are some of the most important mainland sites in Australia. Wildlife officers and scientists are generally on hand to ensure that the turtles are not harassed.

Gladstone is an industrial town, with no particular tourist attractions. It is mainly a stepping stone to the reef.

The **Heron Island Dive Festival**, held every second year in November, features night dives on the reef, courses and talks by acclaimed speakers.

Whale-watch ship at sunset in Hervey Bay.

THE KEPPEL ISLANDS

Lying close to the Tropic of Capricorn, the Keppel Islands consist of two large continental island masses, Great Keppel and North Keppel, around which is a number of smaller islands, rocks and reefs. They are located some 520km (325 miles) north of Brisbane and 48km (30 miles) east of Rockhampton, one of Queensland's major provincial cities. The closest coastal township is Yeppoon, 40km (25 miles) northeast of Rockhampton. Much of the coastal area here is national park, as are many of the islands.

The Keppel Islands were first discovered by Captain James Cook on 28 May 1770 and named in honour of Rear Admiral Augustus Keppel. A small band of Aborigines inhabited Great Keppel Island at the time. A homestead was later built by a family called Leeke who grazed sheep on the island from the 1920s to the 1940s.

Today, Great Keppel, the largest in the Keppel Island complex, has a thriving tourist resort which can accommodate up to 500 people. There are cabins and tents at Keppel Haven and camping is available in other designated areas.

The island is serviced daily from the Rosslyn Bay boat harbour near Yeppoon by the Great Keppel Island tourist services catamaran (which lands right on the beach), or by plane from Rockhampton airport to the strip at Great Keppel Island. These flights integrate with normal domestic flights. Undercover parking is available for cars at Rosslyn Bay.

Great Keppel is a large, thickly forested continental island around 7km (4½ miles) long, with 17 beautiful sandy beaches, and a wealth of natural landscape to explore. The resort offers a variety of day and night activities. The islands, rocks and reefs in the Keppel Island complex support fascinating underwater flora and fauna.

Diving and snorkelling can be done everywhere around the islands and reefs. Even the sandy bottoms and soft-bottom trenches between the islands support a great diversity of marine life – it's just a little more difficult to find for the untrained eye. Many excellent sites around Great Keppel Island, such as Egg Rock, Outer Rocks, Hannah Rock and Halfway

Left: The foreshore of Humpy Island, south of Great Keppel Island.
Above: The Keppel Islands are famous for their fringing coral reef formations.

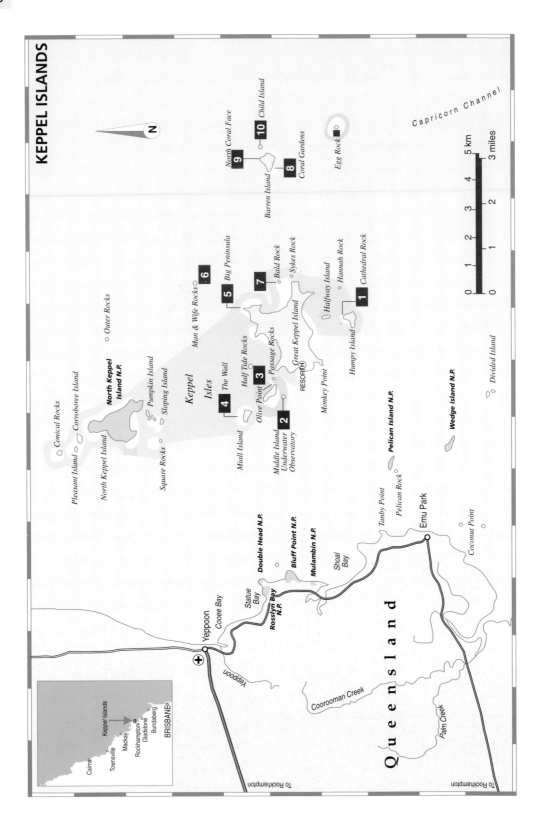

KEPPEL ISLANDS

Island and the islands around North Keppel, are not dived regularly as they are far from the resort or only accessible during slack tides.

Daytrips depart from the mainland at Rosslyn Bay boat harbour in Yeppoon and stop at Great Keppel Island on the way to Barren Island on the inner Barrier Reef. These trips include snorkelling, viewing from a glass-bottomed boat, morning and afternoon tea and a smorgasbord lunch, with scuba diving as an optional extra. Halfday-trips depart from Great Keppel Island. Connections are available from the mainland to the many surrounding reefs and islands in the Keppel Bay.

1 CATHEDRAL ROCK

★★★★☆☆

Location: Eastern side of Humpy Island, 18km (11 miles) from Rosslyn Bay.
Access: Approximately 20min from Great Keppel Island. By charter boat, around 1½hr from the boat harbour at Rosslyn Bay.
Conditions: Stationary boat dive site. No buoys present. Average visibility 15m (50ft).
Minimum depth: 6m (20ft)
Maximum depth: 12m (40ft)
Although not as spectacular as others, this is a nice dive spot. What it lacks in big fish and deep water it makes up for with its beauty and interesting caves, ledges and swim-throughs. The fringing coral reef is not as high as in other locations. Along the ridges and rock formations, encrusted corals and soft corals with egg cowries cover most of the hard bottom. There are many smaller fish beneath the ledges with sponges, ascidians and nudi-branchs on the sides of the gutters. Burrowing clams inhabit the tops of some older coral formations.

2 MIDDLE ISLAND UNDERWATER OBSERVATORY

★★★★

Location: Southwest side of Middle Island, 12km (7 miles) from Rosslyn Bay.
Access: Approximately 20min from Great Keppel Island Resort. By charter boat, around 1½hr from the boat harbour at Rosslyn Bay.
Conditions: Stationary dive from jetty. No buoys present. Average visibility 8m (25ft).
Minimum depth: 6m (20ft)
Maximum depth: 6m (20ft)
Always a good dive, the waters around the Observatory teem with fish. Huge schools of trevally patrol and at feeding time, sergeant majors, wrasse and schools of rabbitfish join in. Several wrecks inhabited by large

Estuary Cod litter the shallow, sandy sea floor. The cod are quite tame and have no qualms about being first to feed, making any dive worthwhile. There are moray eels and resident lionfish as well as a host of smaller fish. Schools of Barrier Reef chromis, a feature of almost every site in the Keppels, abound and groups of sweetlips hang head-first into the slight current.

3 OLIVE POINT

★★★★★☆

Location: Northern side of Middle Island, 12km (7 miles) from Rosslyn Bay.
Access: Approximately 20min from Great Keppel Island. By charter boat, around 1½hr from the boat harbour at Rosslyn Bay.
Conditions: Stationary boat dive site, excellent for beginners. No buoys present. Average visibility 15m (50ft).
Minimum depth: 5m (16ft)
Maximum depth: 14m (45ft)
A luxuriant coral reef peninsula extending from the exposed northern aspect of Middle Island, this fringing reef area has thick stands of staghorn coral and, due to its geography, is easily navigated. Besides schools of resident damsels, there are butterflyfish, angelfish, schools of parrotfish, wrasse, brightly coloured gorgonian sea fans and batfish, and sheltering under the corals on the sandy sea floor, Blue-spotted Fantail Rays. This is a good snorkelling spot.

PARROTFISH

Besides algae and sea grasses, parrotfish eat quantities of dead and living hard corals and, to a lesser extent, soft corals. Dead coral skeletons and coral rock are ideal settling places for filamentous algae which infiltrate the porous surface of coral structures. They also scrape flesh and tissue from the surface of *Porites* corals, bite the ends off staghorn corals and some *Sarcophyton* soft corals.

QUEENSLAND GROPER

The Queensland groper is the largest reef fish, up to
3m (10ft) long and weighing over 250kg (600 pounds).
They are brownish-grey with faint mottled markings

④ THE WALL
* * * * * *

Location: Northern side of Miall Island, 10km (6 miles)
from Rosslyn Bay.
Access: Approximately 20min from Great Keppel Island.
By charter boat, around 1½hr from the boat harbour at
Rosslyn Bay.
Conditions: Stationary boat dive, no buoys present.
Average visibility 15m (50ft).
Minimum depth: 5m (16ft)
Maximum depth: 14m (45ft)
This site has a sloping wall. The bottom has good coral
cover and a wealth of invertebrates, including molluscs,
echinoderms, sponges, sea anemones, zoantharians, sea
fans, and soft corals. Groves of sea whips live on the
sandy fringe in the deepest area where the current is
strongest. As the site is shallow, there is time to look for
smaller creatures such as nudibranchs, flatworms and fan
worms. There are coral trout on the ledges, and resident
leatherjackets, butterflyfish, wrasse and parrotfish.

⑤ BIG PENINSULA
* * * * * *

Location: Northeastern tip of Great Keppel Island, 18km
(11 miles) from Rosslyn Bay
Access: Approximately 20min from Great Keppel Island.
By charter boat, around 1½hr from the boat harbour at
Rosslyn Bay.
Conditions: Stationary boat dive, no buoys present.
Average visibility 15m (50ft).
Minimum depth: 5m (16ft)
Maximum depth: 12m (40ft)
Sheltered by Great Keppel Island, this site can be dived
even during adverse sea conditions. During spring tides
the current can sometimes be strong. Schools of pelagics
such as trevally often patrol the reef. The coral, sea fans
and sea whips are luxuriant and well developed. There
are sea anemones, schools of damsels, parrotfish,
wrasse, goatfish and butterflyfish. On the sand at the
reef edge are flounder, gobies, lots of sea cucumbers
and sand-dwelling sea whips.

⑥ MAN & WIFE ROCKS
* * * * * * * *

Location: Northeast from Great Keppel Island between
Sloping Island and Great Keppel Island, 22km (13 miles)
from Rosslyn Bay.
Access: Approximately 20min from Great Keppel Island.
By charter boat, around 2hr from the boat harbour at
Rosslyn Bay.
Conditions Stationary boat dive, no buoys present.
Average visibility 20m (65ft).
Minimum depth: 6m (20ft)
Maximum depth: 20m (65ft)
Because of its isolated position, this is one of the best
coral dives around the Keppel Islands. It is a beautiful
plateau of rich coral reef with extensive varieties of hard
and soft corals. Staghorn corals are prolific and as some
of these are delicate but quite brittle formations, divers
must take care when finning around. A number of sea
anemones with resident clownfish can be seen here, and
large schools of pelagic fish swim by. There is a drop of
approximately 18m (60ft) at the edge of the plateau,
where large sponges, sea fans, sea snakes and wobbegong sharks can be encountered. Watch out for currents
during spring tides.

⑦ BALD ROCK
* * * * * *

Location: Eastern side of Great Keppel Island, 20km
(12 miles) from Rosslyn Bay
Access: Approximately 20min from Great Keppel Island
By charter boat, around 1½hr from the boat harbour at
Rosslyn Bay.
Conditions: Stationary boat dives, no buoys present.
Average visibility 15m (50ft).
Minimum depth: 6m (20ft)
Maximum depth: 15m (50ft)
There is a fairly large area of shallow fringing reef at this
dive site, with a spectacular array of colourful coral
species, from staghorns to needle corals. Quite a large
section of the area displays prolific colonies of soft corals,
with leathery soft corals, spiky soft corals and sea fans in
residence. Sea anemones with anemonefish are common
and towards the deeper areas, nudibranchs, sponges,
flatworms, ascidians and zoantharians occur. There are
resident schools of reef fish, batfish, angelfish, butterflyfish, leatherjackets, damsels and Monocle Bream.
Underwater photographers have an excellent opportunity
to try their skills here, whether shooting macro photographs of nudibranchs or wide-angle scenes of corals
and fish life.

8 CORAL GARDENS

✲✲✲✲✲✲✲

Location: Southern side of Barren Island, 25km (15 miles) from Rosslyn Bay.
Access: Approximately 40min from the resort at Great Keppel Island. By charter boat, around 2hr from the boat harbour at Rosslyn Bay.
Conditions: Stationary boat dive. No buoys present. Average visibility 20m (65ft).
Minimum depth: 6m (20ft)
Maximum depth: 20m (65ft)
This sheltered cove offers both experienced and novice divers a large area of diverse habitats and interesting marine life. The island rockface drops down to a ledge at around 8m (25ft), where banks of compacted dead staghorn coral form long mounds. These are carpeted with pink and green and blue corallimorphs. At 20m (65ft), coral encrusted boulders with colonies of huge balloon anemones around their bases lie on the coarse coral-sand bottom. There is a large cave with an easy entry and exit, and at high tide, a smaller entrance, which is suitable only for experienced divers, can be negotiated. Schools of butterflyfish and sea cucumbers, sea stars and feather stars can be seen.

9 NORTH CORAL FACE/BARREN ISLAND

✲✲✲✲✲✲✲✲

Location: Northern side of Barren Island, 25km (15 miles) from Rosslyn Bay.
Access: Approximately 40min from Great Keppel Island. By charter boat, around 2hr from the boat harbour at Rosslyn Bay.
Conditions: Stationary boat dive. No buoys present. Average visibility 20m (65ft).
Minimum depth: 6m (20ft)
Maximum depth: 15m (50ft)
It may be barren on top, but underwater it's certainly not! This is a brilliant dive site with giant table corals dominating the landscape all along the steep rockface. Green, blue and purple hard corals, and green, yellow and brown soft corals with egg cowries can be seen everywhere. Schools of golden-striped butterfly-fish, wrasse, parrotfish, leatherjackets, angelfish and families of Long-nosed Butterflyfish forage along the reef. Pink, blue and green beaded corallimorphs grow in sheets over the clumps of dead coral rubble and there are huge balloon anemones in the deeper water. Clams, sea stars, sea cucumbers, sea urchins and bright-red feather stars are seen together with moray eels and sponges.

The Red-margined Glossodoris, discovered in 1969.

10 CHILD ISLAND

✲✲✲✲✲✲✲

Location: Eastern side of Barren Island, 25km (15 miles) from Rosslyn Bay.
Access: Approximately 40min from Great Keppel Island. By charter boat, around 2hr from the boat harbour at Rosslyn Bay.
Conditions: Stationary boat dive. No buoys present. Average visibility 20m (65ft). Some current during spring tides.
Minimum depth: 10m (33ft)
Maximum depth: 30m (100ft)
This is the deepest dive offered by Keppel Reef Scuba Adventures and although the lower depths are suitable only for experienced divers, the magnificent coral forma-tions and shallower waterlife, the Gulch cave, forests of sea whips and many sea fans at the 15m (50ft) level are enough to keep any novice happy. For experienced divers exploring the Gulch drop-off, the large schools of pelagic fish which cruise around the island are really worth see-ing, particularly when they encircle. Giant groper and cod, giant trevally and wobbegong sharks can be found on the bottom, and nudibranchs live on the ledges. Child Island can only be visited during periods of relative calm.

Flatworms may bear a superficial resemblance to nudibranchs, but these belong to an entirely different phylum, Mollusca. Due to their soft bodies and vibrant colours, flatworms and nudibranchs can be difficult to preserve in their natural shape, and their colours almost impossible to retain in alcohol or formalin unless a great deal of care is taken and expertise applied. The best way to see them, therefore, is in their natural habitat and the best way to record them is by close-up photography.

They belong to the phylum Platyhelminthes, which has two classes, Turbellaria and Acoela. Most of the marine flatworms divers see are found in the order Polycladia. There are five main genera, *Pseudoceros, Pseudobiceros, Thysanozoon, Acanthozoon* and *Eurylepta*. They are wafer-thin, bilaterally symmetrical creatures that crawl with a gliding motion; most can also swim.

Flatworms do not have any external gills, although some have marginal folds at the 'head' end which may contain groups of tiny 'eyes' or light receptors. Others have true tentacles further back in the vicinity of the brain. These organisms feed on gorgonians, oysters, tubeworms and bryozoans, sometimes by protruding their pharynx and engulfing their prey; food wastes are expelled from the mouth. Flatworms have no circulatory system and respire by diffusing oxygen into the body from the sea water.

Sex
Flatworms are hermaphrodites with complex male and female sex organs. Mating and cross-fertilisation occur between two individuals. Copulation is quite an interesting event: each flatworm stabs the other anywhere in the body with its sharp penis situated just below the mouth in the 'chest' region. In the genus Pseudobiceros, the penis stylets are paired.

During courtship, the worms may circle each other, crawl all over each other or face up to each other bringing the front part of their bodies up off the bottom 'penis to penis', The body stab leaves quite a hole in the recipient! After copulation, eggs are laid on the substrate, under rocks or coral or near a food source. The flatworm eggs are laid in spiral ribbons which are somewhat similar to those of some nudibranchs and other molluscs.

Linda's Flatworm was first discovered by the author in Papua New Guinea in 1981 and was only described in 1995.

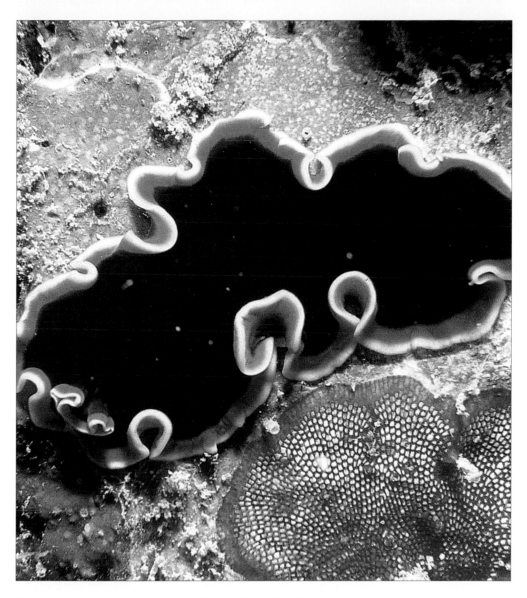

Flatworms are rarely seen by day, but crawl across the reef at night.

Although flatworms don't reproduce asexually, they can reconstruct two flatworms from one bitten in half, and a badly damaged one can re-grow. Sometimes the new growth does not follow the original pattern or design.

Predators
With such fantastic colour patterns and designs, it is thought that some species have toxic properties, and that visual predators such as fish are repelled when trying to eat one for the first time. Older, wiser fish learn either to avoid them, or how to wash out the toxic taste and eat them anyway.

Colour
Few mobile invertebrates exhibit even a fraction of the incredible diversity of colour that flatworms display.

Rockhampton and the nearby town of Yeppoon are the gateways to the Keppel group of islands. Rockhampton is located 726km (450 miles) north of Brisbane. Yeppoon is located 41km (25 miles) northeast of Rockhampton on the shores of Rosslyn Bay. The easiest way to reach Rockhampton is to fly there with one of the regional airlines, Flight West or Sunstate, which offer numerous daily flights. One can also travel by train, coach or motor car, depending on your budget and the time you have available. From Rockhampton to Yeppoon you can use the train or bus service. Fly to Great Keppel Island from Rockhampton airport or catch the launch which leaves several times a day from Yeppoon.

Water sports are some of the great attractions of resorts.

WHERE TO STAY

Great Keppel Island Resort has a range of facilities and accommodation.

The Oceanview Villas have four-star rooms, sleeping two to four, with air-conditioning, TV, refrigerator, washing machine and drier. The garden units and beachfront units sleep two to six people with most of the facilities of the villas except airconditioning. The resort has a restaurant, night club, convention centre, pool, spa, squash and tennis courts, and golf course and offers a range of watersports. Contact Great Keppel Island Resort, PO Box 108, Rockhampton, 4700, tel 079-395 044, fax 079-391 775.

Keppel Haven Resort is a budget resort on Great Keppel Island and offers accommodation in cabins and tents. The cabins are self-contained and sleep up to six, the tents sleep four and have communal toilets and showers. The resort has a restaurant, a camp kitchen and barbecue and numerous watersports are available here. Contact Keppel Haven Resort, tel 079-336 744, fax 079-336 429.

On the mainland there is a wide range of accommodation in the Rockhampton and Yeppoon area.

High Price Range
Capricorn International Resort, Farnborough Rd, Yeppoon, tel 079-395 111, fax. 079-395 666. This large resort offers suites, hotel rooms and apartments. All are airconditioned and have a TV and video player, and the better units have cooking and laundry facilities. The resort has a pool, gym, sauna, tennis court, golf course, restaurant and convention centre, and offers horse riding, archery, catamarans, windsurfing and diving.

Medium Price Range
Cattle City Motor Inn, 139 Gladstone Rd, Rockhampton, tel 079-277 811, fax. 079-225 448. This two-storey complex has a restaurant, pool, convention centre and barbecue area. The rooms are airconditioned and have a TV, video

player, microwave and mini bar. The suites have spa baths.

Bayview Tower, Adelaide St, Yeppoon, tel 079-394 500, fax 079-393 915, offers ocean views and self-contained rooms with TV, video player and airconditioning. There is a restaurant, pool, sauna, spa and convention centre.

Lower Price Range
Southside Caravan Village, Lower Dawson Rd, Rockhampton, tel 079-273 013, fax 079-277 750. The village consists of villas, cabins and on-site van accommodation, with a pool, half-court tennis, kiosk, barbecue, camp kitchen and communal toilets and showers.

Capricorn Palms Holiday Village, Wildin Way, Mulambin Beach, Yeppoon, tel 079-336 144, fax 079-336 266 has villas and cabins which sleep up to seven people, and a pool, spa, kiosk, camp kitchen, barbecue, and communal toilets and showers.

WHERE TO EAT

There is a fine selection of restaurants and take-away places in Rockhampton and Yeppoon on the mainland, where you can choose from a wide variety of cuisines, including Chinese, char grill, Italian, seafood, Indian, French, and Malaysian; you can also have a light meal at a café or pub. Aussie steaks are available at pubs or steak houses.

DIVE FACILITIES

Keppel Reef Scuba Adventures, Great Keppel Island, tel 079-395 022, fax 079-395 022. Keppel Reef Scuba Adventures offer daily trips to local dive sites, and extended trips to the inner reefs. A PADI facility, they offer dive and resort courses, and have a range of retail and hire gear.

Capricorn Reef Diving, 189 Musgrave St, North Rockhampton, tel 079-227 720, fax 079-227 933.

Inner Space Images, 17 Caroline St, Yeppoon, tel 018 458 602.

Rockhampton Diving, 61 High St, North Rockhampton, tel 079-280 433.

Tropicana Dive, 12 Anzac Pde, Yeppoon, tel 079-394642, fax 079-394 662.

Keppel Tourist Services, Rosslyn Bay Boat Harbour, Yeppoon, tel 079-336 744.

Capricorn Coast Charters, 12 Poplar St, Cooee Bay, tel 079-394 949.

FILM PROCESSING

Print film can be processed at a number of camera stores in the area; for E6 processing try **Casey's Cameras**, Denham St, Rockhampton, tel 079-227 331.

HOSPITALS

Rockhampton Hospital, Canning St, Rockhampton, tel 079-316 211.

Yeppoon Hospital, Anzac Pde, Yeppoon, tel 079-393 511.

For any emergency, fire, police or ambulance tel 000

RECOMPRESSION CHAMBER

For any diving accident anywhere in Australia, contact DES (Diving Emergency Service) on 1800 088 200. For more information see 'Diving Accidents', page 169.

LOCAL HIGHLIGHTS

Rockhampton, the beef capital of Australia, probably has more statues of bulls than anywhere else in the world.

Cammoo and **Olsen's Caves** are 22km (14 miles) north of Rockhampton and are definitely worth a visit. There are daily tours to the caves, which have stalagmites, stalactites, fossils and columns formed by thick tree roots.

Other attractions include a crocodile farm, historic cottages and museums, the Mt Morgan copper mine and the Mt Hay Tourist Park where one can buy gems or search for one's own, Children love 'mining' here.

Yeppoon's beaches are peaceful, charming and tree-lined, but its main claim to fame is the World Cooee Championships which are held here each August.

SWAIN REEFS AND POMPEY REEF COMPLEX

The southern end of the Swain Reefs is the start of the real barrier reef wall that runs all the way to Papua New Guinea. This barrier has been a shipping hazard for centuries, from Captain Cook's journeys in 1770 to giant oil tankers operating today. Some safe passages have been charted, but in many areas the reefs are so dense that they remain uncharted and a threat to unwary vessels.

The Swain Reefs and Pompey Reef Complex is one such area. The reefs form an endless maze and most haven't been named. They are a diver's paradise. Nearly all of them offer great year-round diving. Most of the reefs have walls to explore and colourful coral gardens in the shallows, and quite a few have sheltered lagoons that offer safe anchorages and excellent night diving. Marine life is generally rich. Schooling pelagic fish and resident fish are found on most reefs, and divers are also likely to encounter sea snakes, reef sharks, Manta Rays and turtles at certain times of the year. Many of the reefs have small sand cays that are worth a visit. These are generally home to nesting seabirds such as gannets, terns and gulls, and are also the breeding sites of turtles.

The Swain Reefs have been a popular destination for fishermen and divers for over 20 years, while the Pompey Reef Complex is still largely unexplored. Charter boats operating to these areas generally leave from Urangan, Gladstone or Bundaberg, and as most of the reefs are over 200km (125 miles) from the mainland, the trip is usually done overnight. The crossing can get a bit rough but once in the reef system, the waters are calm and sheltered. Drift dives can be done in the currents which sometimes occur between tides. Strong currents can reduce visibility, which varies from 10m (33ft) to 30m (100ft).

The Swain Reefs and Pompey Reef Complex fall within the boundaries of the Great Barrier Reef Marine Park Southern Section (Mackay and Capricorn Sections). Most of the reefs are zoned for general use, but there are preservation areas and a number of reefs have seasonal closures, so keep this in mind when planning your trip.

Left: Sea snakes are a feature of the Swain Reefs.
Above: Kunie's chromodoris nudibranch.

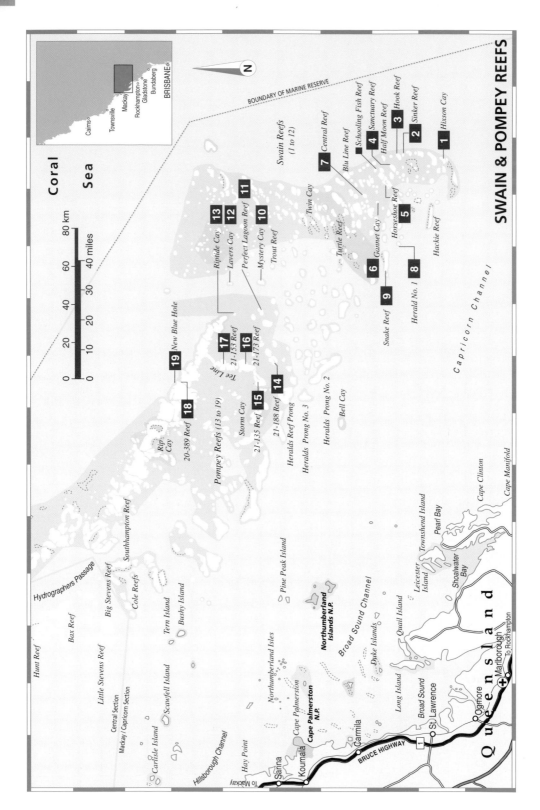

SWAIN & POMPEY REEFS

Swain Reefs

The Swain Reefs have been a popular location for diving and fishing for many years and fishing has certainly taken its toll on popular table fish such as coral trout and sweetlips. The Swain Reefs are very colourful: most of the drop-offs are decorated with soft coral and gorgonians, and you are also likely to find black coral trees, forests of sea whips, delicate hydrocorals and some very large sponges. Sea snakes are common in the area, as are turtles, stingrays, barracuda, trevally, batfish, moray eels and reef sharks. A number of reefs are visited by Manta Rays, and divers have also seen Bottlenose Dolphins, Humpback and Minke whales in the area.

Most of the charter boats only make a few trips to the Swain Reefs each year. There are also no set itineraries, but the majority work around the southern end of the Swain Reefs with sea conditions determining which reefs to explore. Many reefs in the Swains haven't yet been dived, thus making exploratory diving and the chance of finding something really spectacular possible. Dive sites are mostly referred to by their reef name.

◾ HIXSON CAY
★ ★ ★ ★ ★ ☆ ☆

Location: The southern end of the Southern Swain Reefs, 200km (125 miles) from Gladstone.
Access: Over 10hr sailing time from Gladstone.
Conditions: Protected by reef, mostly calm, slight currents. Average visibility 25m (80ft).
Minimum depth: 3m (10ft)
Maximum depth: 60m (200ft)
There is a variety of dive sites around Hixson Cay. At the edge of the reef are drop-offs with gorgonians, soft corals and sea whips. Batfish, reef sharks, mackerel, trevally, fusiliers and sweetlips are common. On the northern side lies a protected lagoon with scattered coral heads. Blue-spotted Fantail Rays, coral trout, angelfish, pufferfish, butterflyfish, filefish and anemonefish are plentiful. Divers are likely to see giant clams, basket stars, tube worms, sea stars, nudibranchs and brilliant flatworms. The lagoon is an excellent anchorage and a pleasant night dive. Snorkellers will find lots to explore.

◾ SINKER REEF
★ ★ ★ ★ ★ ☆ ☆

Location: The eastern edge of the Southern Swain Reefs, 220km (130 miles) from Gladstone.
Access: Over 11hr sailing time from Gladstone.
Conditions: Generally calm as it is protected by the reef. Average visibility 25m (80ft).
Minimum depth: 1m (40in)
Maximum depth: 20m (65ft)

The northern side of Sinker Reef is a maze of coral formations that have created caves, gullies, overhangs and swim-throughs. The coral is very rich in these shallow waters and supports a wide range of reef fish, including angelfish, flutemouth, triggerfish, filefish, wrasse, batfish, anemonefish, damsels and parrotfish. The bottom of the gutters are littered with coral rubble which is home to spider and cone shells, nudibranchs, Mantis Shrimps, hermit crabs and reef octopus. At the edge of the reef, divers are likely to see barracuda, trevally, gropers and shy Whitetip Reef Sharks.

◾ HOOK REEF
★ ★ ★ ★ ★ ☆ ☆

![diving icons]

Location: The eastern edge of the Southern Swain Reefs, 220km (130 miles) from Gladstone.
Access: Over 11hr sailing time from Gladstone.
Conditions: Protected by reef, mostly calm, slight currents. Average visibility 25m (80ft).
Minimum depth: 3m (10ft)
Maximum depth: 20m (65ft)
There is an extensive shallow reef on the northern side of Hook Reef with numerous pinnacles everywhere. The coral is very colourful and there are plenty of fish and other marine creatures, making this a haven for photographers. Estuary Cod, Barramundi Cod, rock cod, coral trout, scorpionfish, unicornfish, parrotfish and fusiliers are common and Olive Sea Snakes search the bottom for food or sleep in the coral. Night dives in the lagoon are wonderful, diving on the sand or on the coral heads that dot the bottom. There are crabs and shrimps of every description, and parrotfish can be seen sleeping in their mucus cocoons. This is also the time when stingrays, sea stars, molluscs and octopuses hunt for food.

4 SANCTUARY REEF

★★★★☆☆

Location: The eastern side of the Southern Swain Reefs, 220km (130 miles) from Gladstone.
Access: Over 11hr sailing time from Gladstone.
Conditions: Protected by reef, mostly calm, slight currents. Average visibility 20m (65ft).
Minimum depth: 3m (10ft)
Maximum depth: 25m (80ft)

The edge of the reef at Sanctuary Reef drops off into deep water. On the drop-off divers will find colourful soft corals, gorgonians, hydroid corals and swaying sea whips. Schools of trevally, fusiliers, sweetlips, batfish, flutemouth, butterflyfish, hawkfish and shy rock cods are usually encountered. Several species of nudibranchs live here. You are also likely to see the destructive Crown-of-Thorns Starfish, but with only a few around there has been little damage to the coral.

CHEMICAL REPELLENTS

Sometimes hunger will drive a fish to a point where it will attempt to eat animals that taste vile. When this happens, the fish instantly spits out the prey, who show hardly a mark, while the predator swims away, often shaking its head and quite noticeably disturbed. Some marine invertebrate chemical repellents are powerful enough to affect a fish's sense of direction and fish have been observed to bump into objects in their path immediately after a taste of the toxin. However, individual fish belonging to at least two families (wrasses and puffers) have learned how to cope with unpalatable invertebrates (such as nudibranchs and flatworms). By repeatedly mouthing and spitting out the invertebrate, the fish eventually succeeds in causing the invertebrate to exude all its chemical repellent into the water. When the invertebrate has been washed clean, the fish is finally able to swallow its prey.

The Splendid Reef Crab is generally only seen during night dives.

5 HORSESHOE REEF
★★★★

Location: In the centre of the Southern Swain Reefs, 220km (130 miles) from Gladstone.
Access: Over 11hr sailing time from Gladstone.
Conditions: Protected by reef, mostly calm, slight currents. Average visibility 20m (65ft).
Minimum depth: 3m (10ft)
Maximum depth: 35m (115ft)
The southern side of Horseshoe Reef offers exciting wall diving. Colourful corals, including spiky soft coral, sea whips, gorgonians and a variety of hard corals decorate the wall. Small reef fish are abundant and you are likely to see Whitetip Reef Sharks, Estuary Cod, Maori Wrasse, trevally, batfish and large coral trout. Green Turtles sleep in ledges and sea snakes glide by. On the northern side the large, sheltered lagoon is a popular anchorage. Night diving is interesting, with many coral heads to explore. By torchlight divers will see coral crabs, shrimps, brittle stars, molluscs, sea cucumbers, tube worms, anemones, small cuttlefish, squid, and Blue-spotted Fantail Rays.

6 GANNET CAY
★★★★

Location: In the centre of the Southern Swain Reefs, 230km (140 miles) from Gladstone.
Access: Over 11hr sailing time from Gladstone.
Conditions: Generally calm as protected by reef, slight currents. Average visibility 20m (65ft).
Minimum depth: 3m (10ft)
Maximum depth: 35m (115ft)
There is a large pinnacle covered in gorgonians, soft corals, black coral trees and masses of sea whips on the southern side. The pinnacle also attracts fish like a magnet – common here are barracuda, coral trout, rock cod, trevally, mackerel, fusiliers, surgeonfish, batfish and Whitetip Reef Sharks. The usual reef fish are in abundance and sea snakes may also occasionally be seen.

7 CENTRAL REEF
★★★★★★★

Location: The eastern side of the Southern Swain Reefs, 230km (140 miles) from Gladstone.
Access: Over 11hr sailing time from Gladstone.
Conditions: Mainly calm as protected by reef, slight currents. Average visibility 20m (65ft).

Spine-cheek Anemonefish rarely leave the protection of their sea anemone hosts.

Minimum depth: 3m (10ft)
Maximum depth: 35m (115ft)
Central Reef offers many good wall dives. The walls are covered with gorgonians, sea whips and brightly coloured soft corals. The fish life is prolific and includes batfish, mackerel, sweetlips, coral trout, rock cod, hogfish, flutemouth, angelfish and parrotfish. At the top many gutters cut into the reef, creating an interesting environment in which to explore. Painted Crays, stingrays, sweetlips, wrasse, butterflyfish and small moray eels are plentiful.

8 HERALD NO. 1
★★★★★★★

Location: The western side of the Southern Swain Reefs, 200km (125 miles) from Gladstone.
Access: Over 10hr sailing time from Gladstone.
Conditions: Protected by reef, mostly calm, slight currents. Average visibility 20m (65ft).
Minimum depth: 6m (20ft)
Maximum depth: 40m (130ft)
There is quite a good wall to be explored on the western side of Herald No. 1. Schooling fish are quite common and include surgeonfish, unicornfish, batfish, parrotfish, fusiliers, and baitfish. Also seen are giant Maori Wrasse, coral trout, mackerel, Painted Crays, and small Green Turtles. The wall is very colourful and provides endless photographic opportunities.

GIANT CLAMS

Giant clams belong to the family of bivalve molluscs called Tridacnidae and there are six species living on the Great Barrier Reef. The Giant clam is the largest known species of bivalve in the world and grows to a size of 137cm (4ft 6in). The shell valves alone can weigh as much as 240kg (580 pounds). Giant clams are sequential simultaneous hermaphrodites, which means that they begin their lives as males and become both sexes when mature. Although large, records of the clam's danger to divers are exaggerated, despite the fact that the valve edges are razorsharp and can inflict painful cuts. Research has shown that they grow faster than was assumed, raising the possibility of mariculture for future commercial exploitation.

9 SNAKE REEF
* * * * * * *

Location: The western side of the Southern Swain Reefs, 200km (125 miles) from Gladstone.
Access: Over 10hr sailing time from Gladstone.
Conditions: Protected by reef, mostly calm, slight currents. Average visibility 20m (65ft).
Minimum depth: 3m (10ft)
Maximum depth: 40m (130ft)
Snake Reef is a long, narrow reef with many drop-offs. On the western side there is a number of pinnacles attached to the wall and the gutters and ledges are certainly worth exploring. Gardens of sea whips and many large gorgonians can be found beyond 20m (65ft). Fish life is very good and includes batfish, coral trout, scorpionfish, sweetlips, angelfish and rock cod.

10 MYSTERY CAY
* * * * * * *

Location: The centre of the Swain Reefs, 250km (150 miles) from Gladstone.
Access: Over 12hr sailing time from Gladstone.
Conditions: Protected by reef, mostly calm, slight currents. Average visibility 20m (65ft).
Minimum depth: 3m (10ft)
Maximum depth: 20m (65ft)
The western side of Mystery Cay is a popular anchorage and a good dive site as there are many pinnacles and canyons that cut into the reef. Fish life is quite rich and common species include trevally, batfish, reef sharks, coral trout, sweetlips, parrotfish, flutemouth, angelfish and anemonefish. Giant turrum, schools of bonito, or even a Maori Wrasse are found here. Olive Sea Snakes are common and safe to dive with as long as they aren't harassed. On the southern side of the reef are more pinnacles, occasionally visited by Manta Rays waiting to be cleaned by the local population of Cleaner Wrasse. When the Manta Rays are around, this can be one of the best dives in the Swain Reef system as they seem to take great joy in swimming circles and even somersaulting over divers, and will stay in the area long after you have run out of air.

11 PERFECT LAGOON REEF
* * * * * *

Location: The western side of the Northern Swain Reefs, 250km (150 miles) from Gladstone.
Access: Over 12hr sailing time from Gladstone.
Conditions: Protected by reef, mostly calm, slight currents. Average visibility 20m (65ft).
Minimum depth: 3m (10ft)
Maximum depth: 20m (65ft)
Forests of staghorn coral dominate the reef edge on the northern side of Perfect Lagoon Reef. A variety of molluscs can be seen including spider shells, cowries, cone shells and clams with brightly coloured mantles. Mainly small reef species are present, like damsels, gobies, blennies, wrasse, butterflyfish, rock cod, hawkfish and hogfish. It is a good spot to encounter Olive Sea Snakes, and up to a dozen can be seen here at once.

12 LAVERS CAY
* * * * * * * *

Location: The western side of the Northern Swain Reefs, 250km (150 miles) from Gladstone.
Access: Over 12hr sailing time from Gladstone.
Conditions: Protected by reef, mostly calm, slight currents. Average visibility 20m (65ft).
Minimum depth: 3m (10ft)
Maximum depth: 20m (65ft)
The northeast corner of Lavers Cay reef is riddled with canyons, gutters, ledges and caves. While the hard and soft coral growth is quite impressive, the fish life is even more so. Two resident giant groper over 2m (6ft) long can usually be seen. They hide in the gutters and can be quite shy if divers try to take photos. Schools of turrum, trevally and bonito charge over the reef hoping to catch some of the masses of baitfish. Also common are coral trout, angelfish, batfish, parrotfish, squirrelfish, surgeonfish and Whitetip Reef Sharks.

Pompey Reef Complex

Joining onto the northern end of the Swain Reefs is the little-dived Pompey Reef Complex. Navigating this area is a nightmare, as great volumes of water pass through the reefs forming giant 'rivers'. These 'rivers' can be over 80m (260ft) deep between reefs that are only 200m (660ft) wide. It can be quite spectacular boating as you pass whirlpools, standing waves, waterfalls and rapids. The southern end of the Pompey Reef Complex is dominated by the Tee Line, a group of tightly packed reefs in the shape of a giant 'T'. While much of the diving is similar to the Swain Reefs, there is a lot more fish life as this area hasn't been as heavily fished. There are two blue holes to explore, although only New Blue Hole is worth a dive as the other, known as Cockatoo Blue Hole, is more like a stagnant pond. Very few trips are made to the Pompey Reef Complex because of the distance and unknown nature of the area. If they take place, they are usually combined with a trip to the northern end of the Swain Reefs.

Divers often encounter huge schools of colourful reef fish on the reefs.

13 RIPTIDE CAY

Location: The south end of the Pompey Reef Complex, 250km (150 miles) from Gladstone.
Access: Over 14hr sailing time from Gladstone.
Conditions: Protected by reef, mostly calm, strong currents. Average visibility 20m (65ft).
Minimum depth: 3m (10ft)
Maximum depth: 15m (50ft)
The northern side of this cay has a patchy coral bottom with many small coral heads and pretty coral gardens. The cay can really live up to its name and is best dived at low or high tide because the strong currents can make diving impossible between tides. Because of these currents the fish life is quite good and includes coral trout, bonito, sweetlips, boxfish, Rainbow Runners, fusiliers, rabbitfish, angelfish and schools of parrotfish. You are also likely to find Blue-spotted Fantail Rays, a variety of sea stars and nudibranchs, and many Painted Crays.

14 21–188 REEF

Location: The south end of the Pompey Reef Complex, 250km (150 miles) from Gladstone.
Access: Over 14hr sailing time from Gladstone.
Conditions: Protected by reef, mostly calm, slight currents. Average visibility 20m (65ft).
Minimum depth: 3m (10ft)
Maximum depth: 35m (115ft)
Most of the reefs in the Pompey Reef Complex don't have names, only reference numbers. There is an impressive drop-off covered in healthy hard and soft coral on the western side of 21–188 Reef. Small reef fish are plentiful and schools of baitfish cover the wall. Trevally and mackerel speed up and down the reef hoping to part the baitfish so they can pick off individuals. Divers will also see coral trout, angelfish, lionfish, flutemouth and perhaps a few Olive Sea Snakes.

15 21–135 REEF

Location: On the Tee Line of the Pompey Reef Complex, 250km (150 miles) from Gladstone.
Access: Over 14hr sailing time from Gladstone.
Conditions: Protected by reef, mostly calm. Average visibility 15m (50ft).
Minimum depth: 3m (10ft)
Maximum depth: 15m (50ft)
On the northeast corner of 21–135 Reef there is a shallow coral bay with small coral walls and pinnacles. The coral growth here is incredibly rich and includes spiky soft coral, gorgonians, sea whips, staghorn coral, plate coral and bottlebrush coral, as well as sponges and ascidians. Reef fish abound – batfish, surgeonfish, filefish, tuskfish, angelfish, butterflyfish, rabbitfish and gobies, amongst others. A number of giant clams also live here. Olive Sea Snakes are quite common and being short-sighted, they will come straight up to divers to give them a thorough inspection.

16 21–173 REEF

Location: On the Tee Line of the Pompey Reef Complex, 250km (150 miles) from Gladstone.
Access: Over 14hr sailing time from Gladstone.
Conditions: Protected by reef, mostly calm. Average visibility 15m (50ft).
Minimum depth: 3m (10ft)
Maximum depth: 12m (40ft)
21–173 Reef has a small sheltered lagoon that is covered in coral growth. There are many small ledges in the coral where crabs, shrimps and even Painted Crays can be found. This is quite a good location for macro photography and divers are likely to find flatworms, nudibranchs, feather stars, sea stars, molluscs, brittle stars and many small reef fish. Sea snakes are as common here as on most of the Pompey Reef Complex.

17 21–153 REEF

Location: On the Tee Line of the Pompey Reef Complex, 250km (150 miles) from Gladstone.
Access: Over 14hr sailing time from Gladstone.
Conditions: Protected by reef, mostly calm. Average visibility 15m (50ft).
Minimum depth: 3m (10ft)
Maximum depth: 15m (50ft)
The north side of 21–153 Reef offers a large sheltered lagoon for anchorage and diving. The sandy lagoon floor is covered with many coral heads, home to crabs, shrimps, brittlestars, nudibranchs, feather stars and a variety of molluscs. The fish here are generally small and boxfish, pufferfish, damsels, gobies and blennies are the most common. At night a wide assortment of creatures can be seen, from sleeping reef fish to many colourful invertebrates.

The Swain Reefs are rich with coral and marine life.

---

18 20-389 REEF

★ ★ ★ ★ ★ ★ ★

Location: The eastern side of the Pompey Reef Complex, 250km (150 miles) from Gladstone.
Access: Over 14hr sailing time from Gladstone.
Conditions: Generally calm in most conditions, slight currents. Average visibility 20m (65ft).
Minimum depth: 3m (10ft)
Maximum depth: 25m (80ft)

There is a number of good dive sites on 20-389 Reef, including a small basin lagoon on the southern side which has prolific coral growth. There are many small caves and overhangs to explore, most of which are lined with gorgonians and soft corals. Anemones with their resident anemonefish are common, as are large volcano sponges. Whitetip Reef Sharks, stingrays, batfish, sweetlips, snapper, rock cod, tuskfish, surgeonfish and coral trout are just some of the fish that can be seen. At night, all the small creatures of the reef appear: molluscs, sea stars, brittle stars, shrimps, crabs, flat worms, sea urchins and hermit crabs. Giant basket stars stretch their arms to catch food particles, and sea snakes patrol the bottom for sleeping fish to eat. On the eastern side of the reef, which is a bit more exposed, there are many pretty coral gardens. Small reef fish are abundant, but divers will also see trevally, coral trout, Blue-spotted Fantail Rays, reef sharks, flutemouth and the odd moray eel.

19 NEW BLUE HOLE

★ ★ ★ ★ ★ ★ ★ ★

Location: The southern end of 20-389 Reef in the Pompey Reef Complex, 250km (150 miles) from Gladstone.
Access: Over 14hr sailing time from Gladstone.
Conditions: Protected by reef, mostly calm. Average visibility 20m (65ft).
Minimum depth: 3m (10ft)
Maximum depth: 90m (300ft)

This fascinating dive site is rarely visited by charter boats. The hole is some 100m (330ft) in diameter, with sheer walls that start to undercut at 50m (165ft) to the bottom at 90m (300ft). While this is well beyond the range of the average diver, the upper reaches can easily be dived by anyone. Some of the many small caves are overflowing with gorgonians and hydrocoral. While the hole itself is sparsely decorated with corals, a number of leaf and thorny oysters can be seen. Sand and sediment can be dislodged from the walls making photography difficult. There is plenty to see down to 45m (150ft) and the hole can easily be circumnavigated as you make your way up. Fish life is surprisingly good, and Whitetip Reef Sharks, batfish, coral trout, squirrelfish and trevally can be found. There are pretty coral gardens in the vicinity where more fish can be seen – unicornfish, Rainbow Runners, parrotfish, hogfish, Maori Wrasse, sweetlips and sharks.

Divers will encounter several species of sharks on the Great Barrier Reef and the Coral Sea. The most abundant species is the Whitetip Reef Shark which patrols the reef and can be found resting in caves. Other cave residents are Tasselled Wobbegong sharks and large Tawny Nurse Sharks, which are generally harmless if left alone. At night, beautifully marked Epaulette Sharks emerge to feed on crabs, worms and shrimps. Growing to a metre (3ft) in length, they almost walk on their fins while crossing the reef. Grey Reef Sharks and Silvertip Sharks are more common in the Coral Sea on drop-offs, and usually come in for shark feeds. Other species of shark seen on the reef include Whale Sharks, Blacktip Reef Sharks, Leopard Sharks, Bull Sharks, Tiger Sharks, Great Hammerheads and even schools of Scalloped Hammerheads.

A Whitetip Reef Shark cruises the reef.

SHARK FEEDS

Shark feeds are a popular attraction in the Northern Coral Sea. A number of operators conduct these controlled feeding displays to bring the sharks in closer, especially for photos. Sharks may no longer be fed by hand. Operators bring the bait down by remote control in large bins, bags or on a rope. You can view sharks from a cage but most divers simply stay a safe distance away, with the crew acting as safety divers. The main species attracted to shark feeds are Whitetip Reef Sharks, Grey Reef Sharks and Silvertip Sharks and the odd Tiger and Great Hammerhead. It is argued that feeding the sharks makes them more aggressive and dangerous. This is true while there is bait in the water, but the sharks are only interested in the bait and quickly leave once they have eaten, much to the annoyance of most divers. A shark feed provides an unrivalled opportunity to see sharks close up

WOBBEGONG SHARKS

There are six species of wobbegong shark in Australian waters, and three have been found on the reef. These bottom-dwelling sharks with their highly patterned skin and flattish bodies are also known as carpet sharks. The most common species on the reef is the Tasselled Wobbegong, which has a light brown or sand-coloured skin, perfectly camouflaging it on the bottom, be it coral or sand. Up to 3m (10ft) long, the Tasselled Wobbegong spends most of its life resting in caves or under ledges. Don't be fooled by their docile appearance, they have very fast reflexes and a set of long, sharp teeth which they will use if provoked. Sometimes it is hard to avoid an encounter, especially if you find yourself face-to-face with one in a dark cave! So always check the bottom of caves before entering, and if left alone, wobbies can be observed and photographed at close quarters.

MATING SHARKS

Sharks mate mostly at night. The male must position his claspers in the oviduct of the female without the aid of arms or legs. He bites into the female's neck, head, gills, side, dorsal fin, back or pectoral fin, and once he has a grip, twists his body around the female's until, after a rather spectacular amount of rolling and thrashing, the pair become quiet and lay in a twisted encouplement for some time.

Many sharks and rays are oviparous, which means that the egg is held within the female's body till the young hatch. The newly-hatched fish stay within the body of the female until the remnants of the yolk sac have been absorbed.

HOW TO GET THERE

A number of charter boats visit the Swain Reefs each year but very few visit the Pompey Reef Complex. To visit these areas you can arrange your own charter or join a group or dive shop that has booked a boat. Charter boats visiting these reefs generally leave from Hervey Bay, Bundaberg and Gladstone. Hervey Bay is 290km (180 miles), Bundaberg 368km (230 miles), and Gladstone 534km (332 miles) north of Brisbane. After flying to Brisbane, you can transfer to any of these destinations on Flight West or Sunstate Airlines. Coach and train travel are probably the most economical if you have the time, or you can hire a car and drive up the Bruce Highway along the coast. Lock-up facilities are available in all towns – ask the dive operator for details.

WHERE TO STAY

If you wish to stay on the mainland before or after your charter trip to the Swain Reefs you will find a good range of accommodation available in Hervey Bay, Bundaberg and Gladstone. For a brief run-down on what is available, refer to the Capricorn and Bunker Group Regional Directory.

WHERE TO EAT

If you stay on the mainland you will never run out of places to eat as there are many take-away places, pubs which serve meals and fine restaurants.

DIVE FACILITIES

Australiana, 45 Hickey Ave, Gladstone, tel 079-783 956. *Australiana* is a 19m- (62ft) long motor vessel that can carry 16 passengers. She can be chartered for trips to the Swain Reefs, the Capricorn and Bunker Groups and the Southern Coral Sea.

Booby Bird, Marine Drv, Gladstone, tel 079-726 990, fax 079-726 990. *Booby Bird* is available for charter throughout the year, running trips to the Swain Reefs, Capricorn Group, Bunker Group and Southern Coral Sea. She is a 24m- (77ft) long motor vessel and can carry 21 passengers.

Boomerang Cruises, 22 Byron St, Scarness, Hervey Bay, tel 071-242 393. *Boomerang* is a 21m- (70ft) long vessel which can carry 22 passengers. She operates to areas at the southern end of the Swain Reefs, and to the Bunker Group and Southern Coral Sea.

Max Allen Cruises, 7 Illawong Crt, Gladstone, tel 079-791 377, operate the charter boats *Kanimbla* and *Spirit of Freedom*. They are both available for charter and do trips to the Swain Reefs, Capricorn Group, Bunker Group and Southern Coral Sea.

Reef Knot Charters, 19 The Esplanade, Gladstone, tel 079-724 129. *Reef Knot* is a 15m (52ft) motor vessel set up for fishing and diving. *Reef Knot* runs charter trips year round to the Swain Reefs and the Capricorn and Bunker Groups.

Sewah Charters, Gayndah Rd, Oakhurst, Bundaberg, tel 071-213 155. *Sewah* is a 15m- (50ft) long vessel which can carry 12 passengers. She runs trips to the Swain Reefs and Capricorn and Bunker Groups.

FILM PROCESSING

There are many camera and photo stores on the mainland.

HOSPITALS

Bundaberg Health Services, Bourbong St, Bundaberg, tel 071-521 222.

Hervey Bay Hospital, Long St, Point Vernon, tel 071-281 444.

Maryborough General Hospital, 185 Walker Rd, Maryborough, tel 071-238 222.

Gladstone Hospital, Kent St, Gladstone, tel 079-763 200.

For any emergency, fire, police or ambulance tel 000.

RECOMPRESSION CHAMBER

For any diving accident anywhere in Australia, contact DES (Diving Emergency Service) on 1800 088 200. For more information, see 'Diving Accidents', page 169. As part of their survey requirements, all dive charter boats must carry oxygen and know how to handle diving accidents.

LOCAL HIGHLIGHTS

There are a a number of activities and sights to see in Hervey Bay, Bundaberg or Gladstone. For a brief rundown of the local highlights, refer to the Capricorn and Bunker Group Regional Directory on page 46.

Sharks can often be encountered off the reef.

THE SOUTHERN CORAL SEA

The Coral Sea is without doubt one of the most exciting dive locations in the world today. Once the peaks of ancient mountains, these reefs rise steeply from the depths in crystal-clear water which is home to a diverse range of marine life. Extending east from Australia and New Guinea and merging with the Tasman Sea in the south, the Coral Sea covers an area of 4 791 000km² (1 886 000 sq miles).

The Southern Coral Sea is far less visited than the popular Northern Coral Sea. Only a handful of charter boats visit these reefs each year and there is still much to be explored. There are generally no set dive sites, moorings, shops or facilities, only wilderness and exciting diving. Saumarez and Marion Reefs are probably the most popular of all the reefs in the Southern Coral Sea. Their large lagoons are scattered with hundreds of pinnacles and many exciting dive sites have been found. Frederick and Wreck reefs also offer many fascinating dive sites. Cato and Kenn reefs are the most remote of the Southern Coral Sea reefs and have therefore hardly been touched.

The coral in the Southern Coral Sea is generally unexciting, but divers don't come all this way just to look at the coral, it's the marine life that will be long remembered, especially the sea snakes. The Southern Coral Sea is the kingdom of the sea snake. At least five species are found here, and on each dive you will encounter a dozen or more snakes. Besides sea snakes, divers will find masses of reef fish, turtles, schools of pelagic fish, a wide variety of molluscs and invertebrates and, of course, sharks.

A visit to the Southern Coral Sea can be difficult to organise. Few charter boats visit the region because of the distance and the off-chance of being caught in bad weather far from home. Charter boats from Urangan, Gladstone, Airlie Beach and Townsville occasionally make exploratory trips. One can, of course, form a group and charter a boat (with an experienced skipper who has visited the area before) to take you to these remote reefs. Either way, you will have a fantastic adventure in untouched, unexplored territory.

Left: With visibility often over 60m (200ft), snorkelling in the Southern Coral Sea is always enjoyable.
Above: Harlequin Tuskfish often follow divers around.

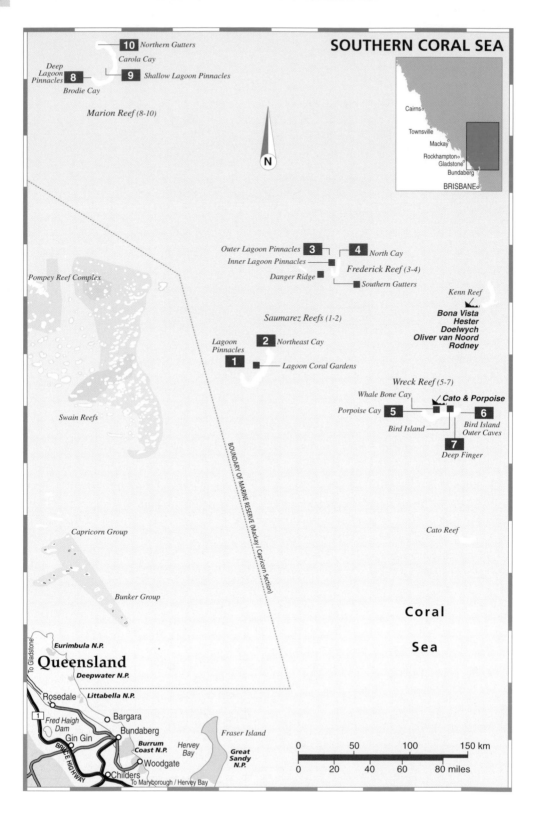

SOUTHERN CORAL SEA

10 Northern Gutters

Carola Cay

Deep Lagoon Pinnacles **8**

9 Shallow Lagoon Pinnacles

Brodie Cay

Marion Reef (8-10)

Cairns

Townsville

Mackay

Rockhampton

Gladstone

Bundaberg

BRISBANE

N

Outer Lagoon Pinnacles **3**

4 North Cay

Inner Lagoon Pinnacles

Danger Ridge

Frederick Reef (3-4)

Southern Gutters

Kenn Reef

**Bona Vista
Hester
Doelwych
Oliver van Noord
Rodney**

Pompey Reef Complex

Saumarez Reefs (1-2)

Lagoon Pinnacles

2 Northeast Cay

1

Lagoon Coral Gardens

Wreck Reef (5-7)

Whale Bone Cay

Cato & Porpoise

Porpoise Cay **5**

6

Bird Island

Bird Island Outer Caves

7

Deep Finger

Swain Reefs

Cato Reef

Capricorn Group

BOUNDARY OF MARINE RESERVE (Mackay / Capricorn Section)

Coral

Sea

Bunker Group

To Gladstone

Eurimbula N.P.

Queensland

Deepwater N.P.

Rosedale

Littabella N.P.

1 Fred Haigh Dam

Bargara

Gin Gin

Bundaberg

Burrum Coast N.P.

Hervey Bay

Fraser Island

BRUCE HIGHWAY

Woodgate

Great Sandy N.P.

Childers

To Maryborough / Hervey Bay

| 0 | | 50 | | 100 | | 150 km |

| 0 | 20 | 40 | 60 | 80 miles |

Saumarez Reefs

The Saumarez Reefs are over 30km (20 miles) long and located more than 300km (200 miles) from mainland Australia. It is easy to see the reef from a great distance as there is a lighthouse on one of its coral cays, but by far the most prominent feature is the wreck of the *Francis Preston Blair*. This massive American liberty ship sits high and dry on the reef top, having been run aground by its captain during World War II in 1945 after being stalked by a Japanese submarine. It is a pity this ship is not submerged as it would make a fascinating wreck dive, but there is still plenty to see. The reefs are colourful, healthy and support a rich diversity of fish and invertebrate life. On nearly every dive you will encounter sea snakes, turtles, reef sharks, stingrays and masses of fish.

Saumarez Reefs are visited by a few charter boats each year and although there are no set dive sites, there are a number that are popular, and many more waiting to be discovered.

▣ LAGOON PINNACLES
★★★★

Location: The northern side of Saumarez Reefs, 300km (200 miles) from Gladstone.
Access: Over 17hr sailing time from Gladstone and Urangan.
Conditions: Generally calm, protected by reef. Average visibility 40m (130ft).
Minimum depth: 12m (40ft)
Maximum depth: 30m (100ft)
There are large pinnacles on the outer edge of the lagoon at Saumarez Reefs which are generally covered in a lush growth of hard and soft corals, long sea whips and some large gorgonian fans. Many are cut with caves and ledges where squirrelfish, pufferfish, Painted Crays, rock cod and well-camouflaged Tasselled Wobbegong sharks can be found. A variety of reef fish add splashes of colour – Fairy Basslets, angelfish, damsels, Blue Tangs, flutemouth and masses of butterflyfish are all commonly seen. The larger fish are spectacular. Lone barracuda drift slowly by, while schools of trevally and surgeonfish dart in and out of the pinnacles, and jobfish and mackerel patrol the outskirts of the pinnacles. Dozens of Olive and Banded sea snakes are encountered at every turn and provide excellent photographic subjects.

▤ NORTHEAST CAY
★★★★★★★★★

Location: The eastern side of Saumarez Reefs, 300km (200 miles) from Gladstone.
Access: Over 17hr sailing time from Gladstone and Urangan.

Conditions: Generally calm, protected by reef. Average visibility 40m (130ft).
Minimum depth: 2m (6ft)
Maximum depth: 20m (65ft)
Along the northwestern side of North East Cay lies an extensive coral garden cut with many deep gutters and caves. The diving here is incredible, the coral rich and varied and the marine life plentiful and exciting. Schools of trevally, Rainbow Runners, surgeonfish, fusiliers and drummer sweep the reef, while below, masses of reef fish swarm over the coral and duck for cover when the predator fish get too close. Blue-spotted Stingrays skip across the sand gutters, sea snakes search the coral for food, turtles cruise the gutters, and barracuda, Maori Wrasse, coral trout and jobfish patrol the reef. Many of the caves are lined with bright hydroid corals, twisted sea whips and beautiful *Tubastrea* corals. Marine life sheltering in the caves includes sweetlips, batfish, black blotched stingrays, Tasselled Wobbegongs, Painted Crays and huge Tawny Nurse Sharks. Small invertebrates and molluscs are quite common and colourful, and will thrill macro photographers. You may also encounter reef sharks, Spotted Eagle Rays and the odd Tiger Shark.

Sea snakes are regular diving companions.

Frederick Reef

Frederick Reef is rarely visited by charter boats, but it is well worth the effort as there is a good variety of marine life and plenty to explore. The reef is over 10km (6 miles) long and there is a long sand cay at its northern end. This cay is no more than 100m (330ft) long and 10m (33ft) wide, but is home to thousands of terns and gannets. Terns eggs are hidden everywhere in the coral rubble and are very hard to see, so each step should be taken with care. Apart from the noisy birds, the cay is dominated by a rocket-shaped lighthouse which is definitely one of the most unusual lighthouse structures in Australia.

With no named dive sites, Frederick Reef offers plenty of exploratory dives. Some will be average, others spectacular, but they will never be dull as there are sea snakes and abundant fish all around the reef.

The rocket-like lighthouse at Frederick Reef.

❸ OUTER LAGOON PINNACLES

★ ★ ★ ★ ★ ★ ★

Location: The northern side of Frederick Reef, 350km (220 miles) from Gladstone.
Access: Over 20hr sailing time from Gladstone and Urangan.
Conditions: Generally calm, sheltered by reef. Average visibility 40m (130ft).
Minimum depth: 10m (33ft)
Maximum depth: 30m (100ft)
The shape of Frederick Reef forms a sheltered lagoon on its northern side. This lagoon is dotted with pinnacles from deep to shallow water. Some of the deep-water pinnacles are covered with sea whips, gorgonians and hard and soft corals, and a few even have large volcano sponges attached to them. Smaller reef fish such as flutemouth, butterflyfish, wrasse, triggerfish, damsels and Fairy Basslets are common. Sea snakes are prolific, and you may also encounter reef sharks, stingrays and shy Estuary Cod. Pelagic fish are also attracted to these pinnacles. Schools of fusiliers, drummer and trevally fly past while mackerel, jobfish and the odd barracuda patrol the area. The clear Coral Sea water is ideal for snorkelling.

❹ NORTH CAY

★ ★ ★ ★ ★ ★ ★

Location: The northern end of Frederick Reef, 350km (220 miles) from Gladstone.
Access: Over 20hr sailing time from Gladstone and Urangan.
Conditions: Generally calm, sheltered by reef. Average visibility 40m (130ft).
Minimum depth: 6m (20ft)
Maximum depth: 20m (65ft)
Off North Cay there is an extensive coral garden consisting of gutters, ridges and pinnacles of healthy hard corals. Small reef fish and colourful invertebrates abound on the reef, making it a good spot for photography. Large fish are common in these coral gardens, including Maori Wrasse, coral trout, trevally, jobfish, surgeonfish, drummer and Estuary Cod. You may even get buzzed by a large Dogtooth Tuna. There is a large population of sea snakes and molluscs, and divers are also likely to encounter Whitetip Reef Sharks, turtles, stingrays and huge Whitespotted Shovelnose Rays that patrol the sandy gutters. Snorkel divers will enjoy the shallows, especially if the visibility is over 60m (200ft), which is quite common.

Cato Reef and Kenn Reef

Cato and Kenn reefs are small, remote and rarely visited. Reports from divers who have dived on these reefs say it isn't worth the effort of getting there. The coral is flat and uninteresting, the fish life sparse and the only redeeming feature is the thousands of sea snakes. There are probably good dive sites waiting to be found, but few charter boats visit the area. The main visitors are fishermen and the odd group of maritime archaeologists who study the wrecks in the area.

Wreck Reef

Wreck Reef has lived up to its name in the past as a number of ships have come to grief along its length. Surrounded by deep water, it is a collection of broken reefs some 30km (20 miles) long. Sheltering close in behind the reef, boats can anchor safely and you can go ashore to explore the many cays or the wealth of marine life. There are pinnacles, coral gardens, the scattered remains of historic shipwrecks, caves, gutters and an impressive wall to be explored. At almost any location divers will be able to see abundant reef fish, sea snakes, a wealth of invertebrates, stingrays, turtles, reef sharks and the odd gathering of pelagic fish.

The wreck of the Francis Preston Blair, *Saumarez Reef.*

The Australian Crown-of-Thorns Starfish, reputed to be destroying the Great Barrier Reef, is just as much a part of Australia's natural heritage as the Reef itself. Named in 1758 by the great naturalist, Carl Linneaus, the Crown-of-Thorns is known in scientific circles as *Acanthaster planci*, and belongs to the phylum Echinodermata or 'spiny skin'. One of the largest starfish in Australia, the Crown-of-Thorns grows larger than 500mm (20in) and, unlike most of its relations, has a large number of arms, usually from 12 to 17.

The back of the Crown-of-Thorns is covered with highly venomous needle-sharp spines up to 25mm (1in) long. Broad and solid at the base and tapering to a fine point, these spines are strong and capable of penetrating wet suits, the soles of dive booties and gloves. Even a minor injury can cause severe pain lasting for hours. A bad spining is serious (especially if it is a puncture wound) and surgery is often necessary to remove the spines which can break off in the wound causing life-threatening secondary complications such as severe infections and the possibility that a limb may be lost. The immune system can also break down. Try at all times to avoid contact.

Thousands of tube feet tipped with powerful gripping suckers weave and curl on the ventral side. These tube feet are hollow and controlled by an extraordinary interconnected water vascular system. Although mainly used for locomotion, the star uses them to grip the coral while it feeds.

The mouth and stomach are at the centre of the underside. The sea star selects a coral colony, preferably staghorn corals, and moving into position, grips tightly with its suckered arms. It then extrudes its stomach over the living coral polyps. The tissue of the coral polyp is broken down and digested outside the starfish's body. It moves over the colony until only the skeleton is left.

Under normal conditions the Crown-of-Thorns is nocturnal, hiding away under ledges and corals during the day. However, when a population explosion has taken hold, they feed almost continuously on different sections of the same reef, less than 500m (164ft) apart.

At the height of summer, sexually mature males and females shed sperm and eggs into the surrounding waters. Some estimates are as high as 20 million eggs per female star. Not all the eggs are fertilised but those that are spend many weeks as planktonic drifters, falling prey to predators such as the giant clam, an inhalant filter feeder, and other species of bivalves. Soft and hard corals, barnacles, crabs and small fish also eat the larvae. Eventually the surviving larvae settle on the bottom and metamorphose. The young starfish grow rapidly for about two years, by which time they have a diameter of 25–30cm (10–12in).

The Crown-of-Thorns doesn't have many enemies. Its speed and armaments put off all but the hungriest of underwater gourmets. Under aquarium conditions, two species of molluscs will attack and eat them. The Giant Trumpet Shell (*Charonia tritonis*) and the Giant Helmet Shell (*Cassia cornuta*) feed almost exclusively on various species of sea stars and sea urchins. Field studies have shown that the Giant Trumpet Shell feeds regularly on the Crown-of-Thorns, but the Giant Triton does not normally occur on the reef.

One report suggested that a small crustacean called the Dancing Shrimp (*Hymenocera picta*), should be introduced to the Great Barrier Reef as a biological control as it has been known to eat the Crown-of-Thorns under aquarium conditions. There is, however, enough evidence to suggest that coral regenerates in the same way as reefs re-establish themselves after fresh-water floods or cyclones and can be left to combat the Crown-of-Thorns on its own. Fears for the future of the Great Barrier Reef could, therefore be unnecessary.

Right: The voracious Crown-of-Thorns Starfish.

A small coral head on Wreck Reef.

5 PORPOISE CAY

Location: On the northern side of Wreck Reef, 350km (220 miles) from Gladstone.
Access: Over 20hr sailing time from Gladstone and Urangan.
Conditions: Generally calm, sheltered by reef. Average visibility 40m (130ft).
Minimum depth: 3m (10ft)
Maximum depth: 15m (50ft)
On the northern side of Porpoise Cay is a wonderful coral garden cut with gutters and many fascinating caves. There are numerous small invertebrates, abundant painted crays, squirrelfish, stingrays and Maori Wrasse in the caves. A huge resident Queensland Groper can sometimes be seen lurking in the dark. Beams of light penetrate the darkness through holes in the roof, making divers feel as if they were performing under spotlights. Also common are small tropical fish, sea snakes, turtles and reef sharks.

6 BIRD ISLAND OUTER CAVES
★★★★ ★ ★ ★ ★

Location: On the eastern tip of Wreck Reef, 350km (220 miles) from Gladstone.
Access: Over 20hr sailing time from Gladstone and Urangan.
Conditions: Mostly calm, behind reef. Average visibility 40m (130ft).
Minimum depth: 3m (10ft)
Maximum depth: 18m (60ft)
Some long and winding caves cut deep into the reef on the southwest side of Bird Island. Ensure you take a torch as you will find that some of the caves are lined with colourful corals and are home to gropers, stingrays, Tawny Nurse Sharks, Painted Crays, pufferfish, crabs, shrimps and a number of molluscs. Some of these caves cut 50m (165ft) into the main reef structure and are incredibly good fun to explore if you use some common sense. On the reef itself, there are reef fish, sea snakes, small reef sharks, schools of parrotfish munching on the coral and the odd turtle resting in a gutter.

7 DEEP FINGER
★★★★★

Location: On the eastern tip of Wreck Reef, 350km (220 miles) from Gladstone.
Access: Over 20hr sailing time from Gladstone and Urangan.
Conditions: Can be rough, quite exposed, slight currents. Average visibility 40m (130ft).
Minimum depth: 10m (33ft)
Maximum depth: 200m (660ft) plus
This is an incredible dive site. The reef is an extension of Bird Island, with the top at 10m (33ft) and a sheer wall dropping to 40m (130ft) in its first step and over 200m (660ft) in the second. The wall is decorated with row upon row of gorgonians, sea whips, small soft corals and sponges. Small reef fish shelter in ledges and crevasses and an amazing collection of pelagic life can be seen off the wall. Barracuda hover in large schools, while masses of trevally, Rainbow Runners and surgeonfish sweep past. Mackerel, tuna, jobfish and sea bass also cruise around the edge of the wall. The most outstanding feature of this site is the sharks. Whitetip Reef Sharks patrol the upper reaches, Grey Reef Sharks buzz divers off the wall, and every now and then a Tiger Shark appears out of the blue. Tiger Sharks generally stay in deep water but lone sharks sometimes rise to inspect divers. Though they appear sluggish, they can put on fast bursts of speed and divers are advised to give them a wide berth.

Marion Reef

Marion Reef used to be visited regularly and was the most popular destination in the Southern Coral Sea, but with the growth of the dive industry in the north, only a handful of charter boats visit this exciting destination each year, each having its special dive sites. Similar to a coral atoll, Marion is a large circular reef some 30km (20 miles) in diameter. The edge of the reef drops into deep water, and numerous pinnacles dot the lagoon floor. Located over 350km (220 miles) from the mainland, this reef is deep in the Coral Sea and has many features to recommend it.

Sea snakes abound at Marion Reef. You will encounter dozens, so many that after a few days you will hardly notice them. Reef sharks will be encoutered on every dive, and there are likely to be turtles, groupers, stingrays, schooling pelagic fish and colourful reef fish in the area. Marion Reef has the best coral growth in the Southern Coral Sea, with large gorgonians, black coral trees, sea whips, hard corals and radiant spiky soft coral. The reef is situated between Gladstone and Townsville, so charter boats can be boarded at any port between these towns.

Huge coral structures have been built up over many years.

Reef-edge drop-off at Marion Reef.

their curiosity. Schooling and lone pelagic fish cruise these pinnacles – trevally, Rainbow Runners, barracuda, mackerel and tuna can be seen on most dives.

9 SHALLOW LAGOON PINNACLES
* * * * * * * *

Location: The northern side of Marion Reef, 350km (220 miles) from Gladstone and Airlie Beach.
Access: Over 18hr sailing time from Gladstone and Airlie Beach.
Conditions: Generally calm, sheltered by reef. Average visibility 40m (130ft).
Minimum depth: 3m (10ft)
Maximum depth: 15m (50ft)
These shallow water pinnacles are covered in a variety of hard corals and are populated with thousands of reef fish. They are also riddled with ledges and caves where divers will find moray eels, squirrelfish, resting turtles, Estuary Cod, Painted Crays, stingrays and the odd Tawny Nurse Shark. Photographers will find clams, anemones, feather stars, tube worms, molluscs, nudibranchs, sea snakes, reef sharks, and turtles in shallow water. At night these pinnacles pulsate with life, hermit crabs come out, moray eels go on the hunt, molluscs appear from the sand and everything looks all the more colourful under torchlight. Divers will also find sleeping fish, hunting sea snakes, shrimps and crabs, lionfish, stingrays and dancing flatworms.

10 NORTHERN GUTTERS
* * * * * * * *

Location: The northern end of Marion Reef, 350km (220 miles) from Gladstone and Airlie Beach.
Access: Over 18hr sailing time from Gladstone and Airlie Beach.
Conditions: Generally calm, sheltered by reef. Average visibility 40m (130ft).
Minimum depth: 6m (20ft)
Maximum depth: 18m (60ft)
At the northern end of Marion Reef is a rich coral garden cut with many gutters and fascinating caves. Some of the twisting caves are over 30m (100ft) long, so take a torch to explore this labyrinth. These caves shelter large coral trout, squirrelfish, spotted cod, stingrays and even Painted Crays. The reef supports a large fish population, including filefish, moray eels, anemonefish, damsels, hawkfish, wrasse, sweetlips, fusiliers, trevally, jobfish and mackerel. Other marine life in the area includes reef sharks, Tawny Nurse Sharks, Potato Cod, turtles, Maori Wrasse, tuna and the ever-present sea snakes.

8 DEEP LAGOON PINNACLES
* * * * * * * *

Location: The northern side of Marion Reef, 350km (220 miles) from Gladstone and Airlie Beach.
Access: Over 18hr sailing time from Gladstone and Airlie Beach.
Conditions: Generally calm, sheltered by reef. Average visibility 40m (130ft).
Minimum depth: 10m (33ft)
Maximum depth: 60m (200ft)
Dozens of pinnacles are scattered over the sandy lagoon floor at Marion Reef. Some lie in deep water at the edge, others in very shallow water, and all are worth exploring. The deeper pinnacles are coated in gorgonians, sea whips and spiky soft corals. These pinnacles are home to a variety of reef fish such as angelfish, Fairy Basslets, moray eels, coral trout, flutemouth, sweetlips, lionfish and giant Maori Wrasse. Grey, Whitetip and Blacktip Reef Sharks appear regularly. Sea snakes sleep under coral, or just probe the reef (or nervous divers) to satisfy

How to Get There

Only a handful of boats visit the remote reefs of the Southern Coral Sea each year. Arrange a charter or join a group. Charter boats generally leave from Hervey Bay, Gladstone and Airlie Beach. Hervey Bay is 290km (180 miles) and Gladstone 534km (332 miles) north of Brisbane. After flying to Brisbane, you can fly with Flight West or Sunstate to these destinations, go by coach or train, or hire a car and drive up the Bruce Highway. Airlie Beach is located over 1100km (682 miles) north of Brisbane and is accessible by plane, car, train or bus. If flying, you will have to fly into Hamilton Island Airport or Proserpine Airport, and transfer to Airlie Beach by water taxi or coach.

Where to Stay

There is a wide range of accommodation on offer in Hervey Bay, Gladstone and Airlie Beach. For a brief rundown, refer to the relevant regional directory.

Where to Eat

On the mainland, you will never run out of places at which to eat.

Dive Facilities

Australiana, 45 Hickey Ave, Gladstone, tel 079-783 956. *Australiana* is a 19m- (62ft) long motor vessel for 16 passengers and can be chartered for trips to the Southern Coral Sea, the Capricorn and Bunker Groups and Swain Reefs.

Booby Bird, Marine Drv, Gladstone, tel 079-726 990, fax 079-726 990. *Booby Bird* is available for charter throughout the year, to the Swain Reefs, Capricorn and Bunker Groups and the Southern Coral Sea. She is a 24m- (77ft) long motor vessel for 21 passengers.

Boomerang Cruises, 22 Byron St, Scarness, Hervey Bay, tel 071-242 393. *Boomerang* is a 21m (70ft), 22 passenger vessel. She operates in the Southern Coral Sea, and makes trips to the Bunker Group and Swain Reefs.

Max Allen Cruises, 7 Illawong Crt, Gladstone, tel 079-791 377, operate the charter boats *Kanimbla* and *Spirit of Freedom,* available for charter to the Swain Reefs, Capricorn Group, Bunker Group and Southern Coral Sea.

Pacific Star Charters, 48 Coral Esplanade, Cannonvale, Airlie Beach, tel 079-466 383, fax 079-466 901, operate the 19m (62ft) motor sailing catamaran *Pacific Star* which does weekly and extended trips to Lihou reef, Diamond Islets, Abington Reef, Flinders Reef, the reefs around the Whitsundays and even Marion Reef in the Southern Coral Sea.

Film Processing

E6 processing is restricted in these areas.

Hospitals

Hervey Bay Hospital, Long St, Point Vernon, tel 071-281 444.

Maryborough General Hospital, 185 Walker Rd, Maryborough, tel 071-238 222.

Gladstone Hospital, Kent St, Gladstone, tel 079-763 200.

Proserpine Hospital, 2 Herbert St, Proserpine, tel 079-451 422.

For any emergency, fire, police or ambulance tel 000.

Recompression Chamber

For any diving accident anywhere in Australia, contact DES (Diving Emergency Service) on 1800 088 200. For more information see 'Diving Accidents', page 169. All dive charter boats must carry oxygen and know what to do if a diving accident occurs.

Local Highlights

There is a number of activities and sights to see at Airlie Beach, Hervey Bay or Gladstone. For a brief rundown, refer to the relevant regional directory.

Shipwrecks

Early mariners were always weary when sailing the waters of the Coral Sea, and many voyages ended in tragedy on uncharted reefs.

The *Cato* and *Porpoise* were lost on Wreck Reef in 1803, the *Bona Vista, Hester, Doelwych, Oliver Van Noord* and *Rodney* were all lost on Kenn Reef between 1828 and 1857, and many others have been lost on other reefs in this region.

Most of these wrecks are fascinating for maritime archaeologist but of little interest to the average diver as they are broken up and hidden in the coral. All wreck sites are protected under the Historic Shipwrecks Act and should remain undisturbed.

A number of ships have been lost at Wreck Reef, including guano ships that were wrecked when Bird Island was mined for guano in the 1860s.

The most famous wrecks are those of the *Cato* and *Porpoise,* lost in 1803 with one of Australia's most famous explorers, Captain Matthew Flinders, on board. On a voyage from Sydney to England the cargo vessels *Bridgewater* and *Cato* were under the escort of HMS *Porpoise.* The *Porpoise* was the first to strike the reef, the other ships turned to avoid disaster, but it was too late for the *Cato.* The *Bridgewater* went wide and then, ignoring the stricken vessels, continued toward England, only to disappear herself after leaving India.

All but three of the crew of the wrecked ships made it safely to one of the islands, with a fair amount of supplies and materials. In an amazing feat of seamanship, Captain Flinders and a few men sailed a long boat back to Sydney, over 1000km (620 miles) to the south. Within two months they returned to rescue the remaining men.

Today all that remains of these shipwrecks is scattered and encrusted in coral. It's best not to remove anything as these are historic wrecks which are still being surveyed by maritime archaeologists.

THE WHITSUNDAY ISLANDS

Created by volcanic turbulence, sculpted by erosion, their valleys drowned by rising sea levels over the last 10 000 years, the Whitsunday group of continental islands is a popular destination for thousands of holiday-makers from all over the world each year. Most of the islands are rugged and heavily wooded, with rocky shorelines, beautiful inlets and white, sandy beaches with reef platforms, fringing coral reefs, good snorkelling and some interesting scuba diving areas.

Originally called the Cumberland Islands, they have since come to be known by the name of the northern passage, which was called Whitsunday's Passage after the festival of Whit Sunday, through which Captain James Cook sailed in 1770. The Whitsunday coast stretches from Mackay in the south to Bowen in the north. Mackay is a large seaport, the port of access to Brampton, Lindeman and Hamilton Islands. Some 203km (127 miles) north of Mackay lies the town of Whitsunday which consists of three villages, Cannonvale, Airlie Beach and Shutehaven. These towns are the main access points to the Whitsundays.

Of the 150 mainland islands, islets and rocks which make up the Whitsunday Islands, only seven have tourist resorts, and although scuba diving and snorkelling can be done at all the resorts, only Hayman, South Molle, Daydream and Hamilton Islands have fully-equipped dive shops. Boats call daily at the other island resorts to pick up divers and snorkellers and take them to the outer reef pontoons where they can enjoy crystal-clear waters and training by experienced diving instructors.

There are some excellent reefs and dive sites which can be accessed by boat from resorts on the Whitsundays. Some islands, such as Long, Hayman and Brampton, have good walking trails maintained by Queensland National Parks. The beaches are spectacular – white, sandy stretches and secluded inlets fringed by coconut trees. However, for most, access is only by boat due to the rugged terrain. Many areas are inaccessible on foot, especially places such as Hook Island, where there are no trails.

Left: Typical fringing reef around the Whitsunday Islands.
Above: Egg cowries feed on soft corals.

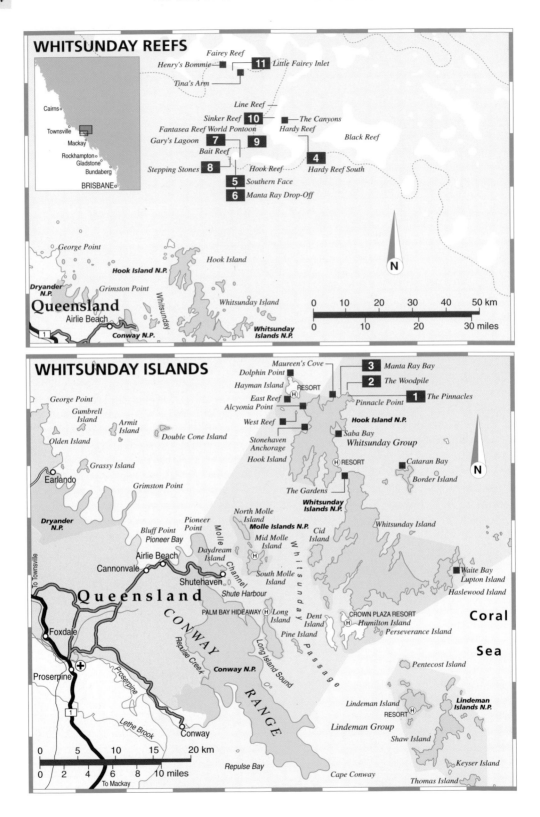

Direct flights from Sydney, Brisbane, Melbourne and Cairns land at Hamilton Island. Air taxi and charter flights from Mackay fly to Brampton Island and the small grass airport at Lindeman Island. All the other islands rely on boats: Hayman Island's launch operates from Hamilton Island, private vessels and charter boats from Mackay, catamaran ferry from Shute Harbour, and water taxis from Hamilton Island and Shute Harbour.

Just south of Mackay is an area known as Broad Sound. The greatest tidal influence on the Australian east coast occurs here, with a maximum range of 10m (33ft). Mackay experiences tides of up to 7m (23ft). Throughout the Whitsundays there are restricted passages with deep, narrow channels and strong tidal currents can make boating and diving difficult, especially during spring tides.

With 150 islands and hundreds of reefs, this vast complex has yet to be biologically assessed in detail. It is known to be extremely rich in marine life, with over 1000 species of fish, over 300 corals and several thousand molluscs.

There is a wide range of easily accessible sites for scuba diving and snorkelling, and due to the high profiles of many of the islands, there are sheltered bays and inlets that can be visited on most days of the year, depending on the weather. The 'real' Great Barrier Reef dive sites on the outer reef are some 60km (37 miles) northeast of the Whitsunday mainland and some 40km (25 miles) from the island resorts.

◼ THE PINNACLES

* * * * * * * *

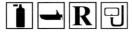

Location: Northeastern point, Hook Island, 35km (20 miles) from Shute Harbour.
Access: By boat, 30min from Shute Harbour.
Conditions: Subject to strong currents on the eastern side of the point, especially during spring tides. Western side generally good, except in northerly winds but can be affected by southerly swells coming around the point. Average visibility 3m (10ft) to 15m (50ft).
Minimum depth: 3m (10ft)
Maximum depth: 18m (60ft)
This shallow-water area is thickly covered with coral and dense thickets of bommies, 5m (16ft) to 18m (60ft) tall. There are a few coral clumps and rubble on the sandy bottom. Most bommies have huge, towering coral heads. Damsels and fusiliers swim above the rich coral, and butterflyfish and wrasse add flashes of colour. The best point of entry is on the western side. Manta Rays occur here in winter (May to September). Snorkelling is excellent off the western end.

◪ THE WOODPILE

* * * *

Location: Northeastern point, Hook Island, 35km (20 miles) from Shute Harbour.
Access: By boat, 30min from Shute Harbour.

Conditions: Exposed to northerly winds and any southeast swells rolling around the point. Strong currents near the point. Visibility 5m (16ft) to 15m (50ft).
Minimum depth: 5m (16ft)
Maximum depth: 30m (100ft)
This site takes its name from the strange shape of the rock wall formations. Thought to be the best wall dive in the Whitsundays, it drops 30m (100ft) to the sandy bottom, with scattered coral patches, and deep-water bommies. However, it's the wall itself, much of which is covered in soft corals and sea fans, which makes it such a spectacular dive. Take a torch to inspect the caves and ledges which are encrusted with invertebrates such as sponges, bryozoans and ascidians and a good range of flatworms, nudibranchs and ovulids. The large black coral trees are amazing and brightly-coloured snake stars are entwined around their branches.

◼ MANTA RAY BAY

* * * * * * * *

Location: Northeastern end of Hook Island, 35km (20 miles) from Shute Harbour.
Access: By boat, 30min from Shute Harbour.
Conditions: Generally excellent, sheltered water except during northerlies. Currents can be strong at the northeastern point. Visibility 3m (10ft) to 15m (50ft).
Minimum depth: 3m (10ft)
Maximum depth: 15m (50ft)
Considered by locals and visitors to be one of the best dive sites in the inshore islands, Manta Ray Bay's rugged terrain features bommies, reefs, valleys and caves dropping down

ROCK LOBSTERS

Tropical Rock and Shovelnose lobsters occur all along the coastal areas, islands, cays and reefs of the Great Barrier Reef and its perimeter. Unlike many other species of rock lobsters found in other parts of the world and in southern Australian waters, the tropical Great Barrier Reef species do not enter lobster pots and can only be taken by diving or trawling. Shovelnose Lobsters are generally only caught by trawling for target species such as prawns or scallops. Slipper Lobsters occur on reefs and must be caught by hand. All species of rock lobsters are nocturnal and only venture out at night for food. Mostly they stay hidden beneath plate corals or in caves, crevices and ledges in deeper water. They can also be seen in holes and crevices in underwater cliffs down to 30m (90ft). Tropical Rock lobsters (crayfish) are not successfully commercially fished on the Great Barrier Reef although live-aboard dive boats usually manage to have a few on the menu. Rock lobsters must never be speared, especially during breeding season, as the females may be carrying eggs and once speared, they cannot be set free to reproduce. Most tropical lobsters feed on molluscs.

to a sandy sea floor with patch reefs, scattered gorgonians and a few black corals. Staghorn corals dominate the shallows and the 12m- (40ft) high bommies reach to within 2m (6ft) of the surface. There is a deep crevasse at the western end of the beach. Manta Rays visit during winter (May to September) and there are huge schools of damsels which feed on plankton. Soft corals, sponges and a wealth of corals abound. Watch out for the resident Maori Wrasse.

◪ HARDY REEF SOUTH

* * * * * * * * * *

Location: Southern ends of Hardy Reef on the outer Great Barrier Reef, 60km (37 miles) from Shute Harbour.
Access: By boat, 2½hr from Shute Harbour, 2hr from Whitsunday Islands.
Conditions: Exposed to southerly winds, swell and strong currents. Visibility 12m (40ft) to 30m (100ft).
Minimum depth: 5m (16ft)
Maximum depth: 30m (100ft)
Hardy Reef South features luxuriant coral in the shallows, although due to the southerly aspect of the reef it is low profile, with lots of table corals and rugged staghorns. The terrain is indented with gullies running into the reef, and there are patches of sand. The slope, rich in coral life, drops off very quickly and is spectacular. Besides

damsels and fusiliers in the shallows, the gullies and walls have butterflyfish, wrasse, angelfish, sweetlips and cod, with pelagic fish sweeping along the deeper reef face. Snorkelling is good in the shallows.

◻ SOUTHERN FACE

* * * * * * * * * *

Location: Southern end of Bait Reef on the outer Great Barrier Reef, 60km (37 miles) from Shute Harbour.
Access: By boat, 2½hr from Shute Harbour, 2hr from Whitsunday Islands.
Conditions: Exposed to southerly winds and swell, and moderate currents. Visibility 5m (16ft) to 30m (100ft).
Minimum depth: 5m (16ft)
Maximum depth: 30m (100ft)
The flat reeftop is covered in a mass of living coral, mostly staghorns. The reef angles down to 30m (100ft) and is cut by weather-worn gullies. These gullies are often lined with gorgonian sea fans and soft corals and have incredibly colourful under-ledge fauna such as soft and hard corals, sea fans, ascidians, bryozoans, nudibranchs, flatworms and sponges. Boxfish, wrasse, butterflyfish, angelfish, damsels, puffers and triggerfish abound, and turtles, Manta Rays, mackerel and barracuda are regular visitors. This is an excellent site for snorkelling.

◻ MANTA RAY DROP-OFF

* * * * * * * * * *

Location: Southern end of Bait Reef on the outer Great Barrier Reef, 60km (37 miles) from Shute Harbour.
Access: By boat, 2½hr from Shute Harbour, 2hr from Whitsunday Islands.
Conditions: Exposed to southerly winds and swells, and prone to strong currents. Visibility 12m (40ft) to 30m (100ft).
Minimum depth: 3m (10ft)
Maximum depth: 36m (118ft)
Manta Ray Drop-off is what many consider to be the ultimate dive site. This is outer reef wall diving at its best: vertical coral walls drop 30m (100ft) straight down, with labyrinths of tunnels, canyons and a chimney on the way. All the walls are covered in sea fans, black corals, 3m (10ft) sea whips, huge spiky soft corals, feather stars, sponges and numbers of fish, big and small – damsels, fusiliers, giant wrasse, trevally, mackerel and the occasional shark venturing up from deeper water. During the winter (May to September), Manta Rays are also seen.

Whitehaven Beach, the Whitsunday Islands.

Lionfish are common throughout the Whitsunday reefs.

There are many species of butterflyfish, parrotfish and wrasse, all of which are colourful photographic subjects. This is definitely wide-angle country. Snorkelling is excellent here, but watch out for currents.

7 GARY'S LAGOON

* * * * * * * *

Location: Eastern side of Bait Reef on the outer Great Barrier Reef, 60km (37 miles) from Shute Harbour.
Access: By boat, 2½hr from Shute Harbour, 2hr from Whitsunday Islands.
Conditions: Inside, the inlet is reasonably protected from all winds except northwesterlies. Outside, wall diving is subject to strong currents during spring tides. Average visibility 10m (32ft) to 20m (65ft).
Minimum depth: 4m (13ft)
Maximum depth: 18m (60ft)
This popular dive site has relatively easy access and a choice of dive profiles. The dive along the outside edge of the reef into the entrance is a deeper wall dive of 10m to 18m (33ft to 60ft) deep. The coral cover is excellent. Large soft corals and gorgonian fans wave in the current. Larger fish are common and cod, trevally, mackerel and coral trout are present. There is hardly any current on the inside of the inlet, making it a good dive for less experienced divers. As it is only 12m (40ft) deep, you will have lots of time to explore the canyons and ledges.

There are many giant sea anemones with resident anemonefish, a resident wobbegong shark and a myriad coral reef fish. Snorkelling is excellent.

8 STEPPING STONES

* * * * * * *

Location: Western side of Bait Reef on the outer Great Barrier Reef, 60km (37 miles) from Shute Harbour.
Access: By boat, 2½hr from Shute Harbour, 2hr from Whitsunday Islands.
Conditions: Exposed to southerly winds and swells with strong currents. Visibility 10m (33ft) to 30m (100ft).
Minimum depth: 3m (10ft)
Maximum depth: 30m (100ft)
A huge divable area, the Stepping Stones consist of 18 or more flat-topped circular coral pinnacles which extend from 25m (80ft) deep to within 1m (40in) of the surface. Each stone is spectacular in its own right and worthy of an entire dive. There is a straight-sided monolith crowned with extraordinary corals and fringed all the way down with bright, soft corals, black corals and sea fans, among which swim every species of colourful fish imaginable. There are resident giant Maori Wrasse, and Manta Rays visit in winter (May to September). Snorkelling across the coral gardens on the tops of the Stepping Stones is exceptional and should not be missed.

9 FANTASEA REEF WORLD PONTOON

******

Location: Western side of Hardy Reef on the outer Great Barrier Reef, 60km (37 miles) from Shute Harbour.
Access: By boat, 2½hr from Shute Harbour, 2hr from Whitsunday Islands.
Conditions: Protected in most conditions except northerlies. Currents especially strong in the channel. Average visibility 8m (25ft) to 18m (60ft)
Minimum depth: 5m (16ft)
Maximum depth: 18m (60ft)
There are good coral growths in the shallow water and a wall down to 10m (33ft) which is undercut with caves and ledges on which small sea fans, sponges and soft corals can be seen. However, like most pontoon dives, it is the fish life that is really superb. The local fish are big and cheeky. One resident giant groper is about 2m (6ft) long and there are schools of trevally and snappers, a

---

Sea fan shells make excellent close-up subjects.

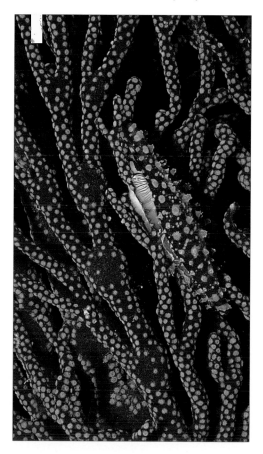

few coral trout and giant Maori Wrasse. Feeding over a period of years has built up numbers and multitudes of smaller species live in the shadow of the pontoon. Snorkelling is excellent.

10 SINKER REEF

****

Location: Small reef at the junction of Line Reef and Hardy Reef, 60km (37 miles) from Shute Harbour.
Access: By boat, 2½hr from Shute Harbour, 2hr from Whitsunday Islands.
Conditions: Protected, but prone to strong currents (drift dive). Visibility 8m (25ft) to 18m (60ft).
Minimum depth: 5m (16ft)
Maximum depth: 30m (100ft)
The top of this small reef is a mass of staghorn coral. As it is a popular site, there is a noticeable amount of anchor damage. The reef drops away quite steeply, with walls full of nooks and crannies, ledges and caves in which rich growths of soft corals, sea fans, ascidians along with sponges can be seen. Feather stars are everywhere and the larger sea fans have spiky brittle stars. Cod, sweetlips, butterflyfish, parrotfish and wrasse are common. Coral trout hide in the shadows and squirrelfish peek out from the deeper ledges. This is an excellent site for fish portraits or wide-angle photography.

11 LITTLE FAIREY INLET

****

Location: Inlet a little south of Henery's Bommie at Fairey Reef on the outer Great Barrier Reef, 60km (37 miles) from Shute Harbour.
Access: By boat, 2½hr from Shute Harbour, 2hr from Whitsunday Islands.
Conditions: Good protection inside the inlet, with some current outside along the deeper wall. Visibility 10m (33ft) to 20m (65ft).
Minimum depth: 5m (16ft)
Maximum depth: 18m (60ft)
This is a wall dive down to 16m (52ft) where the inlet begins. There are hard corals and soft corals, and sea fans along the wall but these tend to pan out below 18m (60ft). Swimming along the wall are butterflyfish, angelfish, parrotfish, wrasse, coral trout, sweetlips and squirrelfish hiding under coral ledges. The sides of the inlet contain a hundred havens and undercuts where sponges, ascidians, hydrocorals, nudibranchs and bryozoans make excellent close-ups. Snorkelling in the shallows, even over the wall edge enables a wealth of corals, surgeonfish, damsels and parrotfish to be seen.

Often referred to as the butterflies of the sea, nudibranchs are among the most colourful ocean creatures. Their bodies are so soft that their true beauty can only be captured by underwater photography as they collapse when out of the water and their colours cannot be adequately preserved. Since they only live a month or two or at the most a year, photographing and studying them is indeed a challenge.

Nudibranchs are found in every habitat, from intertidal rock pools down to 100m (305ft), and almost every sedentary colonial organism from sponges to soft corals can be a potential food source. There are diurnal nudibranchs and nocturnal nudibranchs, some live under the sand and some under rocks. Some actually even live inside sponges and ascidians.

All nudibranchs are functional hermaphrodites with reproductive pores on the right side of their necks. They mate with any mature individual of the same species and sometimes have communal mating groups. At the time of mating, both are males. They impregnate each other by swapping sperm packets, after which both produce eggs. Quite often, egg masses are laid on, or near, food sources. Some larger species produce up to a million eggs at a time. Most have planktonic larval dispersal, hatching as minute larvae in embryonic shells. They drift around until they make contact with their food organisms; they then settle and metamorphose into crawling juveniles. A few species, such as *Hypselodoris bennetti*, have direct development, hatching from their eggs as crawling juveniles.

Nudibranchs feed by means of a flexible, toothed, ribbon-like tongue called a radula, which is covered with minute teeth arranged in rows. Each species of nudibranchs has a different radula tooth pattern.

Nudibranchs have no shell to protect their soft parts but although they appear defenceless, this is hardly the case. Most nudibranch predation takes place in the plankton before the young settle to the bottom. Once they have metamorphosed, they have to contend with fish, molluscs, crabs and sea stars.

The creatures defend themselves with cryptic camouflage or toxic substances which they obtain from their food source and which gives them a bad taste. Many of the brightly-coloured nudibranchs manufacture their own chemical defences, while the aeolids, which feed on cnidarians, actually eat their host's stinging cells (nematocysts), ingest them without discharge, and store them in the knobs (cerrata) on their backs for their own defence. Some nudibranchs mimic defensive species and other toxic invertebrates such as flatworms.

Left: Nudibranchs move around the reef.
Right: The Spanish Dancer is the largest nudibranch in the southern hemisphere.

HOW TO GET THERE

Airlie Beach and Mackay are the gateways to the Whitsunday Islands. Mackay is 975km (610 miles) north of Brisbane, with regular domestic flights by Sunstate and Flight West Airlines. It is possible to reach Mackay by train, coach or car. From Mackay there are daily flights and launch services to Brampton Island. To reach Airlie Beach you have to fly, or catch a train or coach to the nearby small town of Proserpine, 1100km (682 miles) north of Brisbane. Proserpine is only 26km (15 miles) from Airlie Beach, and is accessible by coach or car. From here there are regular water taxi and launch services to the islands. The other option is to fly directly to Hamilton Island, on either Qantas or Ansett, and catch a water taxi to the island you are staying on.

WHERE TO STAY

Resort Islands

Brampton Island Resort, tel 079-514 499, fax 079-514 097. Two-storey complex with 108 units sleeping up to three people. All rooms are airconditioned, self-contained and have TV, video player and queensize beds. Facilities include a restaurant, nightclub, pool, gym, tennis court and golf course. Activities include bushwalking, fishing, sailing, water-skiing, archery, windsurfing, snorkelling and diving.

Daydream Island Travelodge Resort, tel 079-488 488, fax 079-488 499. The resort offers three types of self-contained unit (over 300 rooms) at varying prices, all with airconditioning, TV, video player and mini bar. The complex includes a restaurant, cocktail bar, convention centre, nightclub, sauna, pool, spa, gym, tennis court and putting green. Activities include fishing, sailing, bush walking, waterskiing, parasailing, windsurfing, snorkelling and diving.

Hamilton Island Holiday Inn Crowne Plaza Resort, tel 079-469 999, fax 079-468 888. With two tower blocks containing 554 rooms, two 60-room lodges and 53 huts, this large complex offers a range of accommodation from penthouse suites to normal units, but all are airconditioned, self-contained and have a TV and mini bar. Facilities include a restaurant, convention centre, nightclub, sauna, spa, pool, gym, squash courts, tennis courts and mini golf, and guests can enjoy fishing, waterskiing, sailing, bushwalking and diving with H20 Sportz.

Hayman Island Resort, tel 079-401 234, fax 079-401 567, is the most exclusive of all the resorts in the area with over 250 units. It offers penthouses, suites and units, and all have TV, video player, mini bar, 24-hour room service and airconditioning. Activities include golf, tennis, fishing, bush walking, waterskiing, windsurfing, parasailing and diving with Barrier Reef Diving Services. Resort facilities include a restaurant, nightclub, convention centre, barbecue area, sauna, pool and gym.

Long Island, Club Crocodile Long Island Resort, tel 079-469 400, fax 079-469 555. This two-storey resort has over 140 self-contained units that sleep up to three people. Resort facilities include a restaurant, cocktail bar, nightclub, pool, spa, sauna, gym and tennis courts. Guests can enjoy sailing, fishing, waterskiing, windsurfing, bushwalking and diving.

Long Island, Palm Bay Hideaway Resort, tel 079-469 233, is a small resort with only 14 cabins and units that sleep up to six people. Facilities at the resort include a restaurant, barbecue, pool, lounge, spa, and activities include boating, fishing, bushwalking, windsurfing and snorkelling.

South Molle Island Resort, tel 079-469 433, fax 079-469 580. This resort has six styles of units (and over 200 rooms) to suit most budgets, all are air-conditioned, self-contained and have a TV and mini bar. Resort activities include squash, tennis, golf, fishing, water-skiing, archery, sailing, windsurfing and diving. The resort complex includes a restaurant, nightclub, pool, sauna, spa and gym.

Should you choose to stay on the mainland you will find a good range of resorts, motels and caravan park units in Airlie Beach and Mackay.

High Price Range

Whitsunday Terraces Resort, Golden Orchid Drv, Airlie Beach, tel 079-466 788, fax 079-467 128, have 112 fully self-contained, airconditioned units with cooking facilities, TV and video player. The complex includes a restaurant, convention centre, barbecue area, pool, spa and communal laundry.

Ocean International Hotel, 1 Bridge Rd, Mackay, tel 079-572 044, fax 079-572 636, is a four-star hotel with restaurant, convention centre, pool, sauna, spa and 24-hour room service. All rooms are fully self-contained, with airconditioning, a TV and video player.

Medium Price Range

Colonial Palms Motor Inn, Shute Harbour Rd, Airlie Beach, tel 079-467 166, fax 079-467 522. All rooms are airconditioned, self-contained and have TV and video player. This motel has its own restaurant, pool, spa and room service.

Coral Sands Motel, 44 MacAlister St, Mackay, tel 079-511 244, fax 079-572 095. This two-storey complex offers a restaurant, convention centre, sauna, pool, room service and laundry. All rooms are airconditioned, and have a TV, video player and mini bar.

Lower Price Range

Airlie Cove Resort Van Park, Shute Harbour Rd, Airlie Beach, tel 079-466 727, fax 079-465 526, have 30 park cabins which sleep up to six people; a number of the cabins are self-contained, with airconditioning, TV and video player, while the rest are basic. Facilities include communal showers and toilets, a barbecue area, pool, spa, tennis court and shop.

Beach Tourist Park, Petrie St, Mackay, tel 079-574 021, fax 079-514 551, has a number of self-contained cabins which sleep up to six people, and there are a few on-site tents. Facilities include a salt-water pool, kiosk, camp kitchen and communal toilets, laundry and showers.

WHERE TO EAT

Many of the resorts offer meal packages at their restaurants. Resort restaurants offer a range of meals, but naturally the more expensive resorts like Hayman Island offer the best food. On the mainland there is a good selection of take-away places and restaurants in Mackay and Airlie Beach, including Chinese, seafood, Italian, and bistros and a number of cafés.

DIVE FACILITIES

A large number of dive shops in the Whitsunday area operate to the islands and reefs.

Barrier Reef Diving Services, The Esplanade, Airlie Beach, tel 079-466 204, fax 079-465 130, operate on Hayman Island and from Airlie Beach. They offer dive courses to instructor level, have a good range of retail and hire gear and run daily and extended trips to the islands and reefs.

Downunder Dive, 11 Iluka St, Cannonvale, tel 079-466 869.

H2O Sportz, Front St, Hamilton Island, tel 079-469 888, fax 079-469 888.

Kelly Dive Whitsundays, Eshelby Drv, Cannonvale, tel 079-466 122.

Mackay Adventure Divers, 153 Victoria St, Mackay, tel 079-531 431, run regular trips to the islands and reef. They are a five-star PADI centre, run dive courses to instructor level and have a good selection of retail and hire gear.

Oceania Dive, Shute Harbour Rd, Airlie Beach, tel 079-466 032, fax 079-466 032, are a five-star PADI facility, and run dive courses and dive trips to the local islands and reefs.

Pro-Dive Whitsunday, Shute Harbour Rd, Airlie Beach, tel 079-466 508, operate daily and overnight trips to the islands and reefs. They are a five-star PADI facility, conduct dive courses to instructor level and have a good range of retail and hire gear.

Aquatic Centre of Education, Shute Harbour Rd, Airlie Beach, tel 079-467 446.

Island Divers, Mandalay Point Rd, Airlie Beach, tel 079-465 650.

Scuba Sport, The Esplanade, Airlie Beach, tel 079-466 204, fax 079-465 130, run daily dives to the reef on their 15m (50ft) catamaran; they also conduct dive courses.

True Blue Dive, 364 Shute Harbour Rd, Airlie Beach, tel 079-466 662.

Whitsunday Diving Services, 34 Manooka Drv, Cannonvale, tel 079-466 811.

Whitsunday Scuba Centre, 5 Garema St, Cannonvale, tel 079-466 865.

Charter boats operating in the Whitsunday area include:

Elizabeth E Coral Cruises, 102 Goldsmith St, Mackay, tel 079-574 281, fax 079-572 268, operate the *Elizabeth E*, a live-aboard vessel that can be chartered for groups to anywhere on the Great Barrier Reef and Coral Sea.

Hamdon Star Charters, Mackay Harbour, Mackay, tel 079-552 490, fax 079-553 209, operate to the islands and reefs.

Maxi *Ragamuffin,* 283 Shute Harbour Rd, Airlie Beach, tel 079-467 777, fax 079-466 941, sail the islands daily and offers snorkelling and diving.

Pacific Reef Charters, 48 Coral Esplanade, Cannonvale, tel 079-466 383, fax 079-466 901, operate the live-aboard vessel *Pacific Star*, they do weekly as well as extended trips to the reefs in the Whitsunday region and to the Northern and Southern Coral Sea.

Reef Enterprise Diving Services, 386 Shute Harbour Rd, Airlie Beach, tel 079-467 228, operate daily and extended trips to the islands and reef and offer dive courses to divemaster level.

FILM PROCESSING

There are a number of one-hour photo stores in the Whitsunday region; a few even do same-day E6 processing.

Tropix Photography, Shute Harbour Rd, Airlie Beach, tel 079-466 639.

Whitsunday Kodak Express, 239 Shute Harbour Rd, Airlie Beach, tel 079-465 404.

HOSPITALS

Mackay Hospital, Bridge Rd, Mackay, tel 079-515 211.

Proserpine Hospital, 2 Herbert St, Proserpine, tel 079-451 422

For any emergency, fire, police or ambulance tel 000.

RECOMPRESSION CHAMBER

For any diving accident anywhere in Australia, contact DES (Diving Emergency Service) on 1800 088 200. For more information see Diving Accidents page 169.

LOCAL HIGHLIGHTS

There are a lot of activities to enjoy in the Whitsunday region, and on these islands you will never run short of things to do and see. On the mainland you may find a sailing adventure around the islands to your taste – charter a yacht which you can sail yourself or hire an experienced skipper.

There are a number of interesting national parks in the area.

The **Eungella National Park**, 84km (53 miles) west of Mackay is a magnificent rainforest region with dozens of walking tracks.

The **Broken River**, which is a platypus habitat, runs through the park, but get there early in the morning so you have a better chance of spotting these unusual creatures.

The **Cape Hillsborough National Park** is located 45km (28 miles) north of Mackay. Wildlife in the park includes wallabies, possums, kangaroos, a number of birds and scrub turkeys. There are many walking tracks and 5km (3 miles) of beach to explore.

TOWNSVILLE WRECKS AND REEFS

Townsville is the third-largest city in Queensland. The city itself is more like a large country town, but does have a variety of shops and restaurants that caters to the tourist market. There is a casino, many motels and hotels and even a large aquarium to whet your appetite for the local diving. Townsville houses Queensland's only recompression chamber.

The area offers the visiting diver a vast number of dive experiences, including shallow coral reefs, pinnacles, deep drop-offs, caves and a number of shipwrecks. There are day-trips to a number of offshore reefs and islands on one of the fast catamarans that leave daily from the harbour. These trips are mainly geared for snorkellers, but also cater for scuba divers who have a tight budget or limited time. They generally visit the inner reefs which are rich with coral and fish and calm in most weather conditions.

Just off the coast of Townsville is Magnetic Island, which is fringed with many shallow reefs. The island has a large resident population and is a very popular holiday and weekend destination for overseas visitors and locals.

There is quite a good collection of reefs off Townsville, in fact, many of the smaller ones have only been numbered. All the reefs provide interesting and varied diving, with the best on the outer edge of the Great Barrier Reef. While the inner and central reefs are thick with coral and fish life, the outer reefs are generally more colourful; they are also washed by clearer water and have dramatic drop-offs. Decorated with spiky soft corals and large gorgonians, the outer reefs are often visited by schools of pelagic fish.

A number of shipwrecks are found on the reefs off Townsville, although most are so badly broken up that they are hardly worth a look. There is one wreck in the inner shipping channel that has become world famous, the *Yongala*. This has been described by many as the best wreck dive in the world, but a more accurate description would be the best marine

---

Left: Gorgonians decorate many of the reefs off Townsville.
Above: 121 people, including this unfortunate soul, died when the Yongala *sank.*

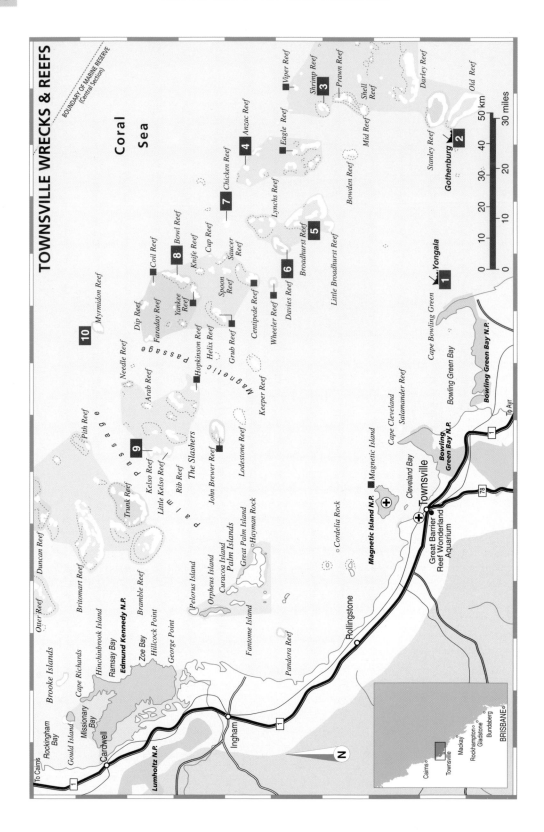

life dive in the world. While the wreck is almost intact and fun to explore, it is the wealth of marine life that makes the *Yongala* unforgettable. Although visibility is nearly always limited to 12m (40ft) or less, most divers don't mind because the fish life is so fantastic.

A number of charter boats operate out of Townsville. Visitors have the choice of day, weekend, four-day or week-long trips. Allow enough time for at least a four-day trip so that you can see a few of the reefs and experience the *Yongala* for yourself. All the operators have their own dive sites. A number of the reefs are also dived by charter boats heading out to the Coral Sea. They generally spend the first day of the trip on one of the outer reefs.

All of the reefs off Townsville fall in the Central Section of the Great Barrier Reef Marine Park. Most have been zoned for general use, but there are a number of preservation areas protected from trawlers and fishermen. With an area of over 75 000km² (47 000 sq miles), there are plenty of reefs just waiting to be explored.

1 *YONGALA* SHIPWRECK
* * * * *

Location: 13km (8 miles) east of Cape Bowling Green.
Access: By boat, about 3hr from Townsville.
Conditions: Located in shipping channel. Not dived in big seas or strong winds; can have strong currents. Average visibility 12m (40ft).
Minimum depth: 15m (50ft)
Maximum depth: 30m (100ft)
Whenever you dive on the *Yongala* you will encounter batfish, tuna, trevally, turrum, barracuda, Spotted Eagle Rays, giant gropers, barramundi cod, coral trout, Maori Wrasse, coral cod, queenfish, cobia (Black Kingfish), Black-blotched Rays, Estuary Cod, pufferfish, stonefish, lionfish, angelfish, surgeonfish and more. Turtles sleep in and under the wreck, sea snakes are everywhere, Estuary Cod peer into your mask, Eagle Rays hover beside you and batfish schools engulf you. There is just so much sea life around the *Yongala* that you will hardly notice the limited visibility.

2 *GOTHENBURG* SHIPWRECK
* * * * * * *

Location: 130km (80 miles) southeast of Townsville, western side of Old Reef.
Access: Over 6hr sailing time from Townsville.
Conditions: Protected by reef, mostly calm. Average visibility 20m (65ft).
Minimum depth: 6m (20ft)
Maximum depth: 30m (10ft)
While not as famous as the *Yongala*, the *Gothenburg* is still a fascinating dive site. Broken up over a wide area, the wreck is still distinguishable though covered in coral. She is also protected under the Historic Shipwrecks Act.

The reef around the wreck provides good diving as there are extensive coral gardens and a number of pinnacles. The corals are quite colourful and there are plenty of reef fish. Pelagic fish cruise through the wreck and even reef sharks are common.

3 SHRIMP REEF
* * * * * * * *

Location: 110km (70 miles) east of Townsville.
Access: Over 8hr sailing time from Townsville.
Conditions: Protected by reef, mostly calm, slight currents. Average visibility 20m (65ft).
Minimum depth: 3m (10ft)
Maximum depth: 35m (115ft)
The eastern side of Shrimp Reef is more exposed to the weather but there is a wonderful drop-off that is covered in soft coral, sea whips and gorgonians. Pelagic fish and reef sharks patrol this drop-off and on a good day you

GOTHENBURG SHIPWRECK

The *Gothenburg* is a 60m (200ft) steel steamer that sank in tragic circumstances in 1875. With a mixed cargo, including $A80 000 in gold and 160 passengers and crew, she was on her way from Darwin to Adelaide when she headed straight into a cyclone and ran aground on the northern end of Old Reef. The lifeboats were smashed onto the reef with all hands lost. Others were swept from the wreck. 14 survivors made land on the remaining lifeboat, and found four of their shipmates there. On the mainland they learned that another lifeboat had also made it, bringing the total number to 21. Salvage divers found her broken in two in 10m (30ft) of water. The gold was successfully salvaged and the wreck forgotten until it was rediscovered in 1967.

will see schools of trevally and barracuda, mackerel, turrum and shy Whitetip Reef Sharks. Red bass, Maori Wrasse and coral trout may also be encountered on this steep reef wall. If conditions don't allow the eastern side to be dived, there are extensive coral gardens at the southern end of the reef. These are cut with many gutters that are fun to explore. Here there are plenty of smaller reef fish and a lot of invertebrate life that make the area perfect for macro photography.

ANZAC REEF

Location: 110km (70 miles) east of Townsville.
Access: Over 7hr sailing time from Townsville.
Conditions: Protected by reef, mostly calm, slight currents. Average visibility 20m (65ft).
Minimum depth: 3m (10ft)
Maximum depth: 35m (115ft)
Anzac Reef has dozens of interesting dive sites, from drop-offs to coral gardens, but the most popular location is a large pinnacle off the main reef. This huge pinnacle, sometimes known as Anzac Bommie, can be circumnavigated in one dive at any depth as its sheer walls drop straight down into 35m (115ft) of water. Its wall is lined with gorgonians, soft corals, sea whips and small black coral trees. Turtles, reef sharks and sometimes Manta Rays swim around the pinnacle and pelagic fish swim along the wall. Trevally, fusiliers, Rainbow Runners and mackerel can all be found here. Reef fish add splashes of colour, complemented by sweetlips, butterflyfish, angelfish, bannerfish, parrotfish, coral trout and hawkfish. The water over the top of the pinnacle is quite shallow, allowing for interesting snorkelling, or for decompression stops at the end of a long dive. After dark, this pinnacle can be seen in all its glory. Nocturnal sealife

SS *YONGALA* SHIPWRECK

The *Yongala* was a coastal steamship that sank in the shipping channel east of Cape Bowling Green during a cyclone in March 1911, taking 121 people to a watery grave. The shipwreck was located in 1958, when hard-hat divers descended to confirm that the wreck was the missing ship. Today the shipwreck is one of the most exciting dives in the world. Most of the structure still remains, and is now protected under the Historic Shipwrecks Act, so divers may not touch or remove any items. The wreck is 110m (360ft) long. Much of it is worth a look – the holds, the passageways, the toilets – but strict rules forbid penetration as the wreck can be damaged. If your reason for diving the *Yongala* is to see fish, you won't be disappointed.

scuttle about in search of food and there are sleeping fish in every hole. If you are lucky, you may even encounter a moray eel on the prowl or a sleeping turtle wedged under a ledge.

BROADHURST REEF

Location: 100km (62 miles) east of Townsville.
Access: Over 6hr sailing time from Townsville.
Conditions: Protected by reef, mostly calm, slight currents. Average visibility 20m (65ft).
Minimum depth: 6m (20ft)
Maximum depth: 30m (100ft)
There is a number of exciting dive sites around Broadhurst Reef, with large pinnacles in deep water and colourful coral gardens in the shallows. Some pinnacles are coated in soft corals, sea whips, gorgonians and black coral, making them interesting locations for photographers. Reef fish are abundant, including coral trout, butterflyfish, anemonefish, parrotfish, hawkfish, angelfish, wrasse, gobies and triggerfish. Larger pelagic fish such as schools of trevally, Rainbow Runners and mackerel can also be seen cruising the reef. The coral gardens in the shallows are definitely worth viewing as the terrain consists of gutters and many small caves lined with gorgonians. Small invertebrates, from nudibranchs and flatworms to molluscs and sea stars abound. Divers will see pipefish, anemonefish, moray eels, lionfish, boxfish, flutemouth, pufferfish and a wide variety of wrasse and butterflyfish. The odd Whitetip Reef Shark or turtle also patrols the gutters, so be ready with your camera.

DAVIES REEF

Location: 100km (62 miles) east of Townsville.
Access: Over 6hr sailing time from Townsville.
Conditions: Protected by reef, mostly calm. Average visibility 20m (65ft).
Minimum depth: 6m (20ft)
Maximum depth: 25m (80ft)
Davies Reef has a number of exciting dive sites, from large pinnacles to prolific coral gardens and small drop-offs. At the southern end of the reef is a number of huge pinnacles coated in soft corals, gorgonians and sea whips. These pinnacles are riddled with small caves where shrimps, squirrelfish, pufferfish, coral crabs and lionfish can be found. The pinnacles are also home to a wide variety of resident reef fish and passing pelagics also sweep the area on occasions. The eastern side of the island has a number of deep gutters cutting through

The toilets are a popular photo stop on the Yongala *wreck.*

the reef. The walls of the gutters are decorated with spiky soft corals and small gorgonians – look closely to find allied cowries on them. Small tropical fish are plentiful. Large numbers of pelagics and other schooling fish congregate in the area, including parrotfish, batfish, surgeonfish, trevally and fusiliers.

⁊ CHICKEN REEF
★★★★☆☆☆

Location: 110km (70 miles) east of Townsville.
Access: Over 8hr sailing time from Townsville.
Conditions: Protected by reef, mostly calm, slight currents. Average visibility 30m (100ft).
Minimum depth: 6m (20ft)
Maximum depth: 30m (100ft)
Chicken Reef has much interesting terrain to be explored, from drop-offs to pinnacles, gutters, caves and shallow coral gardens. The pinnacles and drop-offs are coated with large gorgonians, spiky soft corals, black coral trees, a variety of hard corals and long, swaying sea whips that are home to tiny shrimps and sea whip gobies. Resident fish life is very dense – parrotfish, surgeonfish, unicornfish, angelfish, sweetlips, Fairy Basslets, rabbitfish, fusiliers, wrasse, angelfish and butterflyfish are

some of the more common fish found here. Divers are also likely to encounter huge Maori Wrasse, reef sharks, Potato Cod, turtles and passing pelagic fish. The giant clams in the area, some over 1m (40in) long, are interesting photographic subjects.

⁸ BOWL REEF
★★★★☆☆☆

Location: 110km (70 miles) east of Townsville.
Access: Over 8hr sailing time from Townsville.
Conditions: Protected by reef, mostly calm, slight currents. Average visibility 30m (100ft).
Minimum depth: 6m (20ft)
Maximum depth: 30m (100ft)
The outer edge of Bowl Reef is quite exposed and rarely dived but the inside has many small and large coral heads that are fun to explore. Dozens of caves and crevasses can be traversed on a dive, so don't forget to take a torch. Large gorgonian fans, sea whips, soft corals and black coral trees live on the deeper pinnacles, and forests of healthy hard corals grow in the shallows. Small reef fish are plentiful but divers will also encounter trevally, parrotfish, surgeonfish, turrum, tuna, sweetlips, gropers, Maori Wrasse and tuskfish. Eagle Rays and reef

NATIONAL PARK ISLANDS

All of us dream of being marooned on a desert island, but we should take the realities into consideration. Very few of the islands on the Great Barrier Reef are inhabited, hardly any have a natural year-round water supply and on many one cannot even land unless the sea is extremely calm. They may be covered in scrub, have no sand for tent pegs to hold or plenty of sand washed by the sea. On some islands the birds have lice and ticks.

CAMPING

Camping is permitted under the jurisdiction of the Queensland Department of Environment and Heritage on approximately 60 of the national park islands. However, all are regularly checked by national park rangers and permits must be obtained and camp fees paid before one may set up camp.

The maximum stay on any national park island is three weeks and though some islands (those regularly visited by tourists and tour operators or resort groups) have tank water, most do not and you will have to take all your provisions with you.

SURVIVAL RULES

There are simple survival rules that make camping holidays a pleasant experience or if ignored... hell on earth.

Plan, anticipate, check and double check
Island camping requires good planning, as many things have to be seen to, organised, anticipated and instigated, especially where diving is concerned.

Once you have decided to visit a certain island, gather every bit of information possible. Ring up and write to the various authorities. Make a list of the things you wish to know and ask advice. Check which are the best times of the year to visit that island, ask about permits, camping fees, and what activities are permitted. It's pointless getting to the island, waving the boat goodbye and finding out you can't use a compressor or generator, or no fishing is allowed, or the water tank is dry after a prolonged drought.

Check with the Great Barrier Reef Marine Park Authority for a zoning map of the area you wish to visit. Check that all your equipment is in good working order – there are no shops or spare parts on islands.

Walking the line
Beachcombing (on islands where it is allowed), is an alluring thought; walking along long, white, sandy beaches with the sand between your toes and loving the freedom of the moment. Watch out – bare feet, however tough, are no match for buried coral, fish spines, broken glass, sharp sticks, thorns or bird skeletons. Walk on the hard sand near the water's edge and watch where you put your feet.

Punctures are the worst kinds of wounds and the only first aid on the island will always be what you remembered to bring. Any accident must be balanced against the cost of rescue. Water taxis, charter boats, helicopters are all expensive.

Salt-water healing is not quite what it's cracked up to be. Good antiseptic and dry light, non-restrictive coverings are best. Cover minor wounds with a plaster to avoid the pain of constant rubbing, sometimes a wound actually feels better when it's wet. Precaution and prevention are the watchwords. When climbing, be exceptionally careful on slippery rocks and loose, shaly hillsides and don't run over volcanic rocks (the round shiny ones at the shore) when the soles of your shoes are wet – it's like walking on glass.

Beware of the biters
All campers should note that camping near the sea on islands (especially continental islands that have mangroves, creeks and aquatic swamps) means contending with a host of creeping, crawling, biting, stinging, annoying, flying, slithering and hopping things, both on land and in the water.

A typical camping site among the She Oaks on a vegetated sand cay.

You can be bitten or stung by creatures such as mosquitoes, bushflies, March flies, midges, sandflies, ticks, scrub mites, bird lice, spiders, centipedes and scorpions, even a snake or two.

Insect repellent will keep most of the flying insects, mites, lice and ticks at bay, and by carefully investigating your shoes, socks and sleeping bag, any unwanted guests can be discovered in time. Never do anything to provoke venomous creatures as many are unpredictable and isolation increases the risk of accidents.

North of Maryborough, large continental islands with inland waterways and extensive mangroves have been known to harbour Saltwater Crocodiles and there have been a number of sightings at sea.

From October to May, any inshore waters should be treated with suspicion, for this is when marine stingers are known to occur. Although these animals have powerful stinging cells and can be lethal, they can't sting through closely woven fabric such as Lycra suits, wetsuits, leotards, gymwear, even a T-shirt.

When swimming or snorkelling, always apply sun screen to all exposed parts as the sun's rays reflect off the water even though it may seem cool at the time. Sunburn is no joke. Don't forget to take Stingose, calamine lotion and antihistamine cream just in case.

CAPRICORN AND BUNKER GROUPS

Typical coral cays of the area, vegetation is dominated by Casuarinas (She Oaks) and Pandanus Palms around the shorelines with pisonia forests inland. Large colonies of sea birds nest in the trees and mutton birds nest in holes in the ground. For anybody who has never lived among thousands of raucous, twittering, screaming, courting birds, the noise can be, to say the least, somewhat disquieting – especially as it gets louder at night and never ceases. Turtles are common and come ashore to lay their eggs in the summer months.

Camping is only permitted in approved areas and as it is a designated Category D site, costs $A2 per person per night. Advance booking is essential and there are toilets, walking tracks, swimming and sailing; fishing and collecting, snorkelling and reefwalking are restricted to certain areas only. All water, cooking facilities, fuel and provisions must be brought with you to the island; no open fires may be lit. No lighting generators are allowed, and compressors for filling scuba tanks are only allowed on Lady Musgrave and North West islands.

Access is mainly by charter boat from Gladstone. There is a seaplane service operating from the Gold Coast, Seair Pacific, which is an excellent way to see the reef at minimum cost. It also caters for scenic trips and snorkelling daytrips.

Big schools of Spangled Emperors congregate beneath some of the outer Barrier Reef daytrip pontoons.

sharks occasionally frequent the area, so have your camera at the ready. At night, the reef pulsates with colour and life. The corals look even more radiant under torchlight, and if you look closely you may find allied cowries, decorator crabs or spider crabs living on the corals. Many sleepy fish can be seen in the coral, while others such as squirrelfish and lionfish are out hunting. Extra dashes of colour are provided by nudibranchs, flatworms, hermit crabs, shrimps, molluscs, Mantis Shrimps and by the hundreds of feeding feather stars.

9 KELSO REEF

★ ★ ★ ★ ★ ★ ★ ★

Location: 110km (70 miles) east of Townsville.
Access: By boat, some 2½hr from Townsville's Breakwater Terminal. (By charter boat, 6hr from Townsville)
Conditions: Sheltered dive sites inside the reef, very little current. Outside reef subject to conditions. Some current, depending on site. Average visibility 20m (70ft).
Minimum depth: 2m (6ft)
Maximum depth: 30m (100ft)
This area is a smorgasbord of luxuriant corals – brain corals, hedge corals, honeycomb corals and plate corals of every colour and hue. Giant Clams live all around the reef, sometimes two or three together. There are swimthroughs, gardens of soft corals and thickets of staghorn corals in purples, blues and greens. Bright blue sea stars, huge pineapple sea cucumbers, horsehoof clams, giant cuttles, octopus, Crown-of-Thorns Starfish, feather stars and golden sea fans abound. Beneath the Pure Pleasure

Reef platform pontoon are hundreds of fish, including a big school of Spangled Emperors, Yellow-tailed Fusiliers, snappers and a couple of large cod. Out in the reefs are wrasse, parrotfish, butterflyfish, damsels and sweetlips. Snorkelling is excellent anywhere on the reef.

10 MYRMIDON REEF

★ ★ ★ ★ ★ ★ ★ ★

Location: 130 km (80 miles) north of Townsville.
Access: Over 9hr sailing time from Townsville.
Conditions: Protected by reef, mostly calm, slight currents. Average visibility 30m (100ft).
Minimum depth: 3m (10ft)
Maximum depth: 30m (100ft)
Very rich coral growth is a feature of Myrmidon Reef as it sits on the edge of the Coral Sea. Steep coral walls cut by long caves fringe the reef and some are packed with gorgonians and soft corals. These caves are fun to explore, so take a torch. The reef itself is heavily decorated with corals, sea whips, sponges and gorgonians. Reef fish are especially abundant, but you are also likely to encounter giant Maori Wrasse, coral trout, sweetlips, surgeonfish, parrotfish, rock cod, fusiliers, mackerel and schools of trevally. On the top of the wall is a number of coral gardens and gutters. Here there are anemones, a variety of molluscs and Giant Clams. Some of these clams are almost 1½m (4ft) long, among the largest found on the Great Barrier Reef. These gutters also shelter schooling reef fish, stingrays and a few juvenile Green Turtles.

How to Get There

Located 1371km (855 miles) north of Brisbane and 438km (272 miles) south of Cairns, Townsville is regularly serviced by domestic flights from Australia's two national airlines, Qantas and Ansett. If you have time to spare, drive or take a coach or train – the train from Cairns follows a scenic route.

Where to Stay

Townsville is a popular destination with accommodation to suit every pocket, from five-star motels to caravan parks.

Upper Price Range
Sheraton Breakwater Casino Hotel, Sir Leslie Thiess Dr, Townsville, Tel 077-222 333, fax 077-724 741. This five-star hotel complex has a casino and all the luxury, service and facilities associated with a five-star hotel.

Medium Price Range
There are over 25 medium-priced motels in Townsville, and several dozen outside the town.

Central City Gardens, 270 Walker St, Townsville, tel 077-722 655, fax 077-211 728, is located next door to Mike Ball Dive Expeditions, and is probably the most popular motel with visiting divers. It is a five-storey complex with airconditioning, TV, video player, pool and your own cooking facilities.

Lower Price Range
Adventurers Resort, 79 Palmer St, South Townsville, tel 077-211 522, fax 077-213 251, is a two-storey complex with excellent facilities, including a salt water pool, spa and barbecue.

Civic Guesthouse & Backpacker Inn, 262 Walker St, Townsville, tel 077-715 381, is located next to Mike Ball Dive Expeditions. Though it has fewer facilities than the Adventurers Resort, it is still comfortable and convenient.

On Magnetic Island you could try **Magnetic Island Holiday Units,** 16 Yule St, Picnic Bay, tel 077-785 246, or **Magnetic Island Retreat**, 17 Hayles Ave, Arcadia, tel 077-785 357, both of which are fully self-contained.

Where to Eat

Townsville has many take-away food places and restaurants offering seafood, Chinese, Japanese, Italian, French, Greek, Malaysian, Mexican, Indian and Thai food or a thick Aussie steak

Dive Facilities

Mike Ball Dive Expeditions, 252 Walker St, Townsville, tel 077-723 022, fax 077-212 152. Established in 1969, MBDE is the biggest dive operation in Australia. They offer dive courses to instructor level, have a large selection of retail and hire gear and operate two live-aboard charter vessels from Townsville. *Watersport* does three-day trips to the reefs off Townsville and the *Yongala*, and *Spoilsport* does longer trips to the Coral Sea and the *Yongala*. They also offer a number of adventure packages, including white-water rafting, rainforest walks and outback safaris.

Pro-Dive Townsville, Shop 4, Great Barrier Reef Wonderland, Flinders St, Townsville, tel 077-211 760, fax 077-211 791. Pro-Dive, a five-star PADI dive centre offering courses to instructor level, has a dive store and operates the live-aboard vessel *Running Free*, which does twice-weekly three-day trips to the *Yongala* and reefs off Townsville.

Pure Pleasure Cruises, PO Box 1831, Townsville, tel 077-213 555, fax 077-213-590, run a 30m (92ft) catamaran daily to their pontoon at Kelso Reef. They also offer diving, snorkelling, ecology tours and dive courses.

Blue Water Scuba Diving, 102a Forrestry Rd, Bluewater, tel 018 779 267.

Sun City Watersports, Tobruk Pool, The Strand, Townsville, tel 077-716 527.

Reef Magic Charters, 5 Barringha Court, Mysterton, tel 016 782 286.

Power Play Charters, Breakwater Marina, Townsville, tel 077-872 666.

Coral Sea Wilderness Expeditions, TSMV Hero, 16 Dean St, Townsville, tel 077-211 155.

Reef Charters, MV Challenger, 20 Tamarind St, Kirwan, tel 077-733 341.

True Blue Charters, 65 Gilbert Crs, North Ward, tel 077-715 474.

Tangaroa, 19 Crowle St, Hyde Park, tel 077-722 127.

Scorpion Charters, 5 Sharp St, Mt Louisa, tel 077-797 568.

Film Processing

Print and E6 processing is widely available in Townsville.

Auscolor, 350 Flinders St, Townsville, tel 077-212 588.

Doug Kemp's Camera House, 401 Flinders Mall, Townsville, tel 077-723 541.

Reef Colour, Flinders Mall, Townsville, tel 077-723 499.

Hospitals

Townsville General Hospital, Eyre Street, Townsville, tel 077-819 211.

Magnetic Island Health Centre, 74 Sooning Road, Magnetic Island, tel 077-785 107.

For any emergency, fire, police or ambulance tel 000.

Recompression Chamber

Townsville has Queensland's only recompression facility. For any diving accident anywhere in Australia, contact DES (Diving Emergency Service) on 1800 088 200. For more information see 'Diving Accidents', page 169.

Local Highlights

The **Great Barrier Reef Wonderland** is an impressive aquarium on the waterfront, with a reef tank, a predators' tank, a touch tank and several smaller ones. Most of **Magnetic Island** is a national park, with many bushwalks, wildlife and beaches. There are regular ferries, and bikes and boats for hire. Other attractions include outback and rainforest tours and parks such as **Cape Cleveland National Park**, 30km (20 miles) south of Townsville.

THE NORTHERN ISLANDS

The Northern islands include the Palm Island Group, the Bedarra Group and Lizard Island. These continental islands are situated just off the mainland and do not always enjoy the same visibility as the outer barrier. However, the waters are rich in vertebrates and invertebrates and have more representatives in some groups than outer barrier areas.

The Palm Island Group is situated some 80km (50 miles) north of Townsville and although the islands are only 24km (14 miles) off the coast, the waters are usually quite clear, reaching over 25m (80ft) visibility. Apart from Orpheus, Fantome and Pelorus, little diving is done around the islands.

A premier Great Barrier Reef resort, Dunk Island is about 160km (100 miles) north of Townsville and 120km (75 miles) south of Cairns. Bedarra, another resort island, is in the vicinity of Dunk Island. These two are the only inhabited islands in the Bedarra Group.

Lizard Island is the northernmost resort island on the Great Barrier Reef, some 270km (170 miles) north of Cairns. It has a beautiful lagoon, picture-postcard views, a wealth of wildlife and excellent fringing reefs, with good diving all around. A boat ride away from Lizard Island are the Ribbon Reefs and the legendary Cod Hole (see the Cairns and Port Douglas section), with giant Potato Cods, huge moray eels, Manta Rays and turtles. Lizard Island is accessible by plane from Cairns and by charter boat from Cairns and Port Douglas.

Orpheus Island

The second-largest island in the Palm Island Group, Orpheus Island (named after a naval survey ship by Captain James Cook in 1770) is a designated national park some 11km (7 miles) long and 1km (⅝ mile) wide. A mainland island of volcanic origins, it lies 80km (50 miles) north of Townsville and 24km (14 miles) off the coast.

Left: There are over 300 species of coral around Orpheus Island and the Palm Islands.
Above: Feather-duster worms come in dozens of different colour combinations.

The only resort in the Palm Island Group, Orpheus Island has been catering for holiday-makers for over 45 years. Fish and goat meat (there were once many wild angora goats on the island) was the fare until at least 1968.

The island is rugged and supports a rich collection of flora and fauna. The highest point above sea level is 172m (570ft). On the eastern, seaward side the ridges are very steep, but can be traversed with care. There are picturesque coves and beaches indenting the shoreline. There is a wide range of vegetation, including dense eucalypt woodland, patches of luxuriant forest in the gullies, natural grassland and mangroves. The fauna comprises 50 species of bird, at least 13 butterfly species, and reptiles including the Red-tailed Skink and geckoes.

All around are extravagant fringing coral reefs and an amazing array of soft corals, which carpet the sea floor throughout the entire Palm Island Group. From the top of the ridge down towards Picnic Bay and out towards the Great Barrier Reef proper, a number of islands making up the Palm Island Group can be seen. Great Palm is the only other inhabited island. The fringing reefs and huge coral heads around these islands offer some really fantastic diving but because it is so vast, little of the area has been explored below water.

As there is no direct flow from any major river systems in the vicinity, the waters around Orpheus Island contain some of the best corals (over 340 species) on the reef. During calm weather, the visibility on the ocean side of the surrounding reef reaches 25m (80ft), the yearly average is 8m (25ft) to 10m (33ft). James Cook University at Townsville established a research station at the southern end of Pioneer Bay where the flora and fauna of the island, the surrounding reefs and their marine life are being studied.

Access is by charter boat from Dungeness, but the best way to get there is by amphibious seaplane operated by Seair Pacific from Townsville airport. During the 30-minute flight there is a wonderful panorama of the Palm Islands, the reefs and the coastline. Helicopters can also be chartered from Townsville.

1 FANTOME HIDEAWAY

★★★★★★★

Location: East side of Fantome Island, 8km (5 miles) from the resort.
Access: 15min by boat from the resort, 45min from Dungeness by charter boat.
Conditions: This is a fairly sheltered site and although there may be some current during tide changes (especially in the spring), it is suitable for beginners and resort divers. Average visibility 18m (60ft).
Minimum depth: 2m (6ft)
Maximum depth: 2m (6ft)
As it is shallow and sheltered with lagoon-like conditions, this site is an excellent choice for beginners and resort divers. The bottom is sandy and flat with clumps of staghorn corals, sea cucumbers, sea stars and lots of damsels, butterflyfish, wrasse, a few parrotfish, surgeons, goatfish and Monocle Bream. There are some Blue-spotted Fantail Rays, gobies and scorpionfish.

2 CORAL GARDENS/PIONEER BAY

★★★★

Location: Pioneer Bay, western side of Orpheus Island, 5km (3 miles) from the resort.
Access: By boat only, 10min from the resort
Conditions: Very sheltered site, no currents, suitable for snorkelling at low or high tide. Average visibility 8m (25ft).
Minimum depth: 4m (13ft)
Maximum depth: 12m (40ft)
With excellent coral cover, lots of bommies and a number of caves, this site has a large area for snorkellers with lots of hard and soft coral species and a good array of fish. Sand pockets among the bommies contain sea cucumbers, sea stars and sea urchins and there are Giant Clams and lots of burrowing clams. All divers, snorkellers and swimmers should be advised that the inshore waters of the Great Barrier Reef around the mainland and continental islands may contain marine stingers from October

Manta Rays and other large sea creatures patrol the reefs.

to May. Wear protective clothing such as a Lycra suit or wet suit to ensure that you don't get stung. Some of these small but venomous jellyfish are almost invisible in the water and can cause severe stings to exposed parts of the body.

3 VOLCANIC S

★★★★☆

Location: North-west point of Pelorus Island, 10km (6 miles) from the resort.
Access: 20min by boat from the resort, 1hr from Dungeness by charter boat.
Conditions: This site is best when dived on the high tide. It is very good for experienced divers but unless conditions are good, is not recommended for beginners. There is some current on the tide change, especially during spring tides. Average visibility 8m (25ft).
Minimum depth: 5m (16ft)
Maximum depth: 22m (70ft)
A large rock face, similar to a mini-wall, dominates this site, dropping down to 50m. There are hard corals and carpets of soft corals in the shallows, and besides the sea fans, whip corals and feather stars, there are parrotfish,

Picnic Bay at Orpheus Island.

wrasse, butterflyfish, chromis and sponges, and schools of trevally sometimes pass by. Turtles and stingrays are regularly seen. As this area's subtidal flora and fauna are only now being accessed, many new nudibranchs, flatworms and ascidians should be discovered.

4 BAT CAVE

★★★★★☆

Location: North-east side of Pelorus Island, 11km (6 miles) from the resort.
Access: 25min by boat from the resort, 1hr by charter boat from Dungeness
Conditions: Often subject to strong currents. Stationary dives can be undertaken during neap tide and drift dives during spring tide. Average visibility 10m (33ft).
Minimum depth: 4m (13ft)
Maximum depth: 18m (60ft)
This site has been named after the colony of bats which inhabits a sea cave that is only open during low tides – one of the unique features of the area. Underwater, the terrain is flat and sandy with large bommies and scattered patches of reef. Large Shovelnose Rays inhabit the bottom. Around the bommies are schools of damsels, parrotfish, wrasse and butterflyfish; under the caves and ledges are cardinals and squirrelfish, and out on the sand, gobies and grubfish.

5 AL'S PLACE

★★★★★★★★

Location: Southern point of Pelorus Island, 8km (5 miles) from the resort.
Access: 15min by boat from the resort, 45min by charter boat from Dungeness.
Conditions: Easy dive for seasoned divers and beginners. Best at high tide, some current during spring tides. Average visibility 8m (25ft).
Minimum depth: 4m (13ft)
Maximum depth: 33m (110ft)
Excellent fringing reefs, with a predominance of staghorn-type corals, especially in the shallows. As at most dive sites in this area, there is an overwhelming number of soft coral fauna, especially where there are moderately strong currents around points and in channels. The soft corals carpet the rock-based reef in masses of colour, particularly greens, yellows and blues. Deeper, reds and pinks appear with sea fans and whip corals. The elusive Allied Cowries live here, their bright colours blending into the colour of their host. Giant Clams are common, and being an established fish-feeding site, this is one of the best areas for fish-watching.

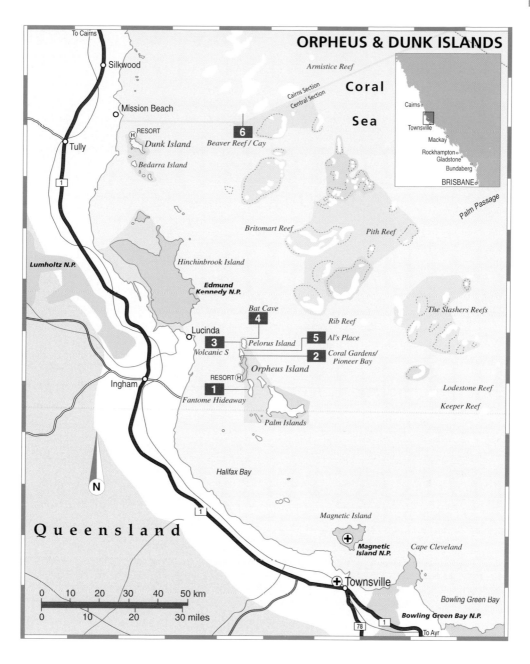

ORPHEUS & DUNK ISLANDS

To Cairns
Silkwood
Mission Beach
RESORT
Dunk Island
Tully
Bedarra Island
Beaver Reef / Cay
6

Armistice Reef
Cairns Section
Central Section
Coral

Sea

Cairns
Townsville
Mackay
Rockhampton
Gladstone
Bundaberg
BRISBANE

Palm Passage

Britomart Reef
Pith Reef

Lumholtz N.P.

Hinchinbrook Island

Edmund
Kennedy N.P.

Bat Cave
4

Rib Reef
The Slashers Reefs

Lucinda
3
Volcanic S
Pelorus Island
5 Al's Place
2 Coral Gardens/
Pioneer Bay

Ingham
RESORT
1
Fantome Hideaway
Orpheus Island

Lodestone Reef
Keeper Reef

Palm Islands

Halifax Bay

Queensland

Magnetic Island

Magnetic
Island N.P.
Cape Cleveland

N

0   10   20   30   40   50 km

0   10   20   30 miles

Townsville

Bowling Green Bay

Bowling Green Bay N.P.

78   1
To Ayr

Dunk Island

Dunk Island is part of the Bedarra Group and the site of a very popular holiday resort. While snorkelling and diving is available, most people come to Dunk Island to relax and enjoy the natural beauty. Little scuba diving is done around the island, but snorkelling is very popular. The Quick Cat catamaran visits the island each day to take guests, divers, and snorkellers out to Beaver Cay. All services are provided by the dive staff, including underwater camera hire.

Lizard Island

L izard Island is without question one of the most remote and exclusive resorts in Australia. This picturesque continental island is located 27km (17 miles) from the mainland at the northern end of the Ribbon Reefs, and was named by Captain Cook in 1770 after the large monitor lizards observed there.

Lizard Island is situated 240km (150 miles) north of Cairns, about a one-hour flight. The entire island is a national park and is home to a marine research station run by the Australian Museum. Visitors are welcome at the station, and will learn a lot about the reef and possible threats to its existence.

Lizard Island is close to some of the best dive sites on the Great Barrier Reef, as the resort is located only an hour's boat ride from the outer edge of the Ribbon Reefs. The dive boat runs out every second day to locations such as Cod Hole (listed in the Cairns and Port Douglas section) for dives at these spots. Some fine dive sites are found around Lizard Island and its neighbouring reefs and islands. Here divers will encounter marine life such as sea snakes, reef sharks, stingrays, turtles, Giant Clams, Manta Rays and many dense schools of reef and pelagic fish.

The Lizard Island Resort is not solely dedicated to diving and only offers two to three dives a day. Most people come to this isolated resort to relax, go fishing, soak up the sun, explore the island and escape from the world.

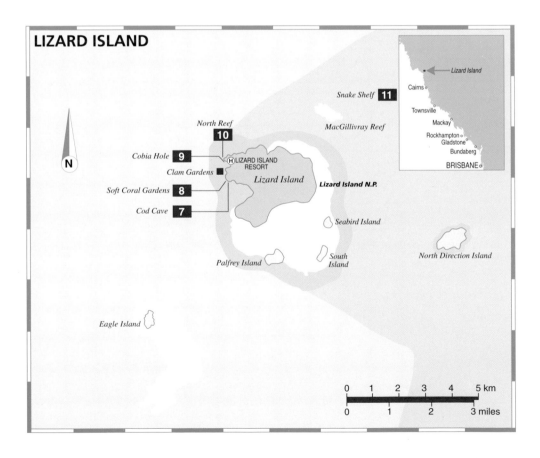

6 BEAVER REEF/CAY

★★★★★★★

Location: 28km (19 miles) east of Dunk Island and 37km (22 miles) from Mission Beach.
Access: By high-speed catamaran (Quick Cat) 20min to Dunk island (stop-over 1hr), then 55min to the reef.
Conditions: Sheltered in most conditions, easy entry from shallow water, mild current. Visibility 10m (33ft) to 20m (65ft).
Minimum depth: 3m (10ft)
Maximum depth: 22m (70ft)

Beaver Reef features an unspoiled fringing reef around the sand cay, with excellent coral formations and a wide variety of species, especially on the slopes and small drop-offs. There are abundant soft corals and large gorgonian sea fans in deeper water and as the area is a protected marine park, fish (even pelagics) are common and unafraid. There are lots of Giant Clams, Helmet Shells and bailer shells on the sandy sea floor. Both Green and Hawksbill turtles are regularly sighted, as are large cod, big schools of Spangled Emperors, fusiliers, Whitetip Reef Sharks, barracuda and trevally. Manta Rays occur in the winter, and anemonefish are common. The snorkelling is extremely good from the cay or boat. Talks and courses on reef ecology and biology are held regularly.

7 COD CAVE

★★★★★★

Location: West of Lizard Island Resort.
Access: Only minutes from the resort.
Conditions: Protected by the island, mostly calm. Average visibility 12m (40ft).
Minimum depth: 3m (10ft)
Maximum depth: 12m (40ft)

The Cod Cave, a relaxing dive just off Lizard Island, will suit all levels of divers and snorkellers. There is a large pinnacle decorated with a variety of corals sheltering small reef fish and a multitude of invertebrates. Deeper down on the pinnacle are several small caves that are worth a look as they are home to gropers, squirrelfish,

---

MONITOR LIZARDS

Commonly known as goannas, monitor lizards are good climbers and have a carnivore's diet of small creatures – insects, birds and other reptiles. Powerful limbs and sharp claws help them to overcome their prey. Species found on Lizard Island include the Lace Monitor which grows up to 2m (6ft) in length.

---

pufferfish, soapfish and a variety of molluscs. Photographers will have a field day as subjects include stingrays, filefish, angelfish, parrotfish, goatfish, moray eels and many wrasse. Most of the fish are very friendly; having been fed in the past, they fearlessly swim up to divers and snorkellers.

8 SOFT CORAL GARDENS

★★★★★★

Location: West of Lizard Island Resort.
Access: Only minutes from the resort.
Conditions: Protected by the island, mostly calm. Average visibility 12m (40ft).
Minimum depth: 3m (10ft)
Maximum depth: 10m (33ft)

Countless rich coral gardens are found along the western side of Lizard Island. Almost anywhere you dive you will find colourful corals teeming with reef fish. The Soft Coral Gardens is an exceptional collection of beautiful soft corals. Take a torch to reveal the colours in all their glory and to help you spot many of the small creatures that live on the reef. Spider crabs, Decorator Crabs, Banded Coral Shrimps, hermit crabs, sea stars, feather stars, brittle stars, flatworms and some beautiful nudibranchs can be found on the reef. Small reef fish are also common, but the macro life will easily keep most divers occupied for the entire dive.

9 COBIA HOLE

★★★★

Location: Northwest of Lizard Island Resort.
Access: Only minutes from the resort.
Conditions: Protected by the island, mostly calm. Average visibility 12m (40ft).
Minimum depth: 12m (40ft)
Maximum depth: 18m (60ft)

The Cobia Hole is a large pinnacle and is interesting because of its many caves, gutters and ledges. The pinnacle is decorated with many beautiful corals, including gorgonians, soft corals, sponges and sea whips, but divers come here principally to see fish, and they are rarely disappointed as this pinnacle seems to attract more than its fair share – schools of batfish, barracuda and trevally swarm around the reef. These schools are constantly moving and will occasionally engulf divers. Also on the pinnacle, divers will encounter Black-blotched Rays hovering in midwater, sweetlips, Red Emperors, goatfish, parrotfish, surgeonfish and even turtles. Do explore some of the caves as you are almost certain to find Estuary Cod, coral trout, squirrelfish, lionfish and

The Great Barrier Reef probably has the most diverse marine fauna in the world. Each of the thousands of fish which seem to move about aimlessly has a certain living space and is territorial or home-ranging. Each species has a specialised role evolved over millions of years. Although to the beginner fish just look like fish, each family has a fairly distinct shape, and recognising them is easier once one can distinguish between the major families according to their shapes, colours and behaviour. There are two major groups of marine fish.

CARTILAGINOUS FISH (SHARKS AND RAYS)

Elasmobranchs, among the most primitive fish, have changed little in the past 200 million years. They have five to seven pairs of gill openings and no bones, but are supported internally by flexible cartilage and externally by a rough, scaleless skin in which millions of minute denticles are embedded. They are a successful group and are found from low-tide level down to many thousands of metres. Because of their voracious appetites and efficient predatory senses, the larger sharks have long been feared by man.

TELEOSTS (BONY FISH)

All modern fish with true bony skeletons belong to this class. They possess one gill opening on each side and most have an outer covering of scales. Their size ranges from gobies a few millimetres long to giant gropers and cod measuring up to 3m (10ft) in length. These fish can be carnivorous, herbivorous or omnivorous and feed on a variety of crustaceans and other fish. The teleosts comprise the bulk of edible fish caught on the Great Barrier Reef and are extremely diverse in their shapes and colours and in the habitats they occupy.

THE FIVE MOST PROMINENT FISH FAMILIES

1. Damselfish (Pomacentridae)
Damselfish are one of the most abundant families inhabiting coral reefs with around 320 species worldwide and some 120 species in Australia. They are generally small and elongated to round, with a continuous dorsal fin and a forked or lunate tail. The scales are large. Many damselfish are territorial. The males protect the eggs and will even attack divers who swim too close. Sizes range from 5cm (2in) to 20cm (8in) and they display remarkable diversity in habitat, feeding habits and behaviour.

2. Wrasse (Labridae)
The second largest family of tropical reef fish, wrasse are perhaps the most complex in colour and range in size from 10 cm (4in) to 230cm (90in) weighing 190kg (418

1

2

pounds). Although wrasse vary considerably – from slender to deep-bodied and short- to long-snouted – they are generally elongated in shape. The dorsal fin is continuous; most adults have convex tails. The teeth are separate, well developed and often protrude. They are daytime fish and normally swim with their pectoral fins, using tail fin and body propulsion for fast movement only.

3. Gobies (Gobiidae)

These small, mostly bottom-dwelling fish are abundant, with over 200 species on the Great Barrier Reef and 1600 worldwide. Gobies generally have an elongated shape and have two dorsal fins with fused or partly-fused pelvic fins. They are seldom longer than 10cm (4in) and some may be the world's smallest vertebrates in the sea at 12mm (½in) long. Most live in burrows in the sand, often in relation with shrimps.

4. Blennies (Blennidae)

Blennies are a large family of small, mostly bottom-dwelling elongated fish with no scales and a single dorsal fin. Most have blunt heads and some have head tentacles. They are mostly territorial and often live in empty worm tubes or shells. The male guards the eggs.

5. Butterflyfish (Chaetodontidae)

Probably the most popular tropical fish, butterflyfish are renowned for their striking patterns and delicate movements. Their body shape is deep and compressed, with scales and a single dorsal fin. They have small protractile mouths and brush-like teeth. Most have convex tails and a vertical stripe through their eyes and some grow up to 30cm (12in) long. Butterflyfish are a daytime species.

1. The Blue Demoiselle is a typical damselfish.
2. The male Yellow-green Wrasse.
3. The Blueband Goby is generally found in pairs.
4. Speckled Blennies are territorial.
5. Beaked Coralfish, one of the best-known butterflyfish.

5

3

4

False Clown Anemonefish with their host sea anemone.

gropers there. Black Kingfish or cobia gather near the reef – from a distance they look like reef sharks when they take off from the bottom. They are very shy and difficult to photograph.This is one of the best dives in the area and is also a fantastic night-dive location.

🔟 NORTH REEF

★★★★☆☆

Location: North of Lizard Island Resort.
Access: Only minutes from the resort.
Conditions: Protected by island so mostly calm. Average visibility 15m (50ft).
Minimum depth: 6m (20ft)
Maximum depth: 20m (65ft)
North Reef offers interesting wall diving with plenty of soft corals, gorgonians and sea whips. Ledges and gutters cut into the reef. Fish life on and off the wall can be dense; angelfish, sweetlips, batfish, trevally, coral cod, lionfish, coral trout, surgeonfish, mackerel and parrotfish are common. Also in the area are Eagle Rays, stingrays and turtles. As the water is generally clear, make sure you take your camera along.

🔢 SNAKE SHELF

★★★★

Location: 10km (6 miles) east of Lizard Island Resort.
Access: 30min from the resort.
Conditions: Generally only dived in calm conditions. Average visibility 15m (50ft).
Minimum depth: 10m (33ft)
Maximum depth: 18m (60ft)
All around Lizard Island are hidden reefs and shoals. Some are home to Manta Rays and reef sharks, others to turtles and sea snakes. The Snake Shelf is a collection of three large pinnacles decorated with lovely soft corals and gorgonians. The pinnacles attract a multitude of fish and surgeonfish, batfish, trevally, mackerel, barracuda are common, while turrum, and White-spotted Eagle Rays cruise around the reef. The top attraction is the dozens of Banded and Olive sea snakes – sleeping under the coral, dashing to the surface for a breath of air or hunting around the reef. Sea snakes are wonderful photographic subjects, as they are curious and will come straight up to a diver. Keep in mind that they are dangerous and should be treated with respect.

How to Get There

Orpheus Island is located over 100km (60 miles) north of Townsville and is accessible by seaplane from Townsville and Cairns. Dunk Island is located halfway between Cairns and Townsville and is accessible by air from both cities. There is a water-taxi service and a daily launch from Mission Beach, 115km (73 miles) south of Cairns, accessible by car or coach. Located 270km (166 miles) north of Cairns is Lizard Island, a one-hour flight from Cairns.

Where to Stay

Orpheus Island Resort, Private Bag 15, Townsville, tel 077-777 377, fax 077-777 533. This island resort is exclusive, private and as no children under 15 years are allowed, peaceful. The resort has four styles of fully self-contained accommodation with airconditioning and mini bar. The price includes all meals. Accommodation ranges from large villas with spa baths and kingsize beds to more basic suites with queensize beds. The resort has a restaurant and dining room, convention centre, pool, spa and tennis court and activities include boating, sailing, bushwalking, waterskiing, windsurfing, whale-watching (in season), snorkelling and diving.

Great Barrier Reef Hotel Resort, Dunk Island, PMB 28, Townsville, tel 070-688 199, fax 070-688 528. This popular two-storey resort has a restaurant, dining room, bistro, nightclub, convention centre, pool, spa, squash court, tennis court and golf course, and activities include boating, bushwalking, fishing, horseriding, waterskiing, archery, windsurfing, sailing, and parasailing. The resort has four styles of self-contained accommodation, all with airconditioning, TV, video player and mini bar. Top of the range are the luxury villas for two, while the basic units sleep up to six. Meal packages are also available.

Lizard Island Lodge, PMB 40, Cairns, tel 070-603 999, fax 070-603 991. The lodge only offers one style of accommodation, namely 32 self-contained villas with airconditioning, room service, king-size beds and mini bar. The lodge has a restaurant, dining room, cocktail bar,

pool and tennis court, and activities include bushwalking, sailing, waterskiing, windsurfing and fishing. All meals are included in the price.

There is a wide range of accommodation on offer in Cairns and Townsville,. Refer to the relevant regional directories. There is also a good range of accommodation at Mission Beach, including resorts, motels and caravan parks.

Castaways Beach Resort, Seaview St, Mission Beach, tel 070-687 444, fax 070-687 429, offers self-contained units and suites on the beach, with a restaurant, cocktail bar, pool, spa and room service.

Dunk Island View Caravan Park, 175 Reid Rd, Mission Beach, tel 070-688 248, has self-contained units, caravans and tents with communal toilets and showers. Facilities include a pool, shop and barbecue.

Where to Eat

The choice of eating places is limited on these islands. Dunk Island has the best range with a restaurant and bistro. On Orpheus Island and Lizard Island meals are included. Cairns and Townsville have a good selection of restaurants. Mission Beach has a number of restaurants and take-away food places.

Dive Facilities

Orpheus Island Diving, tel 07-3852 2026 or 079-395 022. Dive packages are available (for guests only) at the dive shop on the beachfront and include fully certified courses, resort courses and individual dives for certified scuba divers. Equipment is available for hire and snorkelling with the Giant Clams is a re-gular feature.

Dunk Island Diving, certified dive courses are available at Mission Beach on Dunk Island by the *Quick Cat* dive operator who runs diving and reef ecology classes on board this daily pick-up service to guests on Dunk Island.

Quick Cat **Dive,** Mission Beach, tel 070-687 289 is a PADI agency offering enjoyable diving to certified divers, resort courses and 'Discover Scuba'

Research Stations

Research stations work on a user-pays system. In general, food must be organised by visitors and accommodation must be reserved well ahead of schedule. There are research stations on One Tree Island (University of Sydney) and Heron Island (University of Queensland). Other stations are run by the Australian Institute of Marine Science at Orpheus Island off Townsville, and the Australian Museum at Lizard Island north of Cairns.

packages to daytrippers. All equipment and dive guides are provided and equipment can be hired. The *Quick Cat* takes divers and snorkellers and outer reef trippers to Beaver cay and reef, and to Dunk Island.

Great Barrier Reef Dive Inn, The Hub Shopping Centre, Mission Beach, tel 070-687 294, fax 070-687 294, operates to dive sites around Dunk Island and the inner reef. They have a well-stocked store, and offer dive courses and local tours.

Dale Skipper Services, 27 Holland St, Mission Beach, tel 070-688 550, offer snorkelling and diving trips around Dunk Island and the inner reef.

Lizard Island Lodge, Private Mail Bag 40, Cairns, tel 070-603 999, fax 070-603 991, run regular resort and open-water courses and daily boat dives to local dive sites around the island and dive sites on the Ribbon Reefs, including the Cod Hole.

Film Processing

There are no film processing facilities on the islands, but print and E6 processing is available at mini-labs and camera stores in Cairns and Townsville.

Recompression Chamber

For any diving accident anywhere in Australia, contact DES (Diving Emergency Service) on 1800 088 200. For more information see 'Diving Accidents', page 169.

THE REEFS AND ISLANDS OF CAIRNS AND PORT DOUGLAS

Cairns is without doubt the heart of the Great Barrier Reef diving scene. It seems as if every street corner has a dive shop, and every other shop is geared to promote the reef to the tourists. Port Douglas is a little less developed than Cairns.

The inner reefs off Cairns and Port Douglas are very close inshore, some only 30km (20 miles) away. The inshore reefs have lagoons, pinnacles, drop-offs and extensive coral gardens. A wide variety of hard corals dominate the shallows, and deeper down on these inner reefs are brilliant soft coral, sea whips, sponges and small gorgonians. The resident fish populations are generally small but pelagic fish can be seen and a few of the reefs have resident Potato Cod and Maori Wrasse. Visibility on these inner reefs is generally 15 to 30m (50 to 100ft) and very few currents are experienced. Considering the large number of visitors to these reefs each year, there is still healthy coral and abundant fish life but naturally, the diving is better the further you travel from the coast.

The outer reefs off Cairns and Port Douglas have dramatic drop-offs, plentiful fish life and fantastic corals. These reefs are remarkably rich and home to a wide variety of reef fish and smaller invertebrate life. Reef sharks, gropers, turtles, stingrays and schooling pelagic fish are common on many of the reefs. The Cod Hole is one of the most famous dive sites in the area, but there are many other exciting locations. Visibility is usually around 30m (100ft) and currents are common, making drift diving a popular activity.

Besides the reefs, three islands in the area are popular with tourists – Fitzroy and Green islands near Cairns, and Low Isles just off Port Douglas. They are mainly popular with snorkellers and divers on open-water dive courses. Daytrips can be made to the islands, or you can stay on Green or Fitzroy islands, both of which offer a variety of accommodation and are great locations for family holidays. Both have dive shops and run daily charters to the inner reefs closest to the islands.

Left. A diver descends on the wall at Briggs Reef.
Above: Leaf Scorpionfish are not often seen during the day.

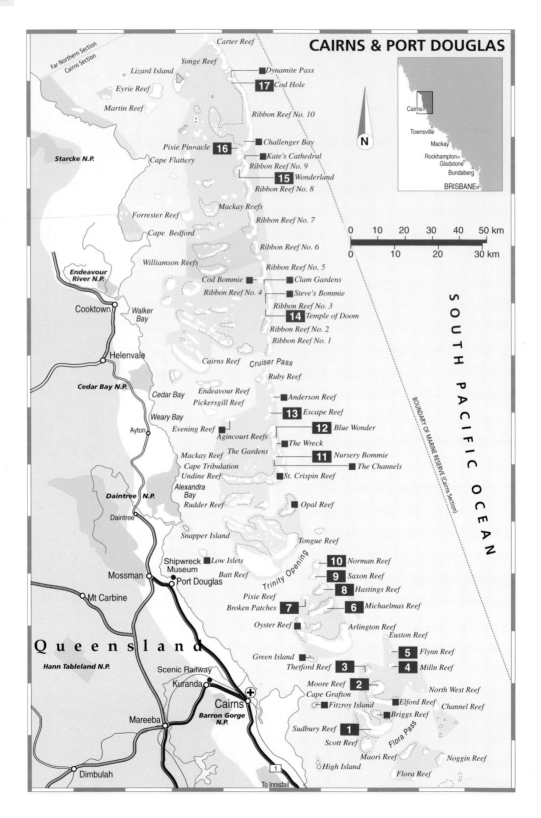

CAIRNS & PORT DOUGLAS

Carter Reef

Far Northern Section
Cairns Section

Yonge Reef
■ Dynamite Pass
Lizard Island
17 ■ Cod Hole
Eyrie Reef

Martin Reef

Ribbon Reef No. 10

N

Pixie Pinnacle **16** ■ Challenger Bay
Starcke N.P.
Cape Flattery ■ Kate's Cathedral
Ribbon Reef No. 9
15 ■ Wonderland
Ribbon Reef No. 8

Mackay Reefs
Forrester Reef Ribbon Reef No. 7
Cape Bedford

Ribbon Reef No. 6

Endeavour River N.P.
Williamson Reefs Ribbon Reef No. 5
Cod Bommie ■ ■ Clam Gardens
Ribbon Reef No. 4 ■ Steve's Bommie
Cooktown
Walker Ribbon Reef No. 3
Bay **14** ■ Temple of Doom
Ribbon Reef No. 2
Ribbon Reef No. 1

Helenvale

Cairns Reef Cruiser Pass
Ruby Reef
Cedar Bay N.P.
Cedar Bay Endeavour Reef
Pickersgill Reef ■ Anderson Reef
Weary Bay **13** ■ Escape Reef
Ayton
Evening Reef ■ **12** ■ Blue Wonder
Agincourt Reefs
Mackay Reef The Gardens ■ The Wreck
Cape Tribulation **11** ■ Nursery Bommie
Daintree N.P. Undine Reef ■ The Channels
Alexandra
Bay ■ St. Crispin Reef
Daintree Rudder Reef

Snapper Island ■ Opal Reef

Tongue Reef

Shipwreck ■ Low Islets **10** ■ Norman Reef
Museum Batt Reef **9** ■ Saxon Reef
Mossman **8** ■ Hastings Reef
● Port Douglas
Mt Carbine Pixie Reef
Broken Patches **7** ■ **6** ■ Michaelmas Reef
Oyster Reef ■
Arlington Reef
Euston Reef

Q u e e n s l a n d
Green Island ■ **5** ■ Flynn Reef
Hann Tableland N.P. Thetford Reef **3** ■ **4** ■ Milln Reef
Scenic Railway
Kuranda Moore Reef **2** ■
Cape Grafton North West Reef
Cairns ■ Fitzroy Island ■ Elford Reef Channel Reef
■ Briggs Reef
Mareeba Barron Gorge
N.P. Sudbury Reef **1** ■
Scott Reef Flora Pass
Dimbulah Maori Reef ■ Noggin Reef
High Island ■ Flora Reef
To Innisfail

Cairns
Townsville
Mackay
Rockhampton
Gladstone
Bundaberg
BRISBANE

S O U T H   P A C I F I C   O C E A N

BOUNDARY OF MARINE RESERVE (Cairns Section)

Trinity Opening

| 0 | 10 | 20 | 30 | 40 | 50 km |

| 0 | 10 | 20 | 30 km |

Mt Carbine

It is up to you how you dive the Cairns and Port Douglas area. If your time is limited, there are many excellent daytrips, some only to the inner reefs, but most of the larger day-trip operators like Quicksilver and Great Adventures can reach the outer reef in under two hours. If you have a few days, consider a live-aboard trip of two to four days to visit the outer reef and explore the Ribbon Reefs and the Cod Hole. If you have longer than a week, a combined Northern Coral Sea/Ribbon Reefs trip would be possible. These are deservedly popular: the boat spends four days exploring Osprey Reef and in the last three days you work your way down the Ribbon Reefs.

Dozens of charter boats operate out of Cairns and Port Douglas, giving the diver a wide range of choices in price and destinations. Booking is recommended but there are generally vacancies on the boats, so shop around if you have a flexible timetable.

All the reefs and islands off Cairns and Port Douglas are located in the northern section of the Great Barrier Reef Marine Park. Most of the reefs have been zoned for general use, but some have been damaged by overdiving. Currently only a few reefs close seasonally, to give them a chance to recover, but with the enormous volume of visitors to this part of the Great Barrier Reef Marine Park, many more may have to be closed in future. At the moment most reefs are quite healthy and well-populated with fish.

1 SUDBURY REEF

✱✱✱✱✱✱

Location: 60km (37 miles) southeast of Cairns.
Access: By boat, over 1hr from Cairns Harbour, ½hr from Fitzroy Island.
Conditions: Generally calm. Average visibility 20m (65ft).
Minimum depth: 2m (6ft)
Maximum depth: 30m (100ft)
Sudbury Reef is a large reef complex with many fine dive sites to suit all levels of experience. There are numerous walls covered in thick growths of hard and soft corals where you are likely to encounter everything from turtles and gropers to schools of fusiliers and parrotfish. Divers will find many colourful corals and reef fish in the shallows. Common are angelfish, flutemouths, lionfish, anemonefish, rock cod, squirrelfish, filefish and blennies. Sudbury Reef is good for both scuba divers and snorkellers, and photographers will find a wide range of subjects. The reef is most commonly dived from Fitzroy Island but other charter boats occasionally stop here.

2 MOORE REEF

✱✱✱✱✱✱

Location: 55km (35 miles) southeast of Cairns.
Access: By boat, over 1hr from Cairns Harbour, ½hr from Fitzroy Island.
Conditions: Generally calm. Average visibility 15m (50ft).
Minimum depth: 2m (6ft)
Maximum depth: 30m (100ft)
Like most of the inner reefs, Moore Reef has sheltered coral gardens at its heart and sloping drop-offs at the edge. There are numerous coral heads and gutters covered in hard coral in the shallows. Here divers will find anemones with their ever-present anemonefish, giant clams, a variety of nudibranchs, an abundance of echinoderms, Blue-spotted Fantail Rays and a wide selection of small reef fish. The drop-offs are decorated with lovely coral growths – the gorgonians and soft corals are the most colourful. Along the drop-off are sheltering reef fish, the odd pelagic and White-spotted Eagle Rays. Whitetip Reef Sharks and Manta Rays sometimes frequent the area to add that extra bit of excitement. Photographers will find that Moore Reef lends itself to macro rather than to wide-angle photography, and snorkellers will have a lot of fun discovering the variety of marine life in the shallows.

3 THETFORD REEF

✱✱✱✱✱✱

Location: 55km (35 miles) east of Cairns.
Access: By boat, over 1hr from Cairns Harbour, ½hr from Fitzroy Island.
Conditions: Generally calm, slight currents. Average visibility 15m (50ft).
Minimum depth: 2m (6ft)
Maximum depth: 30m (100ft)
At Thetford Reef, the shallows are dominated by hard corals, and the sloping reef walls decorated with colourful soft corals and fans. There is a number of pinnacles off the main reef. Fish life is generally good. Divers will

find angelfish, parrotfish, butterflyfish, anemonefish, rock cod, damsels, surgeonfish, wrasse, lionfish and the odd pelagic. For the macro photographer there are nudibranchs, flatworms, tube worms, echinoderms, molluscs, shrimps, crabs, small reef fish and many lovely corals to photograph.

4 MILLN REEF

★★★★☆☆☆

Location: 5km (35 miles) east of Cairns.
Access: By boat, over 2hr from Cairns Harbour.
Conditions: Generally calm. Average visibility 25m (80ft).
Minimum depth: 2m (6ft)
Maximum depth: 30m (100ft)
There are many excellent dive sites around Milln Reef. The Three Sisters at the far northern tip has a series of pinnacles sloping off into deep water. These pinnacles are cut with gutters and swim-throughs, and teem with fish – resident and pelagic – including mackerel, tuna, fusiliers and barracuda. There are also likely to be Green Turtles, White-spotted Eagle Rays, Whitetip Reef Sharks, Grey Reef Sharks and the odd Manta Ray. The corals coating these pinnacles are also spectacular, including spiky soft corals, gorgonians, sea whips, black coral and sponges. Other popular dive sites are the Swimming

Pool, where divers can explore extensive coral beds in shallow water, and Whale Bommie, a deep-water pinnacle covered in coral and with abundant fish life.

5 FLYNN REEF

Location: 55km (35 miles) east of Cairns.
Access: By boat, over 2hr from Cairns Harbour.
Conditions: Generally calm, slight currents. Average visibility 25m (80ft).
Minimum depth: 2m (6ft)
Maximum depth: 30m (100ft)
Flynn Reef is on the outer edge of the Cairns reef system and has many exciting dive sites. Gordon's Mooring consists of a series of coral heads in 15m (50ft) of water. These coral heads are cut by many caves and crevasses, and coloured by many wonderful hard and soft corals. Reef fish are plentiful in the area, sweetlips, parrotfish, angelfish, butterflyfish, anemonefish, rock cod, lionfish, pufferfish, gobies and numerous species of wrasse are common. Whitetip Reef Sharks can sometimes be found sleeping in caves, resting in gutters, or just patrolling the reef. Other popular dive sites are at the Coral Gardens and Northern Moorings, where divers will see a variety of reef fish and many brilliant invertebrate species.

Mimic Leatherjacket sleeping next to a spiky soft coral.

6 MICHAELMAS REEF

★★★☆☆

Location: 45km (28 miles) northeast of Cairns.
Access: By boat, over 2hr from Cairns Harbour.
Conditions: Generally calm. Average visibility 15m (50ft).
Minimum depth: 4m (13ft)
Maximum depth: 20m (65ft)
Michaelmas Reef is a popular location with scuba and snorkel divers. Thousands of seabirds nest at the sand cay at the southern end of the reef. Just off this cay are some lovely coral gardens and large numbers of pinnacles. Wayne's Bommie consists of dozens of pinnacles which seem to be packed with corals and fish life. You are likely to find giant clams nested on the bottom, shy cuttles, turtles, Whitetip Reef Sharks, Blue spotted Fantail Rays wedged under plate corals and even Manta Rays. There are more towering pinnacles at the Coral Gardens which seem to attract a large selection of pelagic fish. Divers regularly encounter Dogtooth Tuna, Spanish mackerel, coral trout, Maori Wrasse, schools of fusiliers and barracuda, and reef sharks. The pinnacles are riddled with small caves and coated with lovely coral growths. Small reef fish are omnipresent and numerous invertebrates hide in the corals.

7 BROKEN PATCHES

★★★☆☆

Location: 50km (30 miles) northeast of Cairns.
Access: By boat, over 2hr from Cairns Harbour.
Conditions: Generally calm, slight currents. Average visibility 20m (65ft).
Minimum depth: 4m (13ft)
Maximum depth: 25m (80ft)
Broken Patches is a collection of fractured reefs that offers some great diving. Paradise Reef is a popular dive site with gutters, pinnacles, walls, caves and shallow reef making it perfect for scuba and snorkel divers. Visitors will discover a wide array of corals, from fields of hard coral to walls of gorgonians and soft corals and patches of sponges and sea whips. Reef fish common in the area include angelfish, lionfish, damsels, triggerfish, surgeonfish, parrotfish, boxfish, pufferfish, anemonefish, sweetlips and rock cod. Larger fish sometimes sweep the area, schools of trevally and barracuda mingle off the deeper walls, Maori Wrasse and groper lurk in caves and Whitetip Reef Sharks can be seen checking the gutters for food. Nearby is a series of pinnacles known as Broken Patches Bommies, where there are gropers and reef sharks.

There are many reefs to explore in the clear blue waters off Cairns and Port Douglas.

8 HASTINGS REEF

★★★★☆

Location: 55km (35 miles) northeast of Cairns.
Access: By boat, over 2hr from Cairns Harbour.
Conditions: Generally calm, slight currents. Average visibility 25m (80ft).
Minimum depth: 2m (6ft)
Maximum depth: 30m (100ft)
Pinnacles, walls, caves and coral gardens are just some of the features of Hastings Reef. The walls and pinnacles are encrusted with gorgonians, soft corals and sea whips, with fragile hydroid corals in the caves and a wealth of hard and soft corals in the shallows. There are plenty of resident reef fish all round the reef and you will also encounter stingrays, Maori Wrasse, triggerfish, turrum, moray eels and schools of barracuda and trevally off the wall. Turtles and reef sharks are also seen in the area. Macro photographers will find fascinating subject matter.

SEA URCHINS

Sea urchins are among the most prolific of the medium-size, mobile invertebrates. A number of species are venomous – avoid those with sharp spines or treat them carefully. The spines consist of brittle, bone-like material. Some species have reverse serrations on the spines which break off and can be extremely painful. Removing them is difficult and if the flesh is badly spined, nothing short of minor surgery will suffice. Several of the larger tropical sea urchins are dangerous and can cause serious, painful wounds, leading to infection and even paralysis. The smaller, finer spines will eventually be dissolved by body fluids. Few precautions can be taken except to be careful in areas where there are urchins. This warning is extended in particular to night divers and people who dive in caves and between ledges lined with sea urchins.

9 SAXON REEF
★★★★★★

Location: 55km (35 miles) northeast of Cairns.
Access: By boat, over 2hr from Cairns Harbour.
Conditions: Generally calm, slight currents. Average visibility 20m (65ft).
Minimum depth: 2m (6ft)
Maximum depth: 30m (100ft)
There are many good diving and snorkelling spots around Saxon Reef. Snorkellers will find masses of small reef fish and the odd turtle in the shallow beds of hard and soft coral. Deeper down, small caves and gutters cut through the reef and coral heads rise from the bottom. The marine life includes nudibranchs, echinoderms, lionfish, anemones, butterflyfish, squirrelfish, goatfish, clams, pufferfish and damsels. Larger fish, generally pelagics, also visit the reef.

10 NORMAN REEF
★★★★★★★

Location: 60km (37 miles) northeast of Cairns.
Access: By boat, over 2hr from Cairns Harbour.
Conditions: Generally calm, slight currents. Average visibility 25m (80ft).
Minimum depth: 2m (6ft)
Maximum depth: 30m (100ft)
Norman Reef is a popular location with a number of charter boat operators. The Great Adventures pontoon is

moored here. There is a range of dive sites – those after a deep dive can drop down a coral wall and poke around the ledges and crevasses that cut into the structure; for shallower, more relaxing diving you can explore the coral heads and gardens of coral in the shallows. Photographers will find macro and wide-angle subjects, including gropers, flatworms, turtles, molluscs, stingrays, sea stars, reef sharks and colourful nudibranchs. Small reef fish are found in abundance but divers may also experience close encounters with trevally, mackerel, turrum, barracuda and giant Maori Wrasse.

11 NURSERY BOMMIE
★★★★★★★

Location: Southern end of Agincourt Reefs, 65km (40 miles) from Port Douglas.
Access: By boat, under 2hr from Port Douglas.
Conditions: Generally calm. Average visibility 20m (65ft).
Minimum depth: 5m (16ft)
Maximum depth: 24m (80ft)
Nursery Bommie is a huge pinnacle, approximately 20m (65ft) in diameter. Divers generally start at the base and work their way up around this large coral head. Two large Leopard Morays that make wonderful photographic subjects live at 18m (60ft). The pinnacle is coated with a fine collection of gorgonians, soft and hard corals and sea whips. Small fish and larger ones such as sweetlips, groper, Maori Wrasse, mackerel, coral cod, batfish, coral trout and striped snapper are prolific. Large anemones house shy anemonefish, delicate shrimps and lovely porcelain crabs. A resident school of barracuda and huge spiky soft corals are found in the deeper waters.

12 BLUE WONDER
★★★★★★★

Location: Eastern side of Agincourt Reefs, 65km (40 miles) from Port Douglas.
Access: By boat, under 2hr from Port Douglas.
Conditions: Generally calm, slight currents. Average visibility 20m (65ft).
Minimum depth: 5m (16ft)
Maximum depth: 40m (13ft) plus
This is one of the best dives at Agincourt Reef, a wall dive with colourful corals, masses of pelagic fish and the odd reef shark. Descending the wall, divers will find a wealth of hard corals in the shallows that quickly gives

Pixie Pinnacle is one of the prettiest dive sites on the Ribbon Reefs.

way to more colourful spiky soft corals, gorgonians and sea whips. Small and large fish shelter along the wall. Schools of barracuda and trevally can be seen with mackerel, jobfish, batfish and fusiliers. Whitetip and Grey Reef Sharks are known to frequent the area but are a little wary of divers. Moving back up the wall there are numerous caves that cut deep into the wall. Explore them for squirrelfish, pufferfish and painted crays. Take your torch.

13 ESCAPE REEF

* * * * * * *

Location: 75km (45 miles) northeast of Port Douglas.
Access: By boat, over 4hr from Port Douglas.
Conditions: Generally calm, slight currents. Average visibility 20m (65ft).
Minimum depth: 6m (20ft)
Maximum depth: 30m (100ft)
At Escape Reef there is a collection of small coral heads that are home to a diverse range of marine life. These coral heads are decorated with soft corals, sponges, sea whips and gorgonians, and many anemones, tube worms and feather stars. Turtles and Whitetip Reef Sharks are encountered in the area, as are coral trout, stingrays, moray eels, sweetlips, surgeonfish and pelagics.

14 TEMPLE OF DOOM

* * * * * * * * *

Location: 110km (70 miles) north of Port Douglas, off Ribbon Reef No. 3.
Access: By boat, over 6hr from Port Douglas.
Conditions: Generally calm, slight currents. Average visibility 30m (100ft).
Minimum depth: 4m (13ft)
Maximum depth: 30m (100ft) plus
Temple of Doom is a massive pinnacle on the western side of Ribbon Reef No. 3. It is over 30m (100ft) in diameter and seems to attract more than its fair share of fish life. As soon as you hit the water you are surrounded by large schools of goatfish, trevally, snapper and fusiliers, tuna, mackerel, barracuda and coral trout. If you can drag yourself away from the fish and explore the deeper reaches of the pinnacle, you will find it covered with gorgonians, black coral trees, sea whips, sponges and some lovely soft corals. A number of small ledges cut into the pinnacle, where you will find moray eels and crays. On the rest of the reef you will see a variety of small reef fish and colourful invertebrates. Whitetip Reef Sharks are also common, as are gropers, stingrays and Eagle Rays.

15 WONDERLAND

* * * * * * *

Location: 160km (100miles) north of Port Douglas, off Ribbon Reef No. 9.
Access: By boat, over 9hr from Port Douglas.
Conditions: Generally calm, slight currents. Average visibility 30m (100ft).
Minimum depth: 4m (13ft)
Maximum depth: 40m (130ft) plus
Wonderland is a small reef on the western side of Ribbon Reef No. 9 with impressive drop-offs populated by a vast array of marine life. Explore this wall on a gentle drift dive – it is decorated with some lovely gorgonians and soft corals and cut by many small caves lined with hydroid and *Tubastrea* corals. Small reef fish and invertebrates are common and numerous pelagics also feed along the wall, scattering the smaller fish. Reef sharks, groper, Eagle Rays and even sea snakes are seen in the area, so have your camera ready.

16 PIXIE PINNACLE

* * * * * * * *

Location: 165km (103 miles) north of Port Douglas, off Ribbon Reef No. 9.
Access: By boat, over 10hr from Port Douglas.
Conditions: Generally calm, slight currents. Average visibility 30m (100ft).
Minimum depth: 4m (13ft)
Maximum depth: 35m (115ft)
Pixie Pinnacle is like a large coral bommie protruding from the bottom, overflowing with colourful corals, and home to a multitude of reef creatures. Many small caves riddle the pinnacle, and each seems to be packed with beautiful, spiky soft corals, hydroid corals, *Tubastrea* corals and small gorgonians. The walls are steep and coated with a wealth of corals, especially sea whips, soft corals and gorgonians. Reef fish, including coral cod, coral trout, Fairy Basslets, rock cod, hawkfish, wrasse, butterflyfish, cardinalfish, squirrelfish, filefish and angelfish, are plentiful and reef sharks, Eagle Rays, barracuda, jobfish, fusiliers, mackerel and batfish swim off the pinnacle. Photographers will find themselves quickly running out of film here. After dark, Pixie Pinnacle is even more colourful under torchlight. Many small reef creatures appear, including Mantis Shrimps, flatworms, coral crabs, molluscs, decorator crabs, coral shrimps and nudibranchs. While most fish sleep in the coral and caves, others such as squirrelfish are out hunting. But the most impressive feature of a night dive is the amazing colours of the corals.

17 COD HOLE

★ ★ ★ ★ ★ ☆ ☆ ☆ ☆ ☆

Location: 190km (120 miles) north of Port Douglas, off Ribbon Reef No. 10.
Access: By boat, over 12hr from Port Douglas.
Conditions: Generally calm, slight currents. Average visibility 30m (100ft).
Minimum depth: 4m (13ft)
Maximum depth: 20m (65ft)

The Cod Hole is one of the most famous dive sites on the Great Barrier Reef. Potato Cod were discovered here in 1973. Today the area is protected, and six to 14 huge Potato Cod live on the sloping reef face at the northern end of Ribbon Reef No. 10. The cod come to greet you as soon as you enter the water, so be ready with your camera. Many of the charter boats hand-feed cod, which can be quite a spectacle. The friendly residents jostle each other and sometimes the divers to get the food – they have to be quick as several Leopard Morays and Maori Wrasse also hang around for easy pickings.

PLANKTON

Plankton, from the Greek meaning 'wanderer', is used to describe all manner of drifting sea life, plants and animals which rely on distribution by current. Many are capable of movement and some engage in the daily pattern of vertical migration from the depths where they spend the daylight hours, to the surface where they spend the night, yet none can swim against the current. They vary in size from microscopic to 10m- (30ft) long giant salps (planktonic communal ascidians). The minute plants called phytoplankton are dominant in the upper layers of the surface where the most light penetrates, while the zooplankton exist throughout the vertical water column. The numbers of zooplankton are bewildering, for not only does this group contain its own specialised fauna, but it also represents all the eggs, spawn, larvae and juveniles of every species of sea creature which has planktonic larval dispersal. Most plankton occur near the shore where there are more nutrients, which is why offshore waters appear clearer.

One of the famous overfed Potato Cod of the Cod Hole.

Mutualism describes what occurs when animals live together and benefit from the association. On the Great Barrier Reef, a number of species live in permanent or transient mutualistic associations with other animals. One of the easiest to observe is the small bottom-dwelling gobies and the alpheid snapping shrimps. Shrimp gobies, alone or in pairs, occupy the burrows of snapping shrimps. The goby guards the shrimp, who has very poor vision. From the entrance of the burrow the goby has a good view over the generally flat, sandy terrain and can spot predators in time. The shrimp spends most of its day cleaning house, carrying sand and coral debris between its pincers almost like a frontloader steam shovel.

CLEANER SHRIMPS

Cleaner shrimps have bright colour patterns, long antennae, special dance routines and swimming postures to attract fish and solicit their submission to cleaning. Each species has its own particular behavioural patterns, and while some are daytime cleaners, others are night-time cleaners, or both. The Banded Coral Shrimp and Grabham's Cleaner Shrimp are tropical species and have conspicuous red and white patterns with long, white antennae. They are generally found in pairs and tend to prefer caves, ledges, holes in rocks, coral bommies or coral slabs as cleaning stations. Most choose stations that have dark interiors, although both species often share a cleaning station and display during daylight hours.

CLEANER WRASSE

The Common Cleaner Wrasse (*Labroides dimidiatus*) is probably the best-known full-time cleaner in Australia. This fish has certain areas or protected places where it sets up what is known as a cleaning station. All fish in the immediate vicinity visit the station. Cleaner Wrasse only operate during the day and have such a close relationship with their hosts that they are able to enter the mouths and gills of large and small

carnivores with impunity. The Common Cleaner Wrasse advertises its readiness to clean by displaying above or near its cleaning station with a series of nod-like swimming movements often called a dance. If the fish host is young or new to the cleaner and a little hesitant to avail itself, the Common Cleaner Wrasse swims out and communicates with a series of touching movements of snout, body and fins. By repeating contact at specific places the Common Cleaner Wrasse can tell its host where it is cleaning and also where it wants to clean, e.g. mouth, behind fins, inside gill plates.

SUCKERFISH

Suckerfish (remora) stick on to larger marine fishes, reptiles and mammals with their modified dorsal-fin suction pads, and are transport symbionts. Although they are mostly dependent on their hosts for mobility, the suckerfish change hosts as they grow and are quite capable of swimming. Suckerfish have the added advantage of leftovers if their host is a carnivore. Some hosts go to great lengths to rid themselves of suckerfish by evasive swimming, jumping out of the water and rubbing the suckerfish on the bottom.

GOBIES

There are at least 20 different species of gobies, which have a protective association with hydrozoans, corals, sea whips, gorgonians and soft corals. Many are coloured in such a way that they are almost undetectable among the fronds and tentacles of their hosts. Gobies live on and in sponges, ascidians, and even on the mantle surface and in the siphons of giant clams. At least two species of gobies live in association with crinoid feather stars and have a similar colour, although they often move between a number of hosts in areas where they are abundant. There is normally a male and female in residence on a host, with one or more juveniles that probably originated hundreds of kilometres away.

Top: Gobies are usually found in pairs and their colouration camouflages them so well that they are often undetectable.
Right: The cleaning stations of Cleaner Shrimp are almost always inhabited by a pair.
Below: Reef fish regularly visit cleaning stations to have parasites and other detritus removed.

HOW TO GET THERE

Cairns is located 1717km (1064 miles) north of Brisbane, has a population of 68 000 and is the capital of Far North Queensland. The town is geared to the tourist market and has an international airport serviced by many airlines. Port Douglas is a small coastal town 75km (45 miles) north of Cairns. There is a regular bus service to Port Douglas, and if you have the time you can hire a car and drive yourself up the coast.

WHERE TO STAY

There are well over 100 motels in Cairns, from five-star hotels to basic backpacker-style accommodation. Port Douglas has a good range of accommodation, with over 30 motels.

High Price Range
Cairns International, 17 Abbott St, Cairns, tel 070-311 300, fax 070-311 801, 16-storey complex in the centre of town with 321 rooms and 18 suites with TV, video player, mini bar and 24-hour room service, a restaurant, pool, spa, sauna, gym and convention centre.

Sheraton Mirage Resort, Port Douglas Rd, Port Douglas, tel 070-995 588, fax 070-985 885, three-storey complex, self-contained rooms with airconditioning, TV, video player and mini bar and the villas have spa baths. Facilities include 24-hour room service, a restaurant, convention centre, tennis court, golf course, pool, spa, sauna and courtesy transport.

Medium Price Range
Cairns Tropical Garden Motel, 312 Mulgrave Rd, Cairns, tel 070-311 777, fax 070-312 605, has 95 units with airconditioning, TV and video player, and a restaurant, convention centre, barbecue, pool, tennis court, sauna and spa.

Port Douglas Motel, 9 Davidson St, Port Douglas, tel 070-995 248, fax 070-995 504, has 19 units, airconditioning, TV, video player, pool and a barbecue.

Lower Price Range
Silver Palm Lodge, 153 Esplanade, Cairns, tel 070-316 099, backpacker-style with a saltwater pool.

Port O' Call Lodge, Port St, Port Douglas, tel 070-995 422, fax 070-995 495, has units, budget rooms and backpacker rooms, a restaurant, cocktail bar, pool, spa, kiosk and communal kitchen.

WHERE TO EAT

The range of eating places in Cairns is incredible. There are take-away places, pub-counter meals, cafés and a wide selection of restaurants where one can try seafood, international cuisine and even barbecues. There are not nearly as many restaurants in Port Douglas but you can still choose between Thai, Italian, Chinese and especially seafood.

DIVE FACILITIES

Cairns Dive Centre, 135 Abbott St, Cairns, tel 070-510 294, fax 070-517 531, operates the charter boat *Coral Reeftel* to the reefs off Cairns; they also offer dive courses and have a good range of retail and hire gear.

Taka Dive, Cnr Lake & Aplin Sts, Cairns, tel 070-518 722, fax 070-312 739, operate the live-aboard vessels *Taka II* and *Taka III* to Ribbon Reefs, Cod Hole and Coral Sea; they also present dive courses, have retail and hire gear and an extensive range of camera gear.

Deep Sea Divers Den, 319 Draper St, Cairns, tel 070-312 223, fax 070-311 210, a five-star PADI facility with courses to instructor level. They have a wide range of retail and hire gear and operate the live-aboard charter boats, *Tropic Queen*, *Tropic Princess* and *Explorer II* to the Ribbon Reefs, Cod Hole and local reefs.

Dive 7 Seas, 129 Abbott St, Cairns, tel 070-412 700.

Don Cowie's *Down Under* Aquatics, Shields St, Cairns, tel 070-311 588, fax 070-313 318, operate daytrips on *Down Under*, they also offer dive courses, retail and hire gear.

Great Diving Adventures, Wharf St, Cairns, tel 070-510 455, operate dive centres at Green Island and Fitzroy Island and hold introductory courses and certified diving packages. The islands and outer reef pontoons at Norman Reef and Moore Reef (which both have complete diving facilities) are serviced daily by the giant luxury catamaran *Reef Queen*. They cater for all levels of diving and snorkelling, with hire gear and sales; return coach pickup from Cairns, northern beaches and Port Douglas.

Just Add Water, Shop 9, Reef Plaza, Spence St, Cairns, tel 070-412 799, are booking agents for *Undersea Explorer* and *Front Runner*, and conduct crocodile dives in the Mitchell River.

Marlin Coast Divers, Novotel Palm Cove Resort, Palm Cove, tel 070-591 144.

Mike Ball Dive Expeditions, 28 Spence St, Cairns, tel 070-315 484, fax 070-315 470, operate the live-aboard vessel *Supersport* on four-day trips to the Ribbon Reefs and Cod Hole, and offer dive courses and retail and hire gear.

Peter Tibb's Scuba School, 370 Sheridan St, Cairns, tel 070-521 266.

Peter Tibb's Dive Shop, 65 Grafton St, Cairns, tel 070-311 586.

Pro-Dive Cairns, Marlin Parade, Cairns, tel 070-315 255, fax 070-519 955, operate two charter boats, *Stella Maris* and *Kalinda,* on three-day trips to local reefs; they are a PADI five-star facility, offer courses to instructor level, and have a good range of retail and hire gear.

S2 Dive, Shop 2 Hides Corner, Lake St, Cairns, tel 070-312 150.

Tusa Dive, Cnr Aplin St & The Esplanade, Cairns, tel 070-311 248, fax 070-315 221, run live-aboard and daytrips on their three dive boats, they also have a well-equipped dive store and offer dive courses.

Auriga Bay II, PO Box 274, Manunda, Cairns, tel 070-581 408, fax 070-581 404, offer live-aboard trips to the Ribbon Reefs, Cod Hole and Far Northern Reefs.

Reef Explorer, PO Box 1090, Cairns, tel 070-939 113, fax 070-939 112, offer live-aboard trips to the Ribbon Reefs, Cod Hole, Far Northern Reefs and Coral Sea.

Rum Runner Charters, Trinity Wharf, Cairns, tel 070-521 388, fax 070-521 488, operate two live-aboards to the Ribbon Reefs, Cod Hole and Coral Sea.

Auspray Yacht Charters, Cairns, tel 018 742 925.

Bali Hai II & *Floreat* **Charter Boats,** 15 Arnhem Cl, Cairns, 070-452 649.

Lady Ruby Charters, Marlin Jetty, Cairns, tel 070-313 528, fax 070-313 554.

Nimrod 3 Dive Adventures, 46 Spence St, Cairns, tel 070-315 566, fax 070-312 431, operate to the Ribbon Reefs, Northern Coral Sea and Far Northern Reefs.

Ocean Spirit Cruises, 143 Lake St, Cairns, tel 070-312 920, fax 070-314 344.

Passions of Paradise, PO Box 2145, Cairns, tel 070-316 465, fax 070-519 505.

Reef Jet Cruises, Pier Market Pl, Cairns, tel 070-315 559, fax 070-315 819.

Sanduria Sail & Dive, 99 The Esplanade, Cairns, tel 070-516 950.

Sea Ray Charters, Marlin Marina, Wharf St, Cairns, tel 018 772 869.

Seastar II, 3 Leoni Cl, Cairns, tel 070-330 333.

Haba Dive, Marina Mirage, Port Douglas, tel 070-995 254, fax 070 995 385; daytrips to the outer Barrier Reef (Opal Reef) on the 15m (50ft) luxury catamaran *Haba Queen*. All services provided, including two dives per day, introductory diving courses, snorkelling with guides and an on-board marine biologist. Hire equipment available and courtesy coach pickup and return service from Cairns and Port Douglas.

Impulse Dive, 51a Macrossan St, Port Douglas, tel 070-995 967, offer daytrips to the outer reefs of Port Douglas on their boat *Impulse II*.

Quicksilver Diving Services, Marina Mirage, Port Douglas, tel 070-995 050,

fax 070-994 065, have a retail shop and offer dive courses and hire gear. They also run two large catamarans daily to Agincourt Reef and Low Isles, and conduct 'Reef Biosearch' tours for divers and snorkellers.

Port Douglas Dive Centre, Prince's Wharf, Port Douglas, tel 070-995 327, fax 070-995 680, offer courses and operate daytrips on their vessel *Freestyle*.

Aristocat Reef Cruises, Suite 6/8 Macrossan St, Port Douglas, tel 070-994 544, fax 070-994 565.

Undersea Explorer, Reef Plaza, Cnr Grafton & Spence St, Cairns, tel 070-512 733, fax 070-512 286, operate out of Port Douglas and run live-aboard trips to the Ribbon Reefs, Cod Hole and Coral Sea.

Outer Edge Dive, Suite 6/8 Macrossan St, Port Douglas, tel 070-994 544, fax 070-994 565.

Phantom Charters, Marina Mirage, Port Douglas, tel/fax 070-941 220, run daytrips on their high speed vessel.

Poseidon Dive Charters, 10 Sonata Cl, Port Douglas, tel 015 162 500, fax 070-994 134, operate daytrips to the reefs off Port Douglas.

Wavelength Reef Charters, 20 Solander Blvd, Port Douglas, tel 070-995 031, fax 070-993 259, operate two boats to Low Isles and the outer reef; they are only set up for snorkelling, but provide guides and marine biology introductions.

FILM PROCESSING

Print film can be processed in Cairns and Port Douglas, and a number of places in Cairns offer E6 processing.

Esplanade Photo Express, 77 The Esplanade, Cairns, tel 070-312 236.

Northern Photo Express, 79 Lake St, Cairns, tel 070-516 804.

Reef Centre Fuji Image Plaza, Lake St, Cairns, tel 070-313 122.

Sunbird Camera House, Sheilds St, Cairns, tel 070-510 222.

Tropical Pics, 61 The Esplanade, Cairns, tel 070-521 844.

Ultrafast Photolab, 67 Abbott St, Cairns, tel 070-515 933.

HOSPITALS

Calvary Hospital, 1 Upward St, Cairns, tel 070-525 200.

Cairns Base Hospital, Esplanade, Cairns, tel 070-506 333.

For any emergency, fire, police or ambulance tel 000.

RECOMPRESSION CHAMBER

For any diving accident anywhere in Australia, contact DES (Diving Emergency Service) on 1800 088 200. For more information see 'Diving Accidents', page 169.

LOCAL HIGHLIGHTS

Cairns is well tuned into the tourist market, and you will never run short of things to do. **White-water rafting** is a popular attraction. A number of companies run half-day, full-day and extended trips on the Tully River. From your motel you are taken to Tully, which is 140km (90 miles) south of Cairns, for a wild ride. You can also bungee jump, go on a rainforest tour, four-wheel drive adventures, outback tours, fishing, sailing, windsurfing, parasailing and more. There are numerous national parks, the scenic **Kuranda railway** which winds up into the mountains and a few volcanic crater lakes surrounded by rainforest where you can swim or enjoy a bushwalk. Port Douglas' main attraction is the beautiful **Daintree Rainforest**, a World Heritage site where you could see everything from crocodiles to giant cassowary, kangaroos and pythons. You can also visit **Ben Cropp's Shipwreck Museum** at Prince's Street wharf where many items from the *Yongala* and *Pandora* shipwrecks are displayed. The **Great Barrier Reef Dive Festival** is held in Cairns in mid-October each year. It offers many exciting activities such as ocean explorer's nights, conferences and free concerts and scuba diving.

THE NORTHERN CORAL SEA

Divers travel halfway around the world to dive in the Northern Coral Sea, and for good reason. The water is warm and exceptionally clear, the reefs are colourful and photogenic and the marine life prolific and spectacular. Some say the best diving in the world can be done here, and with drop-offs 1km (⅝ mile) deep, pinnacles the size of office blocks, countless numbers of caves, huge gorgonians and soft corals, sharks, Manta Rays and schooling pelagic fish, it is hard to argue the point.

The only negative aspect of diving in the Northern Coral Sea is the distance and the time it takes to reach the reefs – some will take longer to reach than your flight to Australia. A number of charter boats make regular weekly and extended trips to Flinders, Boomerang, Holmes, Bougainville and Osprey reefs. Crossings can be rough as boats have to cross open ocean. If you suffer from sea sickness, take medication and try to sleep. Luckily, all crossings are done overnight, and once on the reef the conditions are generally calm even in strong winds and big seas. Any discomfort is soon rewarded.

The Northern Coral Sea reefs are completely different to most of those those found in the south. There are few sea snakes but a wealth of other features. All of these reefs are the tips of ancient mountains, long covered by rising seas. Some form large lagoon basins, others are just towering columns of coral, but all drop quickly into deep water and being so far from the mainland, offer extraordinary visibility, averaging 40m (130ft).

Even though the closest reefs have been extensively dived, there is still much to be explored and new sites are being found all the time. Most of the outer reefs (such as Moore Reef, Willis Islet and Magdelaine Cay) have barely been touched and await further exploration. Only a limited number of charter boats have visited these outer reefs and as such, they offer virgin diving territory and the chance to see the unexpected. A few charter operators are starting to run exploration trips to these outer reefs and although they can be quite costly due to the distances involved, the experience will be well worth the expense.

Left: Snorkelling at Flinders Reef.
Above: Watanabe Bommie.

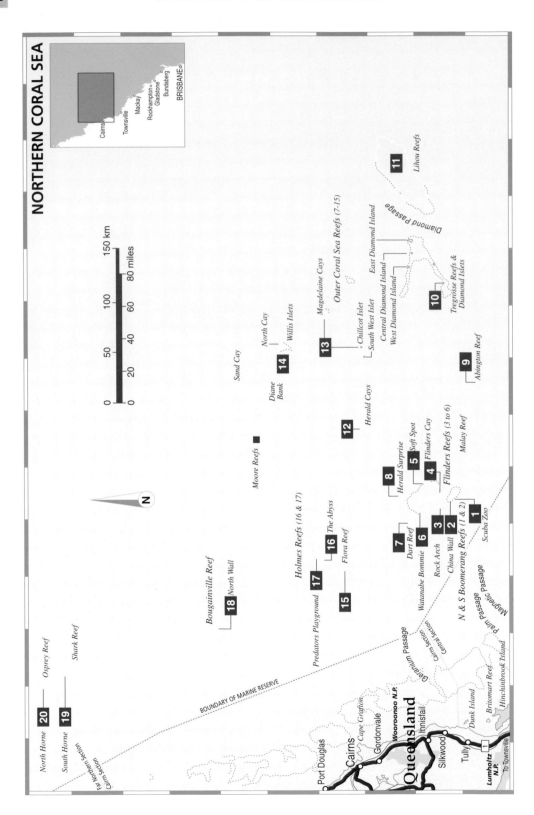

NORTHERN CORAL SEA

North and South Boomerang Reefs

The Boomerang Reefs are an off-shoot of Flinders Reef, located about two hours to the south. Being less protected and with dramatic drop-offs all round the reef, they offer plenty of exciting action. Most diving at Boomerang Reefs is wall diving. These sheer walls drop into 1km (⅝ mile) of water and are encrusted with hard and soft corals, sea whips and gorgonians. You are likely to encounter only a scattering of reef fish, but pelagic fish such as tuna, mackerel, jobfish, barracuda, Rainbow Runners and trevally are plentiful in the area. Mike Ball Dive Expeditions have been doing regular shark feeds here for almost ten years, so sharks are especially common. Divers will see Whitetip, Grey and Silvertip reef sharks and the odd Hammerhead and Tiger Shark.

Boomerang Reefs offer little in the way of safe anchorages, so it is generally done from Flinders Reef for the day, but you will find the short journey well worth the effort.

1 SCUBA ZOO

★★★★★

Location: The western side of South Boomerang Reef, 230km (145 miles) from Townsville.
Access: Over 12hr sailing time from Townsville.
Conditions: Strong winds can make conditions rough. Slight currents. Average visibility 40m (130ft).
Minimum depth: 13m (43ft)
Maximum depth: 20m (65 ft)
Scuba Zoo is where the crew of *Spoilsport* do their regular shark feeds from the safety of their purpose-built shark cage. Sharks gather as soon as the boat arrives. The divers quickly swim down to the cage while the bait is being lowered in a bucket. Over a dozen Whitetip Reef Sharks, Grey Reef Sharks and Silvertip Reef Sharks gather for the free feed. The lid of the bucket is opened by remote control and the sharks rush in to devour the contents. Exciting photos can be taken from the viewing ports in the cage. Once the food is finished, most of the sharks leave and the divers can swim safely back to the boat. This is an exhilarating dive that gives the diver a close view of sharks at their most savage.

2 CHINA WALL

★★★★★★★

Location: The northern end of North Boomerang Reef, 230km (145 miles) from Townsville.
Access: Over 12hr sailing time from Townsville.
Conditions: Can be rough in strong winds, slight currents. Average visibility 40m (130ft)
Minimum depth: 3m (10ft)
Maximum depth: 100m (330ft) plus

The China Wall is a sheer wall that drops into deep water. Cruising along this wall, which undercuts itself in some places, all you see is black water below. Gentle currents wash the wall while soft corals, sponges, gorgonians, sea whips, feather stars and numerous hard corals feed. Large pelagic fish 'fly' past – tuna, mackerel, Rainbow Runners and trevally amongst others. At the end of the dive you can swim into the shallow lagoon through one of the numerous caves that cut into the face of the wall. This sandy lagoon is dotted with small coral heads and is home to parrotfish, triggerfish, pufferfish, Maori Wrasse, coral trout, gobies, blennies and various molluscs and sea stars.

Schools of Big-Eye Trevally are found around pinnacles in the Northern Coral Sea.

Spiky soft coral on a Holmes Reef wall.

Flinders Reef

Flinders Reef is the most popular and regularly visited of all the Coral Sea Reefs. It is by far the most accessible, being only 220km (137 miles) from Townsville, and offers good all-weather anchorages. With over 1000km² (600 sq miles) of reef to explore, there are many exciting dive sites. Flinders Reef is like a huge lagoon basin and part of its structure has a fringing reef offering good protection. The lagoon is dotted with hundreds of small and large pinnacles – some break the surface, and others sit in deep water. Most of the dive sites are located within this lagoon, which is a safe all-weather anchorage and offers unparalleled diving.

3 ROCK ARCH

* * * * * * * *

Location: The southern end of Flinders Reef, 220km (137 miles) from Townsville.
Access: Over 12hr sailing time from Townsville.
Conditions: Protected by reef, mostly calm. Average visibility 40m (130ft).
Minimum depth: 3m (10ft)
Maximum depth: 100m (330ft) plus

The Rock Arch is a very impressive wall that drops into almost 1km (⅝ mile) of water. On this sheer wall branching gorgonians, sea whips, encrusting sponges and spiky soft corals provide splashes of colour. Numerous long caves cut into the wall, one of which winds right back into the lagoon. Grey Reef Sharks, Whitetip Reef Sharks, tuna, trevally and other large pelagic fish patrol the area. Some of the best diving is done in the shallow lagoon on the top of the wall which is dominated by numerous large pinnacles, nearly all of them riddled with caves. One of these forms an arch covered by a screen of the largest gorgonians you will ever see. Fish life is plentiful around the pinnacles with parrotfish, surgeonfish, trevally, unicornfish, sea bass, butterflyfish and colourful Fairy Basslets. In the caves are squirrelfish, Moorish Idols and even Whitetip Reef Sharks. The lagoon offers good snorkelling, and there is also a small coral cay to explore.

4 FLINDERS CAY

* * * * * * * *

Location: The southern end of Flinders Reef, 220km (137 miles) from Townsville.
Access: Over 12hr sailing time from Townsville.
Conditions: Always calm, protected by reef. Average visibility 30m (100ft).
Minimum depth: 3m (10ft)
Maximum depth: 18m (60ft)

This tiny cay houses an automatic weather station. It is populated by hundreds of seabirds and Green Turtles nest here and is surrounded by a large lagoon with many small coral heads. These clumps of coral are home to lionfish, moray eels, coral trout, cardinalfish, butterflyfish, nudibranchs, shrimps and coral crabs. Colonies of garden eels, numerous molluscs, gobies, triggerfish and stingrays live on the sandy bottom. Turtles regularly call here and divers have even reported observing them mating in the shallows in summer. At night, a whole new world of creatures emerges from the reef around Flinders Cay. All manner of invertebrates and a number of nocturnal fish can be seen by torchlight.

5 SOFT SPOT

★★★★★★★★

Location: The eastern side of Flinders Reef, 220km (137 miles) from Townsville.
Access: Over 12hr sailing time from Townsville.
Conditions: Mostly calm, protected by reef. Average visibility 40m (130ft).
Minimum depth: 6m (20ft)
Maximum depth: 40m (130ft)

It is easy to see why this reef was named Soft Spot. There are spiky soft corals in reds, oranges, pinks, purples and yellows wherever you look. They grow in every available spot on the pinnacles and gutters and are huge – up to 3m (10ft) long. It is amazing that the trunks are strong enough to anchor them to the reef. This is a paradise for photographers as trevally, tuna, reef sharks, mackerel, parrotfish and coral trout also visit the site. At night, the colours seem even brighter by torchlight. Shrimps, decorator crabs, arrow crabs, feather stars, brittle stars, allied cowries and tiny gobies live in the coral and on every outcrop there seem to be basket stars waving their arms to catch food. Hermit crabs, cuttles, lionfish, squirrelfish, squid and many sleeping reef fish can also be seen hiding in the coral.

6 WATANABE BOMMIE

★★★★★

Location: The western side of Flinders Reef, 220km (137 miles) from Townsville.
Access: Over 12hr sailing time from Townsville.
Conditions: Generally calm, except in strong winds. Average visibility 40m (130ft).
Minimum depth: 12m (40ft)
Maximum depth: 50m (165ft)

This giant bommie is one of the most action-packed dive sites in the Coral Sea. Watanabe Bommie is a towering pinnacle coated with wonderful corals, but few divers study it as they spend all their time watching the fish. Constantly circling above and around the bommie are schools of barracuda, Big-eye Trevally, Rainbow Runners, oceanic coral trout, Dog-tooth Tuna, surgeonfish, clouds of fusiliers and the resident Grey Reef Sharks. Divers can observe pelagic fish feeding, be engulfed in a whirlpool of circling barracuda or watch reef sharks chasing the fish.

Silvertip Whalers are encountered in the Northern Coral Sea.

Outer Coral Sea Reefs

Anyone looking for virgin diving territory should look no further than the outer reefs of the Northern Coral Sea. These reefs and cays offer similar diving to the more popular and accessible reefs like Flinders and Holmes but there seems to be more of everything. The soft corals appear to be twice as big, the gorgonians twice as wide, the pelagic fish twice as thick, and the reef sharks twice as bold.

A number of these outer reefs (including Dart, Abington, Diamond Islets and Lihou reefs) are now regularly visited by charter boats. For endless visibility, amazing marine life and incredible photo opportunities, a visit to any of these reefs will give you the diving experience of a lifetime.

7 DART REEF

* * * * * * * *

Location: Two hours north of Flinders Reef, 230km (145 miles) from Townsville.
Access: Over 12hr sailing time from Townsville.
Conditions: Exposed and only divable in calm conditions. Average visibility 40m (130ft).
Minimum depth: 6m (20ft)
Maximum depth: 100m (330ft) plus

Dart Reef is an incredible pinnacle of coral. It is an offshoot of Flinders Reef located some two hours north of the Flinders Reef system. Roughly 3km (2 miles) across, the reeftop barely breaks the surface at low tide, making it difficult to anchor and exposed in rough weather. A number of good dive sites have been discovered around here, but the southern wall is the most popular location. Caves and deep crevasses riddle the wall on the southern side of the Reef. Exploring these caves with a torch you will find gropers, squirrelfish, pufferfish, butterflyfish, lionfish and the odd Painted Cray. Some of the caves are impossible to enter because of the masses of gorgonians that shield the entrance. Anywhere along this wall divers

Most sea fan brittle stars are purple; this one is yellow.

will find spectacular coral growth, giant soft corals, row after row of gorgonians, sponges, hydroid corals and plenty of hard coral. Small reef fish are common but are overshadowed by some of the larger residents such as Maori Wrasse, Potato Cod, coral trout, Red Bass and sweetlips, trevally and barracuda. Fast, sleek Grey Reef Sharks stalk the wall, adding an element of excitement to the dive. They are too timid to come close to divers, so are quite difficult to photograph.

8 HERALD SURPRISE

* * * * * * * *

Location: Two hours north of Flinders Reef, 250km (165 miles) from Townsville.
Access: Over 12hr sailing time from Townsville.
Conditions: Exposed and only divable in calm conditions. Average visibility 40m (130ft).
Minimum depth: 6m (20ft)
Maximum depth: 100m (330ft) plus
Herald Surprise is similar in size and structure to Dart Reef but as it is even more exposed it is rarely dived. This reef offers incredible diving – sheer walls plummet into the depths, caves cut into the walls and colourful corals hang from every available spot. Many fish cruise these waters: pelagics, gropers, Maori Wrasse and reef sharks. It is only occasionally visited, exciting to explore and definitely worth a side trip from Flinders Reef if time and weather permit.

9 ABINGTON REEF

* * * * * * * *

Location: 320km (200 miles) east of Townsville.
Access: Over 14hr sailing time from Townsville.
Conditions: Exposed and only divable in calm conditions. Average visibility 40m (130ft).
Minimum depth: 6m (20ft)
Maximum depth: 100m (330ft) plus
Abington Reef offers exciting and unpredictable wall diving. Numerous caves and swim-throughs cut into the wall. Take a torch or you might miss seeing gropers, Tawny Nurse Sharks, Painted Crays, Tasselled Wobbegongs, schools of squirrelfish and the odd turtle. Many of the caves are lined with delicate corals such as purple hydroid coral, pink lace corals, encrusting sponges and pockets of *Tubastrea* coral. Small invertebrates shelter in the caves, including hermit crabs, spider crabs, flatworms, banded coral shrimps, molluscs, brittle stars and some lovely nudibranchs. Deeper down the wall is the usual assortment of Coral Sea life, the soft corals, gorgonians, sea whips, pelagic fish and reef sharks.

Spider crabs can be seen on night dives at Osprey Reef.

10 TREGROSSE REEFS & DIAMOND ISLETS

* * * * * * * *

Location: 440km (275 miles) east of Townsville and 360km (225 miles) east of Airlie Beach.
Access: Over 20hr sailing time from Townsville.
Conditions: Sheltered inside the reef system. Average visibility 40m (130ft).
Minimum depth: 6m (20ft)
Maximum depth: 100m (330ft) plus
This is a large, wishbone-shaped reef, and most of the reef top is permanently under water. Much of the reef remains unexplored, but many walls and pinnacles here offer great diving. One of the best dive sites is on a large coral head near East Diamond Islet which sits in only 10m (33ft) of water on the edge of the lagoon, but attracts plenty of marine life. While the resident reef fish are worthy of attention, they are overshadowed by larger visitors. The pinnacle is sometimes covered with schools of sweetlips, trevally and goatfish, turrum, tuna and jobfish. Eagle Rays 'fly' past, with reef sharks bringing up the rear. At the base of the coral head there are caves and ledges where stingrays, turtles and Tawny Nurse Sharks can be found.

Brilliant spiky soft corals are a feature of the Northern Coral Sea.

⑪ LIHOU REEFS

* * * * * * * *

Location: 500km (312 miles) east of Townsville and 420km (262 miles) east of Airlie Beach.
Access: Over 20hr sailing time from Airlie Beach.
Conditions: Calm and sheltered inside the reef. Average visibility 40m (130ft).
Minimum depth: 6m (20ft)
Maximum depth: 100m (330ft) plus

It is only recently that Pacific Star Charters have included the Lihou Reefs in their Coral Sea trips out of Airlie Beach. Lihou is a large reef system some 90km (55 miles) long by 40km (25 miles) wide. There are numerous cays along the entire length of the reef that are home to prolific seabird populations and that are the nesting site of many Green Turtles. The edge of the reef at Lihou drops into very deep water, and the large lagoon at the centre of the reef is dotted with hundreds of pinnacles. The wall diving here is spectacular – incredible corals colour the walls with masses of small reef fish. Pelagic fish are common, and there are also likely to be stingrays, Eagle

Rays, turtles and especially sharks in the area. As soon as you hit the water you will be surrounded by Whitetip and Grey Reef Sharks which, although incredibly exciting, can be quite unsettling. You will find that you get used to seeing them and eventually end up treating them just like any other fish.

⑫ HERALD CAYS

* * * * * * * *

Location: 350km (220 miles) east of Townsville and Cairns.
Access: Over 17hr sailing time from Townsville.
Conditions: Sheltered and generally calm inside reef. Average visibility 40m (130ft).
Minimum depth: 6m (20ft)
Maximum depth: 100m (330ft) plus

The twin reefs of Herald Cays are surrounded by drop-offs, with a sheltered lagoon between them. The drop-offs are packed with a wide variety of hard and soft corals, including delicate hydroid corals, *Tubastrea* corals black coral trees, spiky soft corals, orange sea fans, gorgonians, sea whips, sponges and many species of hard coral. The resident reef fish are quite abundant and large schools of pelagic fish, gropers, Maori Wrasse or Eagle Rays visit. Reef sharks become constant companions, and you may even find the odd Whitetip Reef Shark sleeping in a cave.

13 CHILCOTT ISLET & MAGDELAINE CAYS
★★★★★★★★

Location: 420km (262 miles) east of Townsville and Cairns.
Access: Over 20hr sailing time from Townsville.
Conditions: Sheltered and generally calm inside reef. Average visibility 40m (130ft).
Minimum depth: 6m (20ft)
Maximum depth: 100m (330ft) plus
This is a large, patchy reef complex with many small cays dotted along its length. There is a choice between steep drop-offs or the numerous pinnacles in the large deep-water lagoon. Most of the reef remains unexplored, but gropers, stingrays, Eagle Rays, pelagic fish and reef sharks have been seen in this area. Turtles are common during the summer months as they nest on the cays. You will see turtles feeding on the reef, resting in caves and gutters or even mating in the shallows.

14 WILLIS ISLETS & DIANE BANK
★★★★★★★★

Location: 450km (280 miles) east of Townsville and Cairns.
Access: Over 20hr sailing time from Townsville.
Conditions: Sheltered and generally calm inside reef. Average visibility 40m (130ft).
Minimum depth: 6m (20ft)
Maximum depth: 100m (330ft) plus
Quite a number of separate reefs make up this large system. Dive trips here have been limited in the past, but a number of pinnacles, coral gardens and drop-offs have been discovered. The coral is thick and healthy, from the hard corals in the shallows to the more colourful gorgonians and soft corals hanging from the walls. The resident reef fish are extremely photogenic – divers will find lionfish, gobies, blennies, flutemouths, moray eels, triggerfish, filefish, butterflyfish and many more. Larger residents include stingrays, turtles, Tawny Nurse Sharks, gropers, pelagic fish and Eagle Rays. Reef sharks are quite common. Whitetip Reef Sharks will inspect most divers, while the Grey Reef Sharks are a bit shyer. Grey Reef Sharks grow to a length of 2m (6ft) and are very territorial. They are usually wary of divers, but some

encountered here are slightly bolder. If threatened they arch their backs, drop their pectoral fins and swim in slow S-movements. This means back off, and it is a good idea to retreat as they have attacked quite a few divers on coral reefs around the world.

15 FLORA REEF
★★★★

Location: 230km (145 miles) from Cairns.
Access: Over 12hr sailing time from Cairns.
Conditions: Can be calm right behind the reef, slight currents. Average visibility 40m (130ft).
Minimum depth: 5m (16ft)
Maximum depth: 200m (660ft) plus
Flora Reef is a small reef just south of Holmes Reef. It is rather unprotected, so charter boats usually only visit this reef when passing, or visit for the day and return to Holmes for the night. The diving at Flora Reef is quite dramatic, with sheer walls plummeting into the depths and numerous caves cut deep into the reef. Flora Reef is well worth a look if conditions allow.

Queensland Sea Stars are only found on the Great Barrier Reef and in New Caledonia.

Holmes Reef

The twin reefs of Holmes Reef are among the more accessible in the Coral Sea, situated only 240km (150 miles) east of Cairns. Holmes Reef covers an area of 450 km² (285 sq miles) and offers incredible diving with walls, caves, pinnacles, colourful corals and a multitude of marine life. On a typical dive you will encounter schools of trevally, reef sharks, a variety of reef fish, invertebrates and spectacular soft corals. On most dives photographers will be overwhelmed with subjects.

A number of charter boats visit Holmes Reef on weekly and extended trips; *Rum Runner*, based in Cairns, is the most regular visitor. They run four-day trips each week and guarantee 30m (100ft) visibility or your money back – they haven't had to pay up yet. *Rum Runner* has over a dozen regular dive sites and they are finding new sites all the time. Holmes Reef offers good protection in rough weather and there are many safe anchorages. Much of Holmes Reef is still unexplored.

16 THE ABYSS

****

Location: South end of Holmes Reef, 240km (150 miles) from Cairns.
Access: Over 12hr sailing time from Cairns.
Conditions: Generally calm in most seas, usually a current. Average visibility 40m (130ft).
Minimum depth: 4m (13ft)
Maximum depth: 100m (330ft) plus

BOX JELLYFISH

Box jellyfish appear along the Queensland coast from October and May each year. The stings of certain species, particularly *C. fleckeri*, are often lethal. The size of the animal, its sexual state, the quantity of venom injected, the age and health of the victim, and the proximity of the sting to vital organs contribute to the severity of the sting. Some sting victims have died within minutes of being stung and others have prominent scars.

The venom has three main effects, the most important being neurotoxicosis or paralysis of the respiratory organs, the circulatory centre or cardiac system. The stings can cause painful weals and lesions. Sting victims should be treated immediately by maintaining respiration and the tentacles should be removed as quickly as possible.

Do not enter the coastal waters of northern Australia without complete protection such as a Lycra body suit, pantyhose or lightweight wetsuit. Due to the turbidity of the water, these transparent animals are almost invisible.

The Abyss is wall diving at its best. This sheer wall is thought to plummet to depths below 1km (⅝ mile). The wall is decorated with gorgonians, sponges, sea whips, and soft and hard corals. Numerous small reef fish live in nooks and crannies – angelfish, butterflyfish, hawkfish, wrasse, anemonefish and blennies. Cruising off the wall and in the depths below are Grey Reef Sharks, large coral trout, jobfish, mackerel, Rainbow Runners and schools of trevally and surgeonfish. The Abyss is usually a drift dive, which allows plenty of time to explore this impressive wall.

17 PREDATORS PLAYGROUND

****

Location: The western side of Holmes Reef, 240km (150 miles) from Cairns.
Access: Over 12hr sailing time from Cairns.
Conditions: Protected by reef so mostly calm. Average visibility 40m (130ft).
Minimum depth: Surface
Maximum depth: 4m (13ft)

Predators Playground is where the charter boat *Rum Runner* presents a unique shark feed with its huge floating shark cage. The cage consists of a net hanging from a giant rubber ring. Divers can either scuba or snorkel to watch the action. After everyone is in the cage, the crew lowers a bait cage and over 20 Grey and Whitetip reef sharks gather under the boat and rush for the food. The crew then throws in fish pieces which the sharks snap up, if the fish don't get to it first. A few of the sharks come in very close to the net, but most stay on the sandy bottom 10m (33ft) below. After half an hour the bait is gone and the sharks slowly leave. This is a spectacular way of seeing feeding sharks up close, and you may be lucky enough to see a Tiger Shark or a Hammerhead.

Bougainville Reef

Bougainville Reef is commonly dived on the way out to the more popular Osprey Reef. If conditions are calm, the charter boat might stay here overnight. Generally, however, Bougainville Reef is only dived for a day before you sail further north to Osprey Reef. Since it is only 4km (2 miles) in diameter there are a few sheltered anchorages in rough weather but most of the reef is rather exposed. Sheer walls of coral populated with resident and pelagic fish drop off all around Bougainville Reef. There are some magic coral gardens on top of the reef and the remains of two shipwrecks partially protrude from from the water. Snorkellers and scuba divers will find plenty to keep them busy here.

Painted Flutemouth using Goldman's Sweetlips as hunting cover.

18 NORTH WALL

★★★★★★★★

Location: The northern end of Bougainville Reef, 230km (145 miles) from Cairns and Port Douglas.
Access: Over 12hr sailing time from Cairns and Port Douglas.
Conditions: Calm behind reef. Average visibility 40m (130ft).
Minimum depth: 6m (20ft)
Maximum depth: 1000m (3300ft) plus

Brilliant wall dives are certainly a feature of all the Northern Coral Sea reefs, and Bougainville Reef is no exception. Floating down this wall it will seem as though you are drifting in space with a black abyss beneath until you are brought back to reality by the appearance of a Grey Reef Shark. Reef sharks (Whitetip and Grey) are common at the northern end of Bougainville Reef, probably because there are more fish there. Schools of barracuda and surgeonfish frequent the area, as do mackerel, turrum, Dogtooth Tuna and jobfish. There are lovely corals and the deeper you go the bigger they get – 2m- (6ft) long spiky soft coral, 3m- (10ft) tall bushy black coral trees and 3m- (10ft) wide gorgonians are common.

Osprey Reef

Osprey Reef is the most northerly of all the Coral Sea Reefs and many people consider it to be the best. The reef is some 20km (12 miles) long and 4km (2 miles) wide. At the centre of the reef is a large deep-water lagoon that offers safe anchorage. The walls are incredibly steep as the water just off the reef is 2km (1¼ mile) deep. Hanging on these walls is a wealth of hard and soft corals. Local reef fish are colourful and varied, and share their home with an interesting collection of gropers, Maori Wrasse, sting-rays, Eagle Rays, Manta Rays, turtles and pelagic fish. Sharks are a feature of Osprey Reef, and at the famous North Horn you have the chance to see Silvertips, oceanic Whitetips and schooling Hammerheads.

A number of charter boats based in Cairns and Port Douglas make regular trips to Osprey Reef. On a normal seven-day charter trip you will stop off at Bougainville Reef then have two or three days at Osprey Reef, and spend the last few days of the trip cruising the Ribbon Reefs.

19 SOUTH HORNE
* * * * * *

Location: The southern end of Osprey Reef, 350km (220 miles) from Cairns, 310km (195 miles) from Port Douglas.
Access: Over 18hr sailing time from Cairns and Port Douglas.
Conditions: Generally calm, slight currents. Average visibility 40m (130ft).
Minimum depth: 6m (18ft)
Maximum depth: 1000m (3300ft)
There are some lovely soft corals and gorgonian fans beyond 30m (100ft) at the South Horne. At this depth you are also likely to meet cruising reef sharks and the occasional school of barracuda or trevally. Mackerel, tuna, Rainbow Runners, fusiliers and jobfish also sweep the area. Moving up the wall there are a number of caverns and ledges to explore. Here you will find more reef fish, a wide variety of invertebrates, stingrays and small, delicate corals.

FLASHLIGHT FISH

Night dives at Osprey Reef can be rather special due to a small species of fish known as the flashlight fish. If you turn off your torch when you enter the water, you will see dozens of little pockets of light moving on the reef – the flashlight fish. There are five species of flashlight fish, but you are most likely to find one-fin flashlight fish at Osprey Reef. The fish have luminous organs under their eyes, which they can turn on and off by closing a dark skin over them. The luminous organ is thought to help the fish to see at night and to attract its zooplankton prey. During the day they hide deep in caves, but at night they feed on the drop off. Dive a few hours after nightfall to give the fish a chance to emerge.

20 NORTH HORNE
* * * * * * * * *

Location: The northern end of Osprey Reef, 350km (220 miles) from Cairns, 310km (195 miles) from Port Douglas.
Access: Over 18hr sailing time from Cairns and Port Douglas.
Conditions: Protected by reef, mostly calm. Average visibility 40m (130ft).
Minimum depth: 6m (18ft)
Maximum depth: 1000m (3300ft)
The North Horne is Osprey Reef's most famous dive site, renowned for its sharks, of which there are plenty. As soon as you enter the water here you will be inspected by six resident Whitetip Reef Sharks and several Grey Reef Sharks. Descending the wall, these sharks are sometimes joined by several large Silvertip Sharks and occasionally by oceanic Whitetip Reef Sharks, Great Hammerheads and the odd lone Tiger Shark, which will certainly make it a dive you will never forget. Some of the charter boats do exciting shark feeds here, but even without the food the shark action is good. Besides the sharks, divers can admire beautiful soft corals, sea whips, gorgonians and other corals. There are also schools of pelagic fish, gropers, Eagle Rays and Manta Rays. One of the most remarkable features of the reef is the population of Hammerhead Sharks. In winter and spring large schools of Hammerheads are seen off the wall. This is thought to be related to mating, but very little is actually known about shark behaviour. To see the sharks you generally have to swim off the wall where, if you are lucky, you may see hundreds of hammerheads swimming in formation.

How to Get There

Many charter boats make regular trips to the Northern Coral Sea from the ports of Airlie Beach, Townsville, Cairns and Port Douglas. Airlie Beach is located over 1100km (682 miles) north of Brisbane, and is accessible by plane, car, train or bus. If flying, you will have to fly to Hamilton Island Airport or Proserpine Airport, and transfer to Airlie Beach by water taxi or coach. Townsville is located 1371km (855 miles) north of Brisbane and is accessible by plane, train, car or bus depending on your time and budget. Cairns is located 1717 km (1064 miles) north of Brisbane. It has a large international and domestic airport, and is also accessible by car, coach and train. Port Douglas is only 75km (45 miles) north of Cairns and there are regular coach services.

Where to Stay

In Airlie Beach, Townsville, Cairns or Port Douglas you will find excellent accommodation – refer to the relevant regional directory.

Where to Eat

All of these towns have an endless number of take-away food places and restaurants.

Dive Facilities

Auriga Bay II, PO Box 274, Manunda, Cairns, tel 070 581 408, fax 070 581 404. *Auriga Bay II* is an 18m (58ft) motor sailer for 12 passengers. Her main area of operation is the Far Northern Reefs, but she also does trips to Osprey Reef, the Ribbon Reefs and Cod Hole.

Taka Dive, Cnr Lake & Aplin Sts, Cairns, tel 070-518 722, fax 070-312 739, operate the 22m (72ft) vessel *Taka II*, which can carry 26 passengers, and the 28m (95ft) vessel *Taka III*. They run year-round trips to Osprey Reef as part of their Ribbon Reefs Tours and four-day trips to Holmes Reef.

Mike Ball Dive Expeditions, 252 Walker St, Townsville, tel 077-723 022, fax 077-212 152, operate the live-aboard vessel, *Spoilsport*, a 30m (100ft) catamaran that caters for 28 passengers and runs regular trips to Flinders Reef,

Boomerang Reefs and the *Yongala,* and a number of extended trips deep into the Coral Sea to Herald Cays, Coringa Islets, Abington and Malay Reefs.

Pacific Star Charters, 48 Coral Esplanade, Cannonvale, Airlie Beach, tel 079-466 383, fax 079-466 901, operate the 19m (62ft) motor sailing catamaran *Pacific Star* that can carry 10 passengers. She does weekly and extended trips to Lihou Reef, Diamond Islets, Abington Reef, Flinders Reef, the reefs around the Whitsundays and even Marion Reef in the Southern Coral Sea.

Reef Explorer, PO Box 1090, Cairns, tel 070-939 113, fax 070-939 112. *Reef Explorer* is a 20m (65ft) vessel that caters for 10 passengers. They run regular trips to Osprey Reef, the Ribbon Reefs and Cod Hole, and Tiger Shark cage trips at Osprey Reef. They also do extended trips to Flinders Reef, Herald Cays, Abington Reef, the Lihou Reefs and Diamond Islets.

Rum Runner Charters, Trinity Wharf, Cairns, tel 070-521 388, fax 070-521 488. *Rum Runner*, a 20m (65ft) motor schooner for 16 passengers and *Rum Runner II*, a 20m (65ft) motor vessel for 18 passengers operate to Holmes Reef, Bougainville Reef, the Ribbon Reefs and Cod Hole.

Nimrod III, 46 Spence St, Cairns, tel 070-315 566, fax 070-312 431. *Nimrod III* is a 20m (65ft) vessel for 16 passengers. She runs trips along the Ribbon Reefs and is available for charter to explore the Northern Coral Sea and Far Northern Reefs.

Undersea Explorer, Reef Plaza, Cnr Grafton & Spence St, Cairns, tel 070-512 733, fax 070-512 286. *Undersea Explorer* is a 25m (80ft) vessel with 11 large two-berth cabins. She runs weekly trips to Osprey Reef, the Ribbon Reefs and Cod Hole, and to Dart Reef, Bougainville Reef and the Far Northern Reefs.

Film Processing

A number of the vessels offer an on-board E6 processing service. Print and E6 processing is available in Airlie

Beach, Townsville, Cairns and Port Douglas. Refer to the relevant regional directory.

Hospitals

Calvary Hospital, 1 Upward St, Cairns, tel 070-525 200.

Cairns Base Hospital, Esplanade, Cairns, tel 070-506 333.

Proserpine Hospital, 2 Herbert St, Proserpine, tel 079-451 422.

Townsville General Hospital, Eyre St, Townsville, tel 077-819 211.

For any emergency, fire, police or ambulance tel 000.

Recompression Chamber

For any diving accident anywhere in Australia, contact DES (Diving Emergency Service) on 1800 088 200. For more information see 'Diving Accidents', page 169. As part of their survey requirements all dive charter boats must carry oxygen, but being such a long way from a chamber it is best to always play it safe.

Local Highlights

For local activities and places to visit refer to the relevant regional directories.

ANTONIO TARABOCCHIA

In November 1961 the Italian freighter *Antonio Tarabocchia* ran full-speed into Bougainville Reef. Stuck high on the reef, the crew tried unsuccessfully to save the ship by running her engines at full astern. A month later her back lay broken and she started to break up. Today the wreck makes a wonderful dive in calm conditions. Much of the 140m- (450ft) long wreck remains to be explored; divers can poke around the boilers, search the buckled steel plates and try to identify the objects they discover.

FAR NORTHERN REEFS

Sharks, walls and pelagic fish, and plenty of them, is the best way to describe the Far Northern region of the Great Barrier Reef. This remote section starts north of Lizard Island and extends all the way to Papua New Guinea.

The reefs of the far north are easily the richest and most diverse of any in Australian waters. In these warm northern seas, hard and soft corals abound, and the wealth and variety of colourful reef fish is unbelievable. Pelagic fish are common as these waters have rarely been fished. There are great numbers of tuna, mackerel, jobfish, turrum, trevally and barracuda. Whales, dolphins, marlin, gropers, stingrays, Eagle Rays, Manta Rays and turtles are found at many of the reefs. The turtle population must be the largest on earth, as there are records of coral cays here where they nest in their thousands, night after night. Probably the most memorable aspect of the Far Northern Reefs is the sharks. Huge numbers are seen, ranging from bottom-dwelling wobbegongs and Leopard Sharks to reef sharks – the Grey, Whitetip and Silvertip – and Hammerheads, Tiger Sharks and even massive Whale Sharks. Most of the charter boats conduct shark feeds.

Currents are commonly experienced as many of the reefs are closely packed. Drift diving along walls and through reef channels is a feature of the area; if it weren't for the currents there wouldn't be such a wealth of incredible coral. Visibility on some of the inner reefs can be low at times, down to 15m (50ft), while on the outer reefs and the detached reefs, it averages 30m (100ft) and can be over 60m (200ft). A number of dive sites in the region have been named but most of them are still unexplored.

A few charter boats call here – most trips last seven days or longer as the reefs are over 400km (250 miles) from Cairns, where most charter boats are based. Boats run out of the Lockhart River with divers flying up from Cairns. From the Lockhart River it is only a few hours' sailing to the heart of the Far Northern Reefs. Divers also fly into Thursday Island and take a dive trip back to Cairns.

Left: Divers will find many colourful and healthy corals on the Far Northern Reefs.
Above: Imperator Shrimps live on Spanish Dancer nudibranchs.

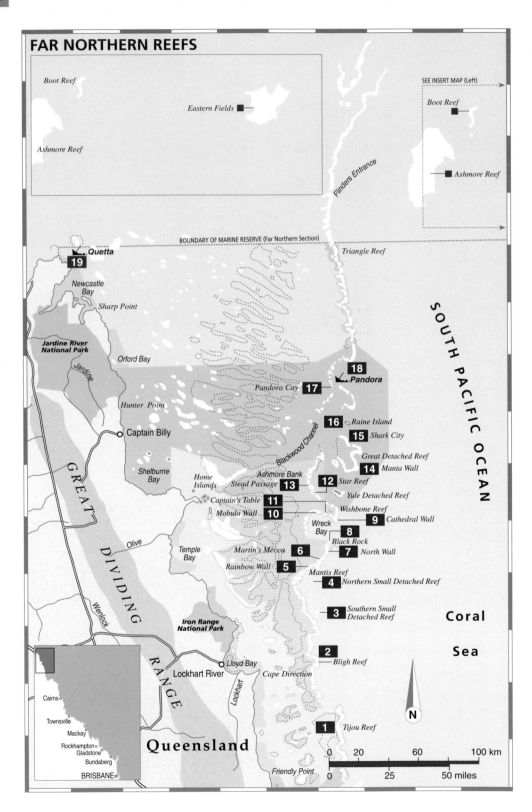

FAR NORTHERN REEFS

Boot Reef

Eastern Fields ■

Ashmore Reef

SEE INSERT MAP (Left)

Boot Reef ■

■ *Ashmore Reef*

Flinders Entrance

BOUNDARY OF MARINE RESERVE (Far Northern Section)

Triangle Reef

■ **Quetta**
19

Newcastle Bay

Sharp Point

Jardine River National Park

Orford Bay

Jardine

Hunter Point

○ **Captain Billy**

Shelburne Bay

Home Islands

Captain's Table

Mobula Wall

Blackwood Channel

18
→ Pandora

Pandora Cay **17**

16 *Raine Island*

15 *Shark City*

Great Detached Reef

14 *Manta Wall*

Ashmore Bank

Stead Passage **13**

12 *Star Reef*

Yule Detached Reef

11

Wishbone Reef

10

9 *Cathedral Wall*

Wreck Bay

8

Black Rock

6

7 *North Wall*

Martin's Mecca

Temple Bay

Rainbow Wall **5**

Mantis Reef

4 *Northern Small Detached Reef*

3 *Southern Small Detached Reef*

Iron Range National Park

Olive

Wenlock

2 *Bligh Reef*

○ **Lockhart River**

Lloyd Bay

Cape Direction

Lockhart

N

1 *Tijou Reef*

○ Cairns

Townsville

Mackay

Rockhampton
Gladstone
Bundaberg

BRISBANE ○

Queensland

Friendly Point

SOUTH PACIFIC OCEAN

GREAT DIVIDING RANGE

Coral Sea

0	20	60	100 km
0	25		50 miles

❶ TIJOU REEF

* * * * * * * *

Location: East of Cape Melville, 100km (62 miles) south of Lockhart River.
Access: Over 10hr sailing time from Lockhart River.
Conditions: Protected by reef, mostly calm, slight currents. Average visibility 40m (130ft).
Minimum depth: 10m (33ft)
Maximum depth: 90m (300ft) plus

The inner side of Tijou Reef offers safe anchorage, and the outer, eastern side offers exciting diving along the sheer coral wall which runs the entire length of the reef. Many small caves and crevasses cut deep into this wall, and all are lined with soft and hydroid corals, sea whips, gorgonian fans and encrusting sponges. Hiding in these caves are pufferfish, flutemouths, squirrelfish, hawkfish and the odd Painted Cray. There are many colourful reef fish, especially in the shallows at the top. Common are angelfish, moray eels, lionfish, rock cod, Fairy Basslets, butterflyfish, sweetlips and wrasse. Pelagics such as turrum and tuna hunt along the wall, and schools of surgeonfish and trevally mingle freely. Reef sharks are constant companions; look up at any time to see them silhouetted against the surface, look down to see their dark shapes patrolling the wall, and out to see them appearing from the blue. The northern tip of Tijou Reef is commonly known as Shark City. Whitetip, Grey and Silvertip reef sharks are always seen cruising along the wall or coming in close to check out divers. Shark feeds are sometimes conducted here.

❷ BLIGH REEF

* * * * * * * *

Location: East of Cape Direction, 60km (37 miles) south of Lockhart River.
Access: Over 6hr sailing time from Lockhart River.
Conditions: Calm in close to the reef, slight currents. Average visibility 40m (130ft).
Minimum depth: 10m (33ft)
Maximum depth: 90m (300ft) plus

Bligh Reef is a long, thin reef with sheltered coral gardens on the inner side and steep walls around the rest. These walls are constantly swept by currents and therefore have an amazing collection of spiky soft corals, gorgonians and sea whips in the deeper water. A number of caves worth exploring cut deep into the walls. Masses of reef fish and pelagics seem to congregate here: surgeonfish, hawkfish, triggerfish, filefish, wrasse, parrotfish, trevally, barracuda, Maori Wrasse and batfish are commonly seen.

❸ SOUTHERN SMALL DETACHED REEF

* * * * * * * *

Location: East of Cape Weymouth, 80km (50 miles) north of Lockhart River.
Access: Over 7hr sailing time from Lockhart River.
Conditions: Protected by reef, mostly calm. Average visibility 30m (100ft).
Minimum depth: 10m (33ft)
Maximum depth: 90m (300ft) plus

There is a number of dive sites on the north-western side of Southern Small Detached Reef, with dramatic drop-offs decorated with incredible coral growths. The south-west corner is a great place to see schooling pelagic fish and whirlpools of trevally and barracuda. Turrum, tuna, mackerel, Rainbow Runners, fusiliers, gropers and Maori Wrasse are all seen in this area. There are also turtles, reef sharks, Eagle Rays and Manta Rays, so don't forget to take your camera. On the northern side, a small sheltered bay, known as Auriga Bay after the charter boat that pioneered trips to this area, has a great collection of hard corals. There is a number of giant clams on sandy patches between the coral. Small reef fish are quite prolific and you will also see Blue-spotted Fantail Rays, small cuttles and even the odd Leopard Shark. The edges of this bay drop off into deep water and some quite good corals grow on the wall.

❹ NORTHERN SMALL DETACHED REEF

* * * * * * * *

Location: East of Cape Weymouth, 90km (55 miles) north of Lockhart River.
Access: Over 8hr sailing time from Lockhart River.
Conditions: Can only be dived in calm conditions. Average visibility 30m (100ft).
Minimum depth: 10m (33ft)
Maximum depth: 90m (300ft) plus

This small reef rises from the depths and just breaks the surface. All around it are steep walls coated with thick coral growths. The northern side of the reef is the most protected and offers some incredible diving. Photographers will be overwhelmed by the number and size of the gorgonians, soft corals and incredibly long sea whips. Adding to the colour are masses of reef fish, from schools of sweetlips and parrotfish to tiny gobies and blennies, and a variety of feather stars, large anemones with their resident anemonefish, nudibranchs, flatworms and delicate shrimps and coral crabs hiding in the soft corals. Off the wall are the usual pelagic fish, mackerel, trevally, barracuda, turrum and fusiliers, and the resident Grey and Whitetip Reef Sharks.

Many reefs are riddled with caves and swim-throughs.

reef sharks. Schooling trevally and barracuda circle the wall, Grey Reef Sharks cruise the depths and mackerel and tuna rush by. The shallows are quite colourful and easily snorkelled. There are masses of reef fish and Whitetip Reef Sharks will come in close to have a proper look.

6 MARTIN'S MECCA

★★★★★★★

Location: Western end of Mantis Reef, 100km (62 miles) north of Lockhart River.
Access: Over 11hr sailing time from Lockhart River.
Conditions: Generally calm. Average visibility 30m (100ft).
Minimum depth: 3m (10ft)
Maximum depth: 25m (80ft)
Martin's Mecca is a colourful pinnacle, teeming with life, that breaks the surface. Reef fish constantly move over the reef, large schooling fish can be seen and there are many tiny invertebrates on the pinnacle itself. The pinnacle is covered in a rich layer of thick, healthy hard corals which shelter many reef creatures such as nudibranchs, feather stars, moray eels, angelfish, butterflyfish, rock cod, Fairy Basslets, filefish, triggerfish, anemones and clams. Sweetlips, parrotfish, surgeonfish, fusiliers and Rainbow Runners school around the pinnacle, which offers excellent snorkelling.

7 NORTH WALL

★★★★★★★★

Location: Northern end of Mantis Reef, 100km (62 miles) north of Lockhart River.
Access: Over 11hr sailing time from Lockhart River.
Conditions: Generally calm, slight currents. Average visibility 30m (100ft).
Minimum depth: 10m (33ft)
Maximum depth: 60m (200ft) plus
Gentle currents wash the northern end of Mantis Reef, making leisurely drift dives along the wall possible. This wall has abundant colourful corals and resident reef fish. Large reef fish usually seen in the area are coral trout, parrotfish, gropers, Red Bass, sweetlips and triggerfish and the pelagics and sharks are memorable. Barracuda, trevally, tuna, mackerel, jobfish, Rainbow Runners and turrum all hunt along the reef face. Reef sharks are common, and Silvertips, Greys and Whitetips are regularly seen. This is also an excellent spot to see Manta Rays, as they congregate in the area to feed in the currents, often coming in quite close to inspect the divers thoroughly.

5 RAINBOW WALL

★★★★★★★★

Location: Southern end of Mantis Reef, 100km (62 miles) north of Lockhart River.
Access: Over 10hr sailing time from Lockhart River.
Conditions: Generally calm, slight currents. Average visibility 30m (100ft).
Minimum depth: 6m (20ft)
Maximum depth: 45m (150ft) plus
Rainbow Wall is at the southern end of Mantis Reef and is generally a drift dive. It is very colourful and covered in spiky soft corals, large gorgonian fans, sponges, ascidians, hydroid coral and hard corals. There are lots of small reef fish and invertebrates, pelagics and

8 BLACK ROCK

★★★★☆☆☆☆

Location: Northern end of Mantis Reef, 100km (62 miles) north of Lockhart River.
Access: Over 11hr sailing time from Lockhart River.
Conditions: Generally calm, slight currents. Average visibility 30m (100ft).
Minimum depth: 10m (33ft)
Maximum depth: 70m (230ft) plus

This is another amazing wall dive with large gorgonians, spiky soft corals and masses of sea whips. Pelagic fish constantly patrol the wall and reef sharks and the odd Hammerhead Shark can usually be seen. There is a lovely coral garden and a large field of sand on the top of the wall where dozens of garden eels poke their heads out of the sand – they are very shy and almost impossible to photograph as they slide into the sand when a diver gets too close. The coral garden is alive with reef fish, angelfish, lionfish, triggerfish, flutemouths, damsels, wrasse, rock cod and sweetlips. This shallow coral garden is also a great location for snorkellers. The corals are healthy and colourful, there are plenty of reef fish and even the odd reef shark.

9 CATHEDRAL WALL

★★★★☆☆☆

Location: Southern end of Wishbone Reef, 110km (70 miles) north of Lockhart River.
Access: Over 12hr sailing time from Lockhart River.
Conditions: Generally calm behind reef, slight currents. Average visibility 30m (100ft).
Minimum depth: 10m (33ft)
Maximum depth: 100m (330ft) plus

At the outer edge of Wishbone Reef sheer drop-offs disappear into the depths, and on the inner edge, a large lagoon is dotted with numerous pinnacles. Cathedral Wall is named after a huge split in the wall that cuts to a depth of 80m (260ft). At 25m (80ft), a coral arch bridges the gap, and there are many caves around the main split. Midday is the best time to dive Cathedral Wall as light filters into the cave, delighting photographers in particular. The rest of the wall has colourful corals and numerous reef fish and pelagics such as tuna, barracuda and mackerel. White-spotted Eagle Rays, Manta Rays and Grey Reef Sharks also cruise the wall. This is a brilliant dive for any photographer, with an endless selection of both wide-angle and macro subjects.

Blue-girdled Angelfish.

🔟 MOBULA WALL

******

Location: Western tip of Wishbone Reef, 110km (70 miles) north of Lockhart River.
Access: Over 12hr sailing time from Lockhart River.
Conditions: Generally calm, slight currents. Average visibility 30m (100ft).
Minimum depth: 4m (13ft)
Maximum depth: 25m (80ft)
Relaxing drift dives can be done at this wall. Take your camera as the wall is decorated by plenty of colourful soft corals, sea whips and gorgonians. A close inspection will reveal nudibranchs, flatworms, brittle stars, basket stars, feather stars, molluscs, sea stars and lots of small reef fish. Moray eels can be seen in a few holes, as can lionfish, triggerfish, squirrelfish, Fairy Basslets and colourful butterflyfish. This dive site was named after the schools of Mobula Rays that sometimes cruise the wall. They are closely related to the Manta Ray but are smaller and their heads project further forward. Mobula Rays are very hard to photograph as they are not as playful as Manta Rays and will quickly leave you behind; it is quite a sight when a large school of these rays 'fly' past.

🔟 CAPTAINS TABLE

****

Location: Western side of Wishbone Reef, 110km (70 miles) north of Lockhart River.
Access: Over 12hr sailing time from Lockhart River.
Conditions: Generally calm. Average visibility 20m (65ft).
Minimum depth: 4m (13ft)
Maximum depth: 33m (110ft)

CYCLONES

Cyclones can disrupt travel, resort operations and diving for up to two weeks. Should an island or cay be in a cyclone's direct path, damage to property and vegetation can be considerable, and to coral reefs even more so. It can take from 10 to 15 years for a reef to regenerate good coral cover and up to 50 and even 100 years to establish long-term structures. Mound corals like some *Porites*, brain and honeycomb corals only grow at a rate of some 2cm (¾in) per year, but staghorn and needle corals grow much faster. After a powerful natural occurence such as a cyclone, corals have been known to grow faster.

The western side of this reef offers safe anchorage and has many pinnacles. Captain's Table is a towering pinnacle rising from 33m (110ft) to break the surface. In the first 10m (33ft) there are thick gardens of hard corals, including plate, staghorn and bottlebrush, which shelter many smaller reef fish, such as damsels, triggerfish, wrasse and butterflyfish. The deeper you dive, the more colourful the coral is, and gorgonians and radiant soft corals decorate the depths. Larger reef fish and pelagics – coral trout, barracuda, surgeonfish, sweetlips, barramundi cod, fusiliers and trevally – are encountered in the deeper water. This is a wonderful location for macro photography as there are many species of nudibranchs and molluscs in the area.

🔟 STAR REEF

****

Location: East of Cape Grenville, 120km (75 miles) north of Lockhart River.
Access: Over 13hr sailing time from Lockhart River.
Conditions: Generally calm, currents. Average visibility 30m (100ft).
Minimum depth: 10m (33ft)
Maximum depth: 50m (165ft) plus
A drift dive at Star Reef can be exciting when a current is running. Cruising along this colourful wall, divers will see schools of trevally and barracuda, gropers, Maori Wrasse, coral trout, large Red Bass and small reef sharks. Masses of small reef fish shelter in the coral or caves. Watch out for mackerel and tuna streaking past. Drift dives can be fun – you hardly use any energy and your air lasts longer, but in such a remote region make sure you carry a safety sausage or expandible Diver's Alert Safety Float.

🔟 STEAD PASSAGE

****

Location: East of Cape Grenville, 125km (80 miles) north of Lockhart River.
Access: Over 14hr sailing time from Lockhart River.
Conditions: Generally calm, currents. Average visibility 25m (80ft).
Minimum depth: 18m (60ft)
Maximum depth: 40m (130ft)
Stead Passage is a channel between two reefs where there is a large pinnacle that can be explored or done as a drift dive. While the corals are pretty and there are plenty of reef fish, it is the pelagics and sharks that will stay etched in your memory. Schools of Rainbow Runners, barracuda and trevally pass by with the current, and zooming around them are large mackerel and tuna.

Coral cod favour caves and the underside of ledges during the day.

Grey Reef Sharks patrol the depths, and Silvertip Reef Sharks suddenly appear out of the blue, check you out and depart. This is an action-packed dive site where the fish are fast and furious.

⑭ MANTA WALL

★★★★★★★

Location: Southwestern tip of Great Detached Reef, 140km (90 miles) north of Lockhart River.
Access: Over 15hr sailing time from Lockhart River.
Conditions: Generally calm behind reef, slight currents. Average visibility 25m (100ft).
Minimum depth: 10m (33ft)
Maximum depth: 60m (200ft) plus

Manta Wall is usually a drift dive. Here divers can drift along a magic wall overflowing with gorgonians, spiky soft corals, sea whips and sponges. Living in and around the corals are nudibranchs, sea stars, feather stars, molluscs, hawkfish, gobies, blennies, rock cod, lionfish, filefish and hogfish. Off the wall, pelagic fish sweep by constantly, whether it is a lone mackerel or Dogtooth Tuna, or massive schools of trevally, barracuda, Rainbow Runners or fusiliers. Following them are the odd Grey and Whitetip reef shark looking for an easy feed. Though not always seen, Manta Rays sometimes cruise the wall either feeding or just seeming to play in the current. They will often hover beside a diver, allowing for great photo opportunities.

⑮ SHARK CITY

★★★★★

Location: Northeastern side of Great Detached Reef, 140km (90 miles) north of Lockhart River.
Access: Over 16hr sailing time from Lockhart River.
Conditions: Generally calm, slight currents. Average visibility 30m (100ft).
Minimum depth: 6m (20ft)
Maximum depth: 27m (90ft)

It is always exciting to encounter sharks and this is a great place to see dozens as the crew of *Auriga Bay II* conduct their regular shark feeds here. The reef is patchy in 10m (33ft) of water, dropping off to 27m (90ft). While the area contains some great soft corals and gorgonians and there are plenty of reef fish, it is the sharks and pelagic fish that everyone wants to see. As soon as the bait is in place, Whitetip, Silvertip and Grey reef sharks

HMS *PANDORA* SHIPWRECK

The HMS *Pandora* shipwreck is one of the most famous of all the shipwrecks in Australian waters. After capturing a number of the mutineers from the infamous HMS *Bounty* on the islands of Tahiti, the *Pandora* was returning to England to put the men on trial. The 14 prisoners, all in irons, were confined to a small wooden cell, known as Pandora's Box. On 28 August 1791 the captain was looking for a passage through the reef when the ship suddenly ran aground. The next morning the ship was washed over the reef and drifting towards another reef when she quickly filled with water. As the boat sank, most of the crew jumped into longboats, leaving the prisoners to die, but the bosun's mate threw the keys to them and 10 escaped. Within minutes the *Pandora* went down, taking 31 crew and four prisoners to the depths. In a remarkable feat of seamanship the survivors under control of Captain Edward Edwards sailed for Batavia in four longboats. In just 11 days the 89 crew and the 10 mutineers reached Timor and soon after, arrived in Batavia without the loss of a single man. They were then taken back to England. The mutineers were all court-martialled. Seven were pardoned and three were later hanged.

appear, circle for a few seconds and charge. Usually Red Bass, Potato Cod, surgeonfish and jobfish feed with the sharks. The photographic opportunities are spectacular as the sharks pass close to the divers.

16 RAINE ISLAND

★★★★★

Location: Northeast of Cape Grenville.
Access: Over 16hr sailing time from Lockhart River, 160km (100 miles) north of Lockhart River.
Conditions: Generally calm. Average visibility 20m (65ft).
Minimum depth: 3m (10ft)
Maximum depth: 60m (200ft) plus
Turtles are the main feature of Raine Island as this island has the greatest number of nesting Green Turtles in the world. Each summer tens of thousands arrive to mate and nest, but there are hundreds in the area at any time of the year. A permit is required to land on the island, but divers may dive on the reefs and the surrounding drop-offs. The northern side of Raine Island is the most popular dive site, as divers can drop down the wall which is riddled with caves and overhangs. Each cave seems to house a sleeping turtle or two, along with squirrelfish, pufferfish and butterflyfish. Along the wall the odd

pelagic fish or Tiger Shark will swim past. Tiger Sharks feed on weak and sick turtles – they even patrol the shore line to snatch turtles re-entering the water after they have laid their eggs. They generally ignore divers, so you can enjoy your dive with the turtles and take some exciting photos of Tiger Sharks.

17 PANDORA CAY

★★★★★★★★

Location: East of Cape York, 175km (110 miles) north of Lockhart River.
Access: Over 18hr sailing time from Lockhart River.
Conditions: Generally calm. Average visibility 25m (80ft).
Minimum depth: 3m (10ft)
Maximum depth: 30m (100ft)
On the northern side of Pandora Cay is a lovely coral garden that supports a wealth of reef fish. Flutemouths, sweetlips, coral trout, damsels, parrotfish, surgeonfish, angelfish and clown triggerfish are all commonly found. Turtles are also extremely common as they nest on the cay; they seem to be in every hole, every cave and every overhang. Some will flee from divers but most will stay, making great photographs of them possible. During summer you may even be lucky enough to see a couple of turtles mating in the shallows. In the area are usually Whitetip, Blacktip and Grey reef sharks, and the odd Tiger Shark looking for a turtle meal. Whale sharks have also been spotted in the vicinity, so you may be fortunate to swim with one of these giant fish.

18 THE *PANDORA* SHIPWRECK

★★★★★★★★

Location: East of Cape York, 175km (110 miles) north of Lockhart River.
Access: Over 18hr sailing time from Lockhart River.
Conditions: Can be rough, though generally calm, slight currents. Average visibility 40m (130ft).
Minimum depth: 30m (100ft)
Maximum depth: 35m (115ft)
The *Pandora* shipwreck lies on a sloping sandy bottom. There isn't a lot to see – it is the link to the infamous mutiny on the *Bounty* (see box) that makes the site such an interesting one, especially when maritime archaeologists are at work there. The Queensland Museum has undertaken a number of excavations since the wreck was discovered in 1977. They have uncovered fascinating artefacts such as cannon, the surgeon's implements, a gold watch, a lead pencil and pumping equipment, all of which are on display at the Queensland Museum in

Soft corals colour many of the walls on the Far Northern Reefs.

Brisbane. Due to the depth, excavation work is limited to 40 minutes per diver per day. The shipwreck is a protected Historic Site, and a permit is required to dive on it. A number of Whale Sharks and Tiger Sharks have been encountered here.

19 THE *QUETTA* SHIPWRECK

* * * * *

Location: Northeast of Cape York, 290km (180 miles) north of Lockhart River.
Access: Over 24hr sailing time from Lockhart River.
Conditions: Generally calm, strong currents. Average visibility 15m (50ft).
Minimum depth: 9m (30ft)
Maximum depth: 18m (60ft)

The passenger liner RMS *Quetta* was on its way to England when she hit an uncharted rock off Cape York in 1890. The rock ripped a hole in the hull and the ship sank within minutes. Today the 116m (380ft) ship lies on her port side in only 18m (60ft) of water, in an area with very strong currents. It is usually only dived on the top of the tide. The wreck is in good condition. A fair bit can be penetrated, including the galley, cabins and many compartments. Portholes, the propeller, bottles and even some personal artefacts can be seen, but this is an Historic Site and nothing may be removed. The wreck now has has a wonderful covering of corals, black coral trees, soft corals, gorgonians, sea whips, *Tubastrea* coral and oysters. Thousands of fish hide in and around it – sweetlips, batfish, Potato cod, coral cod, coral trout, Estuary Cod, angelfish, butterflyfish, cardinalfish, trevally, barracuda and Tasselled Wobbegongs. There is so much life on the wreck that many divers have rated the *Quetta* a better dive than the *Yongala*.

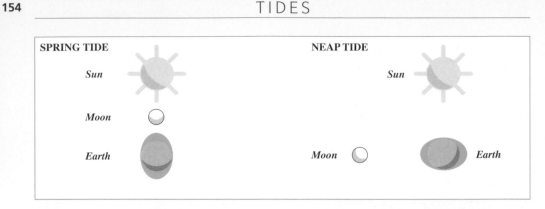

SPRING TIDE

Sun

Moon

Earth

NEAP TIDE

Sun

Moon

Earth

Tides are caused by the gravitational pull of the moon as it travels around the earth, and as the moon and earth travel around the sun. The moon exerts gravitational pull on the part of the earth facing it, causing the water in the oceans to bulge towards it. At the same time, the water on the other side of the earth is also bulging towards the moon, causing troughs in the oceans.

Tidal Cycles

These bulges and troughs are called lunar tides and consist of high and low tides. There are four tides every day, generally two in the day and two at night. The difference between high and low tide is called the tidal range.

Spring and Neap Tides

When it is new moon or full moon, the earth, moon and the sun come into alignment. This occurs twice a month. At this time, the greatest gravitational pull is exerted on the earth and the oceans bulge a little further, causing extra high and low tides.

For the intertidal explorer these times are a boon, as great expanses of subtidal areas are exposed. However, divers and snorkellers don't welcome spring tides. This is because they are often accompanied by bad weather and strong currents, caused by the stronger magnetic influences brought about by alignment of the planets. This makes diving impossible at many sites. Underwater photography is extremely difficult in strong currents and snorkellers must beware

of being swept away. The large volumes of water running out of lagoons pick up sediment and empty it out through the channels and reef exits causing reduced visibility and turbidity, especially near the shore.

Neap tides occur when the earth and the moon are at right angles to the sun. This is when the gravitational pull is weakest, causing lower high tides and higher low tides. During neap tides snorkelling and diving are easiest in waters subject to strong tidal influence.

In general the highest and lowest tides and the largest movements of water in the southern hemisphere occur in tropical regions.

Safety Hints

1. When drift diving, always carry a safety sausage or Diver's Alert Safety Flag to ensure pick-up.
2. In areas of medium tidal movement, always plan the dive against the current.
3. When diving in a current area on the slack tide, take into account that the current direction may reverse when the tide changes.
4. If caught in a current on a soft bottom or sand, one can move forward by stabbing the flat side of a diver's knife into the bottom and using it as an anchor and leverage to pull oneself along.
5. Underwater photographers must be extra careful when diving in strong currents, as the drag caused by a housed camera and strobes will inhibit progress and can contribute to exhaustion.

How to Get There

Only a limited number of charter boats make trips to the Far Northern Reefs each year. All boats visiting this remote section of reef leave from the Lockhart River, which is a small settlement over 500km (300 miles) north of Cairns. Lockhart River has a small airstrip for light planes, and the flight from Cairns takes about 90 minutes. The operators who work in this region arrange all the flights and connections. You only have to get to Cairns Airport.

Where to Stay

See the Cairns and Port Douglas regional directories for information about accommodation.

Where to Eat

Cairns has an endless number of take-away food places and restaurants.

Dive Facilities

Auriga Bay II, PO Box 274, Manunda, Cairns, tel 070-581 408, fax 070-581 404. *Auriga Bay II* is an 18m (58ft) motor sailer that can carry 12 passengers. She runs trips to this region from April to December and also operates to the Ribbon Reefs, Cod Hole and the Northern Coral Sea.

Reef Explorer, PO Box 1090, Cairns, tel 070-939 113, fax 070-939 112. *Reef Explorer* is a 20m (65ft) vessel catering for 10 passengers that does extended trips to the Far Northern Reefs from October to January. During the rest of the year trips are made to the Ribbon Reefs, Cod Hole and the Coral Sea.

Nimrod III, 46 Spence St, Cairns, Tel 070-315 566, fax 070-312 431. *Nimrod III* is a 20m (70ft) long vessel for 16 passengers. She operates to the Ribbon, Reefs, but is also available for charter to the Far Northern Reefs.

Undersea Explorer, Reef Plaza, Cnr Grafton & Spence St, Cairns, tel 070-512 733, fax 070-512 286. *Undersea Explorer* is a 25m (80ft) vessel with 11 large two-berth cabins. Her skipper, John McGregor, has years of experience on the Great Barrier Reef and Coral Sea. They run a few exploration charters to the Far Northern Reefs each year, and do regular trips to the Ribbon Reefs, Cod Hole and the Northern Coral Sea.

Mike Ball Dive Expeditions, 28 Spence St, Cairns, tel 070-315 484, fax 070-315 470. MBDE has made a number of exploration trips to the Far Northern Reefs on *Spoilsport*, a 30m (100ft) catamaran catering for 28 passengers which is based in Townsville and does trips to the Northern Coral Sea and the *Yongala*.

Film Processing

If you have the time you can get print and E6 processing done in Cairns. For a rundown of photo and camera stores, refer to the Cairns and Port Douglas Regional Directory.

Hospitals

Calvary Hospital, 1 Upward St, Cairns, tel 070-525 200.

Cairns Base Hospital, Esplanade, Cairns, tel 070-506 333.

For any emergency, fire, police or ambulance tel 000.

Recompression Chamber

For any diving accident anywhere in Australia, contact DES (Diving Emergency Service) on 1800 088 200. For more information see 'Diving Accidents', page 169. All dive charter boats must carry oxygen for diving accidents, but as it is such a long way from a chamber, it is best to always play it safe.

Local Highlights

For more information refer to the Cairns and Port Douglas regional directory.

Thousands of seabirds breed on the sand cays of the Far Northern Reefs.

THE MARINE ENVIRONMENT

Marine Conservation on the Great Barrier Reef

The Great Barrier Reef is one of the most important biological treasures in the World Heritage listings.

Although guano mining did disturb and destroy surface vegetation on some cays during the early years of Queensland's history, fortunately today these cays have all been able to revegetate.

Apart from fishing, both recreational and commercial such as trawling for prawns and scallops, handlining and spearfishing for reef fish, and smaller additional minor fishing activities such as collecting aquarium fish, coral, shells, bêche-de-mer, trochus and a few traditional Aboriginal fisheries, the Great Barrier Reef has never been intensively exploited for human subsistence.

For this reason it stands apart from tropical reef systems in other parts of the world.

Hazards to the Marine Environment

In the natural course of events, storm-driven waves may cause destruction of reefs, a process which is particularly common in coral reefs in the cyclone belt. The silt load from flooding rivers may smother and sometimes even totally destroy reefs near their mouths. Many human activities are similarly destructive, especially pollution, blast fishing and the indiscriminate collection of shells and corals to sell as marine curios.

Overfishing, too, can be a serious hazard to reef environments, and has already led to perilously declining populations of target species in some areas. This, like any environmental imbalance, can cause grave damage. For example, decreasing the populations of herbivorous fish can lead to an explosive increase in the algae on which those species feed, which may then in turn cause corals and other invertebrates on the reef to be smothered or overgrown.

Some areas are also being damaged by pollution, especially where reefs occur close to large centres of human population. Corals and other reef creatures are sensitive to dirty, sediment-laden water, and are at risk of being smothered when silt settles on the ocean floor. Sewage, nutrients from agricultural fertilisers and other organic or inorganic materials washed into the sea may encourage the growth of one or more species of fauna or flora over others, thus potentially altering the delicate ecological balance of offshore reefs.

The only activities not allowed within the boundaries of the park are commercial limestone mining, mining the sea floor in general and oil drilling.

However, shipping and port activities are important to the region, but with some 2200 ships plying the reef waters every year, dumping their refuse over the sides, flushing their bilge tanks and spilling up to 10 tonnes of oil into reef waters each week, foreign vessels and local authorities have much to improve in this area.

There are no facilities on hand to prevent, contain, or even cope with any major oil spill in the waters of the Great Barrier Reef Marine Park at the moment.

Tourism

With around 2 000 000 visitors per year the Great Barrier Reef Marine Park generates around $A1000 million per year for the Queensland and Australian economy and as such is one of the country's greatest industries. All tourist operators are subject to permits and user-pays fees relative to their activities.

There is also a fee of $A1 per head per night charged to all visitors which goes towards the general upkeep of the reef.

Tourism is seen as a relatively clean industry and now that efforts are being made to transfer all waste and rubbish back to the mainland from the island resorts, instead of the disposal-at-sea methods of the past, this should mean a vast improvement in the future.

Left: Giant clams are found in the shallows of Myrmidon Reef, Townsville.

Water Quality

Due to high rainfall run-off from the adjacent coastal agriculture (namely sugarcane farms) and the heavy siltation (some 15 million tonnes of sediment per year and 88 000 tonnes of nitrogen and phosphates are estimated to be discharged into the Great Barrier Reef Marine Park area), there is general agreement from all relevant authorities that the coastal reef ecosystems of the Great Barrier Reef are deteriorating.

While nutrient levels within the Great Barrier Reef Marine Park are poorly understood, it is known that elevated levels of nutrients can be withstood by the reef system from time to time. However, high levels of nitrogen in the Great Barrier Reef Aquarium at Townsville have caused some of the corals in the aquarium to die.

The work continues to upgrade sewage disposal systems within the park. All tourist resorts on the reef islands now comply with high standards of treatment.

Divers and the Marine Environment

Although, as divers, we simply wish to enjoy ourselves and are, as a rule, conscious of conservation issues and take steps to reduce any deleterious effects of our presence, tourism and development in general have created many problems for the underwater environment. Harbours, jetties and sea walls are, on occasion, built so close to reefs — sometimes even on top of them — that the environment is drastically altered and populations of reef organisms plummet. Hotels, seaside homes and resorts are often built on dunes, thereby necessitating stabilisation which destroys the natural cycle of beach erosion and build-up.

Visiting boats often damage the underwater environment through inadvertent grounding or careless anchoring, and divers themselves, once they get in the water, may cause damage as they move about on the reef.

Although divers, as well as many dive operators and resort management teams, have been at the forefront of the move to protect reefs and marine ecosystems, we all need somewhere to eat and sleep and, no matter how hard we try, we will always have an impact on the environments through which we pass. We should try, however, to minimise the negative and maximise the positive impact.

A number of dive sites on the Great Barrier Reef are buoyed to save anchor damage to the corals, which in some cases is horrific. However, these are only in areas where sites have been established over a long period of time, such as Heron Island and the Cod Hole. With over 300 commercial fishing boats, 24 000 speed-boats (recreational fishing), 150 charter vessels and thousands of yachts plying the reef and anchoring day after day, anchor damage is now becoming a noticeable problem, especially in frequently-visited sites.

Plans are underway to survey many of the regular sites, especially in the Whitsunday Islands where there is very heavy visitor and boat traffic. However, due to the many authorities involved, placing buoys on dive sites in some areas will be impossible because of the threat of propeller damage to the boat traffic in the area or the risk of being wrecked by encountering buoy rope around a propeller during rough seas.

Those dive sites close to the reef edges or in bays may have the best chances of protection.

There is also growing enthusiasm for divers to be trained to be more responsible for their actions underwater by becoming more aware of their effect on the marine environment. PADI's Project AWARE has been instrumental in promoting this theme and applying its weight along with the **Australian Marine Conservation Society** which has been in the frontline protecting the Great Barrier Reef against threats for over 30 years.

Eco-tourism

Growing awareness of environmental issues has given rise to the still somewhat nebulous concept of *ecotourism*. The main underlying principle is often summarised as 'take nothing but photographs, leave nothing but footprints', which, in the diving context can be translated to 'take nothing but photographs, leave nothing but bubbles'. This definition is not complete though, as it is inevitable that we will make an impact on the environments in which we live and dive. A much more constructive way to think of ecotourism is in terms of managing tourism and the tourists themselves, in such a way as to make the industry ecologically, financially, socially and politically sustainable.

In order to achieve this end, try to spend your money with local dive operators and support local businesses, especially the smaller ones.

Plastic

Another major threat to marine environments worldwide, is the indiscriminate use of plastic packaging. Very often this is not properly disposed of or, even if it is, the refuse disposal authorities in many cities of the world do not take sufficient care that dumps are sited where refuse cannot be blown away. Any litter or refuse which is not properly disposed of is quite likely to end up in the stormwater drain system. This will take it to the nearest river and hence to the sea. Turtles, one of the most popular and endangered inhabitants of tropical reefs, are at great risk of being killed by plastic litter. They mistake floating plastic for jellyfish and eat it. Please, therefore, be aware of your use of packaging and, where possible, avoid the use of plastic carrier bags.

Conservation as a Way of Life

A vacation to a pristine environment (and that's what every dive is) should serve to remind us of the need for conservation in our daily lives. Conservation is an attitude which we can nurture by approaching everyday decisions in a thoughtful way. Concerned divers should, therefore, consider the effect their day-to-day lifestyle has on the marine environment, even if they live thousands of miles away from the sea.

Some Tips on Responsible Diving

Here are just some of the ways in which you, as a diver, can help preserve the reefs:

• Try not to touch living marine organisms with your body or your equipment. Be particularly careful with your fins as their size and the force of kicking can damage the reef. Don't use deep fin-strokes near the reef – the surge of water can disturb delicate organisms.

• If your console is dragging across the reef, hold it in your hand or tuck it into your B.C. or weight belt straps.

• Learn the skills of good buoyancy control — divers descending too rapidly or crashing into the living reef while trying to adjust their buoyancy may cause irreparable harm. Make sure you are properly weighted and learn to achieve neutral buoyancy.

• If you haven't dived for a while, practise buoyancy control in a pool before you go on a real dive.

• Avoid kicking up sand. Clouds of sand settling on the reef can smother corals and other invertebrates. Snorkellers should be careful not to kick up sand when treading water in shallow reef areas.

• Never stand on corals, however robust they may seem. Living polyps are easily injured by even the slightest touch. Never pose for pictures by standing inside giant basket sponges or barrel sponges.

• If you need to, steady yourself with your fingertips on exposed rock or on a part of the reef which is dead.

• If you need to adjust your mask or any other part of your diving equipment, do it on the surface beforehand or in mid-water.

• Don't collect or buy shells, corals or any other marine souvenirs.

• On any excursion, whether it is with an operator or privately organised, make sure you take your garbage back for proper disposal on land, and please remember to pick up any litter that you may find.

• Take great care in underwater caverns and caves. Avoid lots of people crowding into the cave, and don't stay there too long; your air bubbles collect in pockets on the roof of the cave and delicate creatures living there could possibly 'drown in air'.

• Don't feed fish. It may seem harmless but it can upset their normal feeding patterns, provoke aggressive behaviour and be unhealthy for them if you give them food that is not part of their normal diet.

• Don't hitch rides on turtles: it causes them considerable distress. When observing marine animals, take into account that they may be resting, feeding or breeding and that our presence may disturb them.

• Spearfishing with scuba is prohibited in the Great Barrier Reef Marine Park.

The beauty of the underwater world.

Coral formation at Kelso Reef, Townsville.

Their young float in the plankton for a few weeks. The shapes corals create as they grow vary enormously according to the species and where on the reef they live.

Colonies range in size from a few centimetres in diameter to giants several metres across and many hundreds of years old. Some are branched or bushy, others tree-like, there are colonies in the form of plates, tables and delicate leafy fronds, and others are encrusting, lobed, rounded or massive.

Microscopic plants called zooxanthellae are very important for the growth and health of corals. Millions of zooxanthellae are packed in the living tissues of most reef-building corals and provide a significant amount of their food, although reef corals also capture planktonic organisms from the water. This is why the most prolific coral growths are found in the shallow, well-lit waters that the zooxanthellae prefer.

TYPES OF REEF
The main types of reef are: fringing reefs; patch reefs, banks and shoals; barrier reefs, and atolls.

Fringing Reefs
Fringing reefs occur in shallow water near land, extending to depths of 15–45m (50–150ft), depending on factors such as the profile and depth of the seabed. Most of the coral cays and the continental islands of the Barrier Reef region have fringing reefs.

Patch Reefs, Banks and Shoals
Reefs develop where the underlying rock has at some time been close enough to the surface for corals to become established. Geological changes such as the lowering of the seabed, result in reefs occuring as isolated mounds or hillocks. Such patch reefs, which vary tremedously in size, can be found in relatively shallow waters around the islands and on continental shelves throughout the Barrier Reef region.

S haped only 60 000 or 70 000 years ago when the sea level stabilised after the last great ice age, the Great Barrier Reef is geologically comparatively young. It forms a barrier between the Pacific Ocean and the Queensland shoreline. Hundreds of tiny reefs and islands dot the huge lagoon between the coast and the outer Barrier Reef. The Coral Sea contains scattered coral reefs and sand islands that are mostly inhabited by large populations of seabirds.

THE NATURE OF CORALS AND REEFS
Tropical reefs consist mainly of coral structures which occur from the mid-tide level down to around 50m (164ft). They develop when incalculable numbers of animals and plants which secrete lime produce intricately connected skeletons, influenced by prevailing conditions of temperature, light penetration, nutrients and oxygenised carbonate-rich water.

Cracks and holes in the reef fill with sand and the calcareous remains of other reef plants and animals; this gradually becomes consolidated, and new corals grow on the surface. Only the outermost layer of the growing reef is alive.

There are about 350 species of reef-building coral in the Great Barrier Reef and the Coral Sea region. Corals grow slowly, adding only about 1–10cm (½–4in) to a reef per year. When mature, they reproduce by releasing sperm and ova into the water.

Barrier reefs

Barrier reefs occur along the edges of islands or continental shelves, and are substantial structures. They are separated from the shore by a wide, deep lagoon. The outer edge of the barrier drops away steeply to the ocean floor. The Great Barrier Reef is the best known example of this type of reef.

Atolls

An atoll is an ancient formation in the form of a ring-shaped reef around a volcanic island. The reef continues to grow although the underlying base gradually subsides beneath the water level. Most of the world's atolls are in the Indian and Pacific oceans.

REEF ZONES AND HABITATS

Reefs can be divided into a number of zones with different features.

The Back Reef and Lagoon

The back reef and lagoon lie between the shore and the seaward reef. The seabed is usually a mixture of sand, coral rubble, limestone slabs and living corals. The water depth varies from a few metres to 50m (165ft) or more, and the size of the lagoon varies from a few hundred to thousands of square metres.

The inside of a lagoon is more sheltered than the seaward reef, and more affected by sedimentation. Here many attractive seaweeds grow and most of the corals are delicate, branching types. Large sand-dwelling anemones are often found, and in places, soft and 'false corals' form mats over the seabed. Extensive beds of seagrass, the only marine flowering plant, occur in currents in this reef zone. Here, too, the longest Sea Cucumbers live. Most typical reef fishes flourish in this habitat, and roving predators – snappers, wrasse, triggerfish, emperors – prowl on the lookout for worms and crustaceans, gastropods, sea urchins and small fish. Bottom-dwelling fish burrow into the sand until completely hidden, emerging only when they need to feed.

The Reef Flat

Reef flats are formed as their associated reefs push steadily seaward, leaving behind limestone areas that have been eroded and planed almost flat by the action of the sea. The reef flat is essentially an intertidal area.

On the sheltered, inner reef-flat, beautiful pools full of corals and small fish can be found. At the outer edge, where wave action is more significant, surfaces are often encrusted with algae on which fish, sea urchins, gastropods and other animals graze. Some fish are permanent inhabitants of this area, retreating to pools if necessary at low tide, but others, like parrotfish and surgeonfish, spend a great deal of their time in deeper water, crowding over the reef flat with the rising tide.

The Seaward Reef Front

The most spectacular features and impressive displays of marine life can be found here. Brightly lit, clean plankton-rich water provides ideal growing conditions for corals, and they in turn create habitats of considerable complexity for other animals. There is an infinite variety, from shallow gardens of delicate branching corals to walls festooned with corals and sea fans.

The top 20m (66ft) are especially rich with sealife. Small, brilliantly coloured damselfish swarm around the coral and butterflyfish show their dazzling array of intricate patterns. Open-water species like fusiliers, snappers and sharks cover quite large areas when feeding, and wrasse often forage far and wide over the reef.

Sedentary reef-dwellers like anemones, cucumbers, sea squirts and sponges live here. There are tiny crabs among the coral branches and spiny lobsters hide in caverns, waiting to hunt under cover of darkness. Some of the most easily spotted mobile invertebrates are the echinoderms, well represented in the Great Barrier Reef region. They include the primitive feather stars with long, delicate arms in colours from bright-yellow to green, red and black.

HEALTH AND SAFETY FOR DIVERS

The information in this section is intended as a guide only. It is no substitute for thorough training or professional medical advice. The information is based on currently accepted health and safety information but it is certainly not meant to be a replacement for a comprehensive manual on the subject. We strongly advise that the reader obtains a recognised manual on diving safety and medicine before embarking on a trip.

Please note that:
• Divers who have suffered a diving-related injury, no matter how minor, should consult a doctor, preferably a specialist in diving medicine, as soon as possible after the symptom or injury occurs.

• If you are the victim of a diving injury do not hesitate to reveal your symptoms, no matter how minor they seem to be. Mild symptoms can later develop into a major illness with life-threatening consequences. It is better to be honest with yourself and live to dive another day.

• No matter how confident you are in formulating your own diagnosis, remember that unless you are a trained medical practitioner, *you are not a doctor*.

• Always err on the conservative side when considering your ailment; if you discover your illness is only minor, the worst that can happen is that both you and the doctor will be relieved.

GENERAL FIRST AID PRINCIPLES

The basis principles of first aid are:
• DOING NO HARM
• SUSTAINING LIFE
• PREVENTING DETERIORATION
• PROMOTING RECOVERY

SAFETY
In the event of any illness or injury, a simple sequence of patient assessment and management can be followed. The sequence first involves assessment and definition of any life-threatening conditions, followed by management of the problems found.

The first things to check are the ABCs:
A — for airway (with care of the neck)
B — for breathing
C — for circulation
D — for decreased level of consciousness
E — for exposure
Ensure both the patient's and your own safety by removing yourselves from the threatening environment (usually the water). Make sure that whatever your actions, they in no way further endanger the patient or yourself.

NEVER ASSUME THAT THE PATIENT IS DEAD.

A. Airway
1. With attention to the neck, is there a neck injury?
2. Is the mouth and nose free of obstruction? Any noisy breathing is a sign of airway obstruction.

B. Breathing
1. Look at the chest to see if it is rising and falling.
2. Listen for air movement at the nose and mouth.
3. Feel for the movement of air against your cheek.

C. Circulation
Feel for a pulse next to the windpipe (carotid artery).

D. Decreased level of consciousness
Does the patient respond to any of the following procedures (AVPU)?:
A — Awake, aware, spontaneous speech
V — Verbal stimuli: Wake up!
P — Painful stimuli: Pinch him/her
U — Unresponsive

E. Exposure
The patient must be adequately exposed in order to examine him properly, so remove clothes as necessary.

NOW, SEND FOR HELP
If you think the patient's condition is serious following your assessment, you need to send or call for help from the emergency medical services (ambulance, paramedics). It is advisable that whoever you send to get help returns to confirm that help is indeed on its way.

Recovery Position

If the patient is unconscious but breathing normally, there is a risk of vomiting and subsequent choking. It is therefore critical that the patient be placed on his/her side in the recovery position.

1. Kneel next to the patient's head on his/her left.
2. Try to maintain the head in line with the trunk.
3. Place the patient's right hand under his/her head with the palm forwards.
4. Cross the left leg over the right leg at the ankle.
5. Fold the left arm over the chest.
6. Grasp the left hip and pull the patient over onto his/her side with your right hand, while supporting the patient's right cheek with the left hand.
7. Now flex the patient's left knee to 90°.
8. Flex the patient's left arm to 90° and place the forearm flat on the ground.
9. The patient is now in the recovery position.

CARDIOPULMONARY RESUSCITATION (CPR)

Cardiopulmonary resuscitation is required when a patient is found to have no pulse. It consists of techniques to:

- VENTILATE THE PATIENT'S LUNGS
(expired air resuscitation)
- PUMP THE PATIENT'S HEART
(external cardiac compression)

Once you have checked and found the patient to have no breathing and pulse, you must apply the ABCs.

A. Airway

1. Gently extend the head (head tilt) and lift the chin with two fingers (chin lift). This will clear the tongue away from the back of the throat and open the airway.
2. If you suspect a foreign body in the airway, sweep your finger across the back of the tongue from one side to the other and if one is found, remove it.

Do not attempt this with a conscious or semi-conscious patient as they will either bite your finger or you will cause them to vomit.

B. Breathing

If the patient is not breathing you need to give expired air resuscitation, in other words you need to breathe into the patient's lungs.

1. Pinch the patient's nose closed.
2. Place your mouth, open, fully over the patient's mouth, making as good a seal as possible.
3. Exhale into the patient's mouth hard enough to cause the patient's chest to rise.
4. If the patient's chest fails to rise you need to adjust the position of the airway. The 16 per cent of oxygen in your expired air is adequate to sustain life.
5. Initially you need to give two full, slow breaths.
6. If the patient is found to have a pulse in the next step continue breathing for the patient once every five seconds, checking for a pulse after every 10 breaths.

7. If the patient begins breathing on his/her own you can turn him/her into the recovery position.

C. CIRCULATION

After giving the two breaths as above, and if the patient still does not breathe or have a pulse you have to give external cardiac compression.

1. Kneel next to the patient's chest.
2. Measure two finger breadths above the notch where the ribs meet the lower end of the breastbone.
3. Place the heel of your left hand just above your two fingers in the centre of the breastbone.
4. Place the heel of your right hand on your left hand.
5. Straighten your elbows.
6. Place your shoulders perpendicular above the patient's breastbone.
7. Compress the breastbone 4–5cm (1½–2in) to a rhythm of one, two, three...
8. Give 15 compressions.

Continue giving cycles of two breaths and 15 compressions, checking for a pulse after every five cycles.

The aim of CPR is to keep the patient alive until more sophisticated help arrives in the form of paramedics or a doctor with the necessary equipment. Make sure that you and your buddy are trained in CPR. It could mean the difference between life and death.

DIVING DISEASES AND ILLNESSES

Acute Decompression Illness

Acute decompression illness means any illness arising out of the decompression of a diver, in other words, by the diver moving from an area of high ambient pressure to an area of lower pressure. It is divided into two groups:

- DECOMPRESSION SICKNESS
- BAROTRAUMA WITH ARTERIAL GAS EMBOLISM

It is not important for the diver or first aider to differentiate between these two conditions because both are serious and both require the same emergency treatment. The important thing is to recognise acute decompression sickness and to initiate emergency treatment. The differences between decompression sickness and barotrauma are described below.

• Decompression Sickness

Decompression sickness, or the 'bends', arises following inadequate decompression by the diver. Exposure to higher ambient pressure underwater causes nitrogen to dissolve in increasing amounts in the body tissues.

If this pressure is released gradually during correct and adequate decompression procedures, the nitrogen escapes naturally into the blood and is exhaled through the lungs. If this release of pressure is too rapid the nitrogen cannot escape quickly enough and physical nitrogen bubbles form in the tissues. The symptoms and signs of the disease are related to the tissues in which these bubbles form and the disease is described by the tissue affected, e.g. joint bend.

Symptoms and signs of decompression sickness include:
• Nausea and vomiting
• Dizziness
• Malaise and loss of appetite
• Weakness
• Joint pains or aching
• Paralysis
• Numbness
• Itching of skin or rashes
• Incontinence
• Shortness of breath

• Barotrauma with Arterial Gas Embolism

Barotrauma refers to the damage that occurs when the tissue surrounding a gaseous space is injured following a change in the volume of air in that space. An arterial gas embolism refers to a gas bubble that moves in a blood vessel usually leading to obstruction of that blood vessel or a vessel further downstream. Barotrauma can therefore occur to any tissue that surrounds a gas-filled space:

• ears	middle ear squeeze	burst ear drum
• sinuses	sinus squeeze	sinus pain, nosebleeds
• lungs	lung squeeze	burst lung
• face	mask squeeze	swollen, bloodshot eyes
• teeth	tooth squeeze	toothache

A burst lung is the most serious and can result in arterial gas embolism. It occurs following a rapid ascent during which the diver does not exhale adequately. The rising pressure of expanding air in the lungs bursts the delicate alveoli, or lung sacs, and forces air into the vessels that carry blood back to the heart and ultimately the brain. In the brain these bubbles block blood vessels and obstruct the supply of blood and oxygen to the brain, resulting in brain damage. The symptoms and signs of lung barotrauma and arterial gas embolism include:
• Shortness of breath
• Chest pain
• Unconsciousness or altered level of consciousness
• Weakness, incoordination and paralysis
• Blurred vision, loss of balance

Treatment
1. ABCs (see p.162) and CPR (p.163) as needed.
2. Position the patient in the recovery position (p.163) with no tilt or raising of the legs.
3. Administer 100 per cent oxygen by mask (or demand valve).
4. Keep the patient warm.
5. Remove to the nearest hospital as soon as possible.
The hospital or emergency services will arrange the recompression treatment required.

Carbon Dioxide or Monoxide Poisoning

Carbon dioxide poisoning can occur as a result of:
• skip breathing — diver holds his breath on scuba
• heavy exercise on scuba
• malfunctioning rebreather systems

Carbon monoxide poisoning occurs as a result of:
• exhaust gases being pumped into cylinders
• hookah systems air-intake too close to exhaust fumes

Symptoms and signs include:
• Headache
• Blue colour of the skin
• Shortness of breath
• Decreased level or loss of consciousness

Treatment
1. ABCs as necessary
2. CPR (p.163) if required
3. 100 per cent oxygen through a mask or demand valve
4. Remove to nearest hospital.

Head Injury

All head injuries should at all times be regarded as potentially serious.

Treatment
The diver should come to the surface, any wound should be disinfected, and there should be no more diving until a doctor has been consulted. If the diver is unconscious, the emergency services should be contacted; if breathing and/or pulse has stopped, CPR (p.163) should be administered.If the diver is breathing and has a pulse, check for bleeding and other injuries and treat for shock (p.165); if wounds permit, put sufferer into recovery position (p.163) with no elevation of the legs and administer 100 per cent oxygen. Keep him or her warm and comfortable, and monitor pulse and respiration constantly.

DO NOT administer fluids to unconscious or semi-conscious divers.

Hyperthermia (increased body temperature)

A rise in body temperature results from a combination of overheating, normally due to exercise, and inadequate fluid intake. The diver will progress through heat exhaustion to heat stroke with eventual collapse. Heat stroke is an emergency and if the diver is not cooled and rehydrated he/she will die.

Treatment
Remove the diver from the hot environment and remove all clothes. Sponge with a damp cloth and fan either manually or with an electric fan. If unconscious place the patient in the recovery position and monitor the ABCs. Always seek advanced medical help.

Hypothermia

Normal internal body temperature is just under 37°C (98.4°F). If for any reason it is pushed much below this — usually, in diving, through inadequate protective clothing — progressively more serious symptoms may occur, with death as the ultimate result.

• A drop of 1°C (2°F) leads to shivering and discomfort.

• A 2°C (3.5°F) drop induces the body's self-heating mechanisms to react, blood flow to the peripheries is reduced and shivering becomes extreme.

• A 3°C (5°F) drop leads to amnesia, confusion, disorientation, heartbeat and breathing irregularities, and possibly rigor.

Treatment

Prevent further heat loss by wrapping him/her in a space blanket, surround the diver with you and your buddies' bodies, and cover the diver's head and neck with a woolly hat, warm towels or anything else suitable. In sheltered warmth, re-dress the diver in warm, dry clothing and then put him/her in a space blanket. If the diver is conscious and coherent, a warm shower or bath and a warm, sweet drink should be enough; otherwise call the emergency services and treat for shock (this page) while deploying the other warming measures noted.

Near Drowning

Near drowning refers to a situation where the diver has inhaled some water. He may be conscious or unconscious. Water in the lungs interferes with the normal transport of oxygen from the lungs into the blood and near drowning victims are therefore often hypoxic.

Treatment

Remove the diver from the water and check the ABCs. Depending on your findings, commence EAR (see Breathing under CPR, p.163) or CPR where appropriate, beginning with EAR in the water if necessary. If possible, administer oxygen by mask or demand valve. All near-drowning victims can develop secondary drowning, a condition where fluid oozes into the lungs causing the diver to drown in his/her own secretions, so all near drowning victims should be observed for 24 hours in a hospital.

Nitrogen Narcosis

The air we breathe is about 80 per cent nitrogen; breathing the standard mixture under compression, as divers do, can lead to symptoms very much like those of drunkenness — the condition is popularly called 'rapture of the deep'. Some divers experience nitrogen narcosis at depths of 30–40m (100–130ft). Up to a depth of about 60m (200ft) — that is, beyond the legal maximum depth for sport diving in the UK, Australia and USA — the symptoms need not (but may) be serious; beyond about 80m (260ft) the diver is likely to become unconscious. The onset of symptoms can be sudden and unheralded. The condition itself is not harmful; dangers arise through secondary effects, notably the diver doing something foolish.

Treatment

The sole treatment required is to return immediately to a shallower depth.

Oxygen Toxicity (Poisoning)

Oxygen, if breathed at a partial pressure of greater than 1.5 atmospheres, can be poisonous to the lung and brain tissue.

• Lung toxicity is a more chronic event and is not commonly seen in sports divers.

• Brain toxicity is common and manifests when breathing pure (100%) oxygen at depths greater than 7msw (metres of sea water) or air deeper than 90msw.

The advent of Nitrox diving (increased oxygen percentage in the breathing mixture) will inevitably increase the incidence of brain oxygen toxicity. The clinical presentation of oxygen toxicity is sudden and unpredictable with unconsciousness and seizures which can be catastrophic under water.

The management revolves around prevention:

• Don't dive on 100% oxygen.

• Don't dive deeper than recommended for a particular Nitrox mix.

• Don't dive deeper than 70m (214ft) on air.

Treatment

Convulsions cannot be treated under water. Bring the diver to the surface and connect him/her to a gas mixture with the correct oxygen content. Prevent the convulsing diver from self inflicting injuries by guiding, not inhibiting, his movements. If possible, put a knotted handkerchief in the diver's mouth to prevent tongue-biting; do not prise the mouth open, but wait for an opportunity to present itself. The diver should be taken to a recompression chamber and a doctor, and kept under observation for at least 24 hours — oxygen poisoning inevitably inflicts neurological damage.

Shock

Shock refers not to the emotional trauma of a frightening experience but to a physiological state in the body resulting from poor blood and oxygen delivery to the tissues. As a result of oxygen and blood deprivation the tissues cannot perform their functions. There are many causes of shock, the most common being loss of blood or hypovolaemic shock.

Treatment

Treatment is directed at restoring blood and oxygen delivery to the tissues, therefore maintain the ABCs and administer 100 per cent oxygen. Control all external bleeding by direct pressure, pressure on pressure points and elevation of the affected limb. A tourniquet should only be used as a last resort and then only on the arms and legs. Unconscious, shocked victims should be placed on their side with the legs elevated.

Diving Rescue

The question is always asked as to what to do if you find your buddy or another diver unconscious underwater. Fortunately this is a rare occurrence as most diving incidents and accidents happen on the surface. The short answer to the question is that incidents and accidents should be avoided as far as possible by the following:

• Thorough training both initially and continuously in personal diving, rescue and emergency care skills.
• Maintaining good physical and mental fitness for diving and avoiding substances like alcohol and drugs that compromise that fitness.
• Equipment maintenance with regular servicing and checks to ensure reliable function. Familiarising yourself with new equipment in the pool before using it in the sea. Diving with equipment appropriate to the complexity of the dive. Wearing appropriate thermal protection.
• Thorough predive checks of equipment.
• Attention to buoyancy ensuring that you are not over- or underweight and that buoyancy control mechanisms are functioning normally.
• Detailed attention to thorough dive planning no matter how apparently routine the dive. Dive planning is an exercise in accident prevention.

If you find yourself in a situation where a diver requires active rescue, the situation can be managed in the following sequence:

1. DIVER RECOVERY
2. DIVER RESUSCITATION
3. DIVER EVACUATION

Diver recovery involves freeing the diver from any entrapment underwater and then providing buoyancy and lift to get them to the surface without further injury. The emphasis is on control of the ascent. The diver must be brought to the surface in a controlled manner to avoid the possibility of barotrauma and air embolism.

To provide positive buoyancy, it may be necessary to release the weight belt, inflate the victim's buoyancy compensator or inflate your own. Take up position behind the diver with your right hand under the chin keeping the airway open and the other hand on the victim's B.C. inflator/deflator hose. Swim up at a controlled, moderate pace, being conscious of your own exhalation and a need not to become exhausted. Once on the surface, resuscitation should be begun in the water with expired air resuscitation while the diver is towed to the nearest boat or land where CPR can begin. Resuscitation is continued while preparations are made to evacuate the injured diver.

Treatment should include:
• EAR or CPR (p.163) as necessary, with or without the assistance of medical equipment.
• Keeping the diver warm.
• 100 per cent oxygen by mask, through a bag, valve or demand valve.
• Maintaining hydration by intravenous therapy if skills and equipment are available.

Evacuation of the diver is by the quickest available means to the nearest resuscitation facility (hospital trauma unit), the options being by sea, land or air, or a combination of the three. The recompression treatment that may be required is arranged from the resuscitation facility once the diver has been adequately assessed.

Ignorance is your greatest enemy in a rescue situation and time and money spent on dive-rescue training is an investment in life. Approach your nearest agency for training in rescue and before going for a dive, find out what rescue facilities are available in the area of the dive and how they are contactable in an emergency.

MARINE-RELATED AILMENTS

Apart from specific diving-related illnesses, the commonest ailments are cuts and abrasions, coral cuts and stings, swimmer's ear, sea sickness, jellyfish stings and sunburn.

Cuts and Abrasions

Divers should wear appropriate protection against abrasions. The prominent areas – hands, knees, elbows and feet – are most commonly affected. The danger with abrasions is that they become infected and all wounds should be thoroughly rinsed with water and an antiseptic, like hibitane in alcohol, as soon as possible after the injury occurs. Infection may progress to a stage where antibiotics are needed. Spreading inflamed areas should prompt the diver to seek medical advice.

Swimmer's Ear

This is an infection of the outer ear canal resulting from constantly wet ears. It is often a combination of a fungal and bacterial infection and especially prevalent in tropical areas.

Treatment
Prevent this condition by always thoroughly drying the ears after diving and, if you are susceptible to the condition, inserting alcohol or acetic acid drops after diving, is the best measure (eg Aqua Ear is a good standby). Never stick anything into your ear (including ear buds) as this will damage the normal lining and predispose the ear towards infection. Once infected, the best possible treatment is by stopping diving/swimming for a few days and seeking medical advice. If you are prone to swimmer's ear and are likely to be in a remote area, carry antibiotic drops with you as recommended by your diving physician.

Sea or Motion Sickness

Motion sickness can be an annoying complication of a diving holiday involving boat dives. If you are susceptible to motion sickness seek medical advice prior to diving.

Treatment
To prevent sea sickness only eat light meals before going to sea and avoid alcohol the night before. Normally a combination of metaclopamide (Maxolon) and an antihistaminic (Valoid) or similar drugs offer a simple preventative solution. Please note that the antihistamine can make you drowsy which may impair your ability to think and act while diving. Limit your diving depth to less than 3m (10ft). A sea-sick diver should not attempt to dive.

SUNBURN

The sun in tropical Queensland is particularly harsh.

Treatment
Wear appropriate wide-brimmed hats and clothing. High-protection-factor sun creams are recommended.

TROPICAL DISEASES

Apart from normal preventative survival vaccinations, all travelling divers should have Hepatitis A and B shots. Malaria has been recorded from the Torres Strait Islands but is not considered a threat with only 600 cases reported in 200 years and many of those were travellers, or visitors from other areas. However, Ross River Fever and Dengue Fever are regularly reported around Townsville, Cairns and Daintree areas on the mainland, so normal precautionary procedures apply towards lessening the possibility of mosquito bites.

MARINE ANIMALS THAT BITE
Sharks

Sharks rarely attack divers but should always be treated with respect. Attacks are usually associated with the spearing of fish and the resultant vibrations released into the water. The Great White, rare in reef waters, is an exception to the rule. It has an unpredictable nature and should be avoided. Leave the water if a Great White makes an appearance. Seals are the normal prey of the Great White and theories have it that divers are often mistaken as such.

Hammerheads, Tiger, Grey Reef Sharks, Silvertips and Whitetip Reef Sharks are commonly spotted in Great Barrier Reef waters. If a shark displays agitated behaviour, such as arching of the back and ventral pointing of the pectoral fins this may be a sign of impending attack and the diver should leave the water.

Treatment
Injuries are normally severe and involve severe blood loss resulting in shock. Blood loss control is the main objective. Control bleeding by applying direct pressure to wounds, pressure on pressure points and by elevating the affected limb. Tourniquets may be used on limbs above an amputation. Preferably use a wide rubber bandage as a tourniquet. The diver should be stabilised as far as possible with the available medical help before being transported to hospital.

Moray Eels

Probably more divers are bitten by morays than by all other sea creatures added together — usually through putting their hands into holes or when feeding them. Often a moray refuses to let go, so, unless you can persuade it to do so with your knife, you make the wound worse by tearing your flesh as you pull the fish off.

Treatment
Thorough cleaning and usually stitching. The bites always go septic, so antibiotics and antitetanus shots are recommended.

Triggerfish

Large triggerfish — usually males guarding eggs in 'nests' – are particularly aggressive, and will attack divers who swim too close. Their teeth are very strong, and can go through rubber fins and draw blood through a 4mm (⅙inch) wetsuit.

Treatment
Clean the wound and treat it with antiseptic cream.

MARINE ANIMALS THAT STING

Scorpion-, lion- and stonefish are venomous. Many venomous sea creatures are bottom-dwellers, hiding among coral or resting on or burrowing into sand. If you need to move along the sea bottom do so in a shuffle, so that you scare such creatures out of the way and minimise your risk of stepping directly onto sharp, venomous spines, many of which can pierce rubber fins. Antivenenes require specialist medical supervision, do not work for all species and need refrigerated storage, so are rarely available when required. Most of the venoms are high-molecular-weight proteins that break down under heat.

Immerse the limb in hot water (use the cooling water from an outboard motor if no other supply is available) at 50°C (120°F) for about two hours, or until the pain stops. Several injections around the wound of local anaesthetic (e.g. procaine hydrochloride) if available will ease the pain. This is known as the **hot water treatment**. Younger or weaker victims may need CPR. Remember that venoms may still be active in fish that have been dead for as long as for 48 hours, in some cases for years.

Cone Shells

Live cone shells should never be handled. The animal has a mobile tube-like organ that projects a poison dart. The result is initial numbness, followed by local muscular paralysis, which may extend to respiratory paralysis and heart failure.

Treatment
Apply a broad ligature between the wound and the body. CPR (p.163) and supportive care may be needed.

Fire Coral
Fire Corals are not true corals but members of the class Hydrozoa, i.e. they are more closely related to the stinging hydroids. Some people react violently from the slightest brush with them, and the resulting blisters may be 15cm (6in) across.

Treatment
Apply vinegar/acetic acid.

Jellyfish
Most jellies sting, but few are dangerous. As a general rule, those with the longest tentacles tend to have the most painful stings. The box jellyfish, or sea wasp, and blue bottle are sometimes encountered. During the months of October till May marine stingers (box jellies) may be present in the waters off mainland Queensland and the inshore continental islands and reefs of the Great Barrier Reef. These animals have killed and/or seriously injured over 60 unprotected swimmers and should be taken seriously — always wear protection when diving or snorkelling. A Lycra suit, a wetsuit or even a T-shirt and pantyhose is sufficient protection against these unseen, but very real coastal inhabitants. Blue bottle and sea wasp stings can be treated with vinegar and alcohol applied locally. Divers commonly develop allergies to these stings and those sensitised should always carry a supply of antihistamines and, if necessary, their injection of adrenalin.

Lionfish/Turkeyfish/Firefish
These are slow-moving except when swallowing prey. They hang around on reefs and wrecks and pack a heavy sting in their beautiful spines.

Treatment
Use the hot water treatment (see p.167).

Scorpionfish
Scorpionfish are less camouflaged and less dangerous than the stonefish but are more common and still quite dangerous.

Treatment
As for Stonefish (see next column this page).

Sea Urchins
The spines of sea urchins can be venomous. They can puncture the skin, even through gloves, and break off, leaving painful wounds that can often go septic.

Treatment
For bad cases give the hot water treatment (see p.167); this also softens the spines, helping the body reject them. Soothing creams or a magnesium-sulphate compress will help reduce the pain, as will the application of flesh of papaya fruit. Septic wounds require antibiotics. Alcohol applied after the heat might prove useful.

Stinging Plankton
You cannot see stinging plankton and therefore cannot take evasive measures. If there are reports of any in the area keep as much of your body covered as possible.

Treatment
Apply vinegar/acetic acid locally.

Stingrays
Stingrays vary from a few centimetres to several metres across. The sting consists of one of more spines on top of the tail; though these point backwards, they can sting in any direction. The rays thrash out and sting when trodden on or caught. Wounds may be large and severely lacerated.

Treatment
Clean the wound and remove any spines. Give the hot water treatment (p.167) and local anaesthetic if available; follow up with antibiotics and antitetanus.

Stonefish
Stonefish are the most feared, best camouflaged and most dangerous of the scorpionfish family. The venom is contained in the spines of the dorsal fin, which is raised when the fish is agitated.

Treatment
There is usually intense pain and swelling. Clean the wound, give the hot water treatment (p.167) and follow up with antibiotics and antitetanus.

Marine Animals that Shock
Electric rays occur on sandy and muddy sea floors and also hunt over reef. They use electric shocks to stun their prey and many divers have been shocked (200 volts) when kneeling on them in the sand especially at night. The voltage generally would not adversely affect a healthy diver but the fright could cause a diving related accident. Ensure buoyancy control over soft, sandy bottoms. There is no specific treatment.

MARINE ANIMALS THAT ARE POISONOUS TO EAT
Eating shellfish can result in gastroenteritis, allergic reactions or paralytic shellfish poisoning. Avoid eating anything but fresh shellfish. Ciguatera poisoning can result from eating reef and game fish contaminated by a dinoflagellate. Obtain local advice on which fish are safe to eat. Puffer- and sunfish are not edible and ingestion of their flesh can result in death. Scromboid poisoning results from eating mackerel and tuna that have been allowed to lie in the sun. Avoid all but the freshest fish.

SCUBA DIVING REGULATIONS, REQUIREMENTS AND PRACTICES FOR DIVING ON THE GREAT BARRIER REEF

1. Any diver wishing to scuba dive on the Great Barrier Reef must have a current medical certificate as provided by a medical practitioner with experience or training in diving medicine. Although such a certificate may be acceptable from a country of origin, it must comply with the form specified in the code of practice and be in English.

2. Certified divers must hold a Certification card from a recognised diver-instruction agency and a current log book to prove their competence.

2a. If competence is not able to be proven, then the prospective diver must undergo a familiarisation dive or dives with a qualified divemaster or instructor for an assessment of skills.

3. Buddy diving is the rule and divers are paired before entering the water.

4. The divemaster or instructor will give a short talk on procedures to all divers before entering the water and advise them about the dangers of overstaying bottom time and so on.

5. Dive computers and/or recognised diving tables are proposed for repetitive diving calculations. Both are managed to apply to the most conservative plan.

6. Divers must be registered for each dive, logged in with entry times and logged out, recording depth bottom time, air consumption and so on. Each diver must then sign the log before leaving the dive site.

7. Divers may be required to complete and sign a deferment of responsibility form which states that they are fully aware of their responsibilities and the dangers involved in scuba diving and agree to abide by the regulations.

DIVING ACCIDENT EMERGENCY INFORMATION

Divers Emergency Service – DES 1 8 0 0 0 8 8 2 0 0

For any diving accident, whether it be decompression sickness, an air embolism or contact with a dangerous marine animal, contact DES and they will offer advice or organise emergency services to get the patient to a recompression chamber or hospital immediately.

• State clearly – 'This is a diving emergency.'
• Give details – Location of patient, name, age, contact name and phone number.
• Accident details – Depth of dive, time of dive, symptoms, first aid applied and the time the sickness started.

Life Threatening Emergencies – 000

In any life-threatening emergency, whether you require fire, police or ambulance, ring 000.
• Ask the operator for the service you need.
• Wait to be connected.
• Once connected, state your phone number, address and your emergency.

This is a free call and a 24-hour service.

UNDERWATER PHOTOGRAPHY AND VIDEO

It is almost impossible to describe to non-divers the incredible beauty of the underwater environment. The best we can do is to take photographs and videos which will also serve to preserve our precious memories for our own pleasure. Neither of these skills is easy, though, and the aspiring photographer or videographer has to be a competent diver, first, and then learn the complexities of photographic equipment and the behaviour of light underwater. You will need perseverance — and a bit of luck — to get really good results but, if you're prepared to persist with this challenging skill, you may well develop a passion that will last for a lifetime of diving.

Buddies

Try to dive with a buddy who understands the photographic process and is prepared to just tag along, allow for your idiosyncrasies, model if necessary, find subjects and generally look after you. If you are doing a shore dive, kit up, get in the water and let your buddy, without fins or tank, hand you your camera from the shallows. When exiting, do the opposite. Wait for him or her to exit, take off tank and fins and then hand it up. Explain to your buddy before the dive that she or he is to stay behind and above you or you may find yourself peering at the reef through a cloud of bubbles or silt.

Power Supplies

Even though torch batteries may fit into your strobe or video camera, buy only camera batteries as they will give you better results. Rechargeable Ni-Cad (nickel-cadmium) batteries are an excellent choice but make sure that you have a sufficient supply so that you can use one set and have a spare while recharging. It might be worth your while, depending on your travel plans, to bring along a charger that can work off the cigarette lighter of a car. Although memory-free batteries are advertised, most still have memory problems. To ensure long life of your Ni-Cads, deep charge them at least every fourth or fifth charge (let them go completely flat and then charge them up to full) and never store them absolutely flat.

The little flat 1.5 or 3 volt batteries for your camera (not the flash) are difficult to get hold of in remote places and take up little room, so take a good supply.

General Hints

• If you have not operated your camera with gloves, practice before the dive. You may find it is easier to dive without gloves, but this can be chilly, especially at night.

• Your mask keeps your eyes distant from the viewfinder. Buy the smallest-volume mask you can wear.

• Refraction makes objects appear one-third closer and larger than in air. Reflex focusing and visual estimates of distances are unaffected but, if you measure a distance, compensate by reducing the resultant figure by one-third when setting the lens focus.

Maintenance

• Follow all the manufacturers' instructions regarding post- and pre-dive preparation, paying particular attention to keeping the sealing surfaces clean and grit-free and the 'O' rings clean, supple and greased.

• Use only silicon grease (never spray and never petroleum jelly) and replace flattened 'O' rings with new plump ones. If possible, store 'O' rings off the camera to prevent their becoming flattened.

• When changing film or tape between dives, ensure that the outside of your camera is completely dry first. It is important to open the camera with the back facing down so that any stray drops of water will fall away from the camera, not into it.

• Never leave your camera lying on its back in the sun without covering the lens, even for a few minutes.

• If you cannot get your camera into fresh water soon after a dive, wrap it in your wet suit and try to keep it wet. If the sea water is allowed to dry, it will be more difficult to remove salt particles.

• Very few Australian dive boats, or even resorts, have dedicated camera tanks or cleaning tables. You may want to purchase a sealable bucket (like those used for cleaning babies' nappies) for this purpose.

Underwater photography is an extremely popular activity.

Still Photography

Underwater photographs are mementos to be treasured. They can be blown up to poster-size to adorn walls, made into greeting cards or even, if they are of sufficiently high quality, sold for publication. One of the major advantages of still photography over video is that each shot is a single entity. Even if most of the photographs are fuzzy blurs, one good shot is well worth the cost of the film, the developing and printing.

Choosing a Camera
When starting out, your major choice will be whether to buy a relatively cheap camera with which you can play around, or to go for an expensive, professional system. Your choice will depend on your budget and ambitions.

There are several waterproof automatic cameras on the market. These range from throwaways (usually manufactured by film companies) to quite sophisticated autofocus and auto-exposure cameras which may operate down to five, or even 10m (16–33ft). As well as buying waterproof disposable cameras, you can obtain a relatively inexpensive perspex housing for the standard, non-waterproof Fuji or Kodak disposable cameras.

If all you want is a few mementos of a wonderful trip, these simple cameras will give you acceptable results in clear, shallow water with colour print film.

For serious underwater photography, you have two options. The first is to splash out on a purpose-built waterproof camera; the second is to buy a waterproof housing for a SLR (single-lens reflex) or land camera, should you already own one or plan to purchase one. Each system has advantages and disadvantages.

Dedicated underwater cameras
The submersible camera used by most professionals is the Nikonos, a 35mm non-reflex camera. The newer models (IV-A and V) have a TTL (through-the-lens) automatic exposure system and the Nikonos V has TTL flash exposure. The older models have no built-in exposure meters but are, nevertheless, excellent, rugged cameras that give good results. You can often buy one of these second-hand for a very good price but will need to acquire a hand-held submersible light meter.

This system, with its specially designed Nikonos lenses, gives sharper results underwater than any housed system, an advantage which (except in the case of very skilled photographers) is usually offset by the lack of reflex focusing. Another disadvantage of this system is the lack of through-the-lens composition. You have to use a little guesswork in composing pictures and you may easily cut off part of a subject. The Nikonos, except with some of the dedicated underwater lenses, also makes an excellent, rugged, weatherproof land camera, with the above-mentioned limitations. Nikon have recently introduced the RS-AF, a fully waterproof reflex

camera with autofocus and dedicated lenses and flashgun, but it is extremely heavy and expensive. If and when the price comes down, this may prove to be a good buy for use as a dedicated underwater camera but it is very clumsy on land.

The most popular rival to the Nikonos is the smaller, lighter and less expensive Sea and Sea range. They have recently brought out the first amphibious camera which allows you to change lenses underwater. Ask a dealer who specialises in underwater cameras to discuss these and other models with you before making this significant financial investment.

Waterproof housings
Specially constructed housings are available for all the popular brands of reflex cameras and even for some of the simpler, present cameras. These may be made from metal, perspex or flexible plastic, each of which has advantages and disadvantages. Metal housings are strong, reliable, work well at depth and last a long time if properly maintained; they are heavier to carry, but are buoyant in water. Their higher cost is justified if your camera is expensive and warrants the extra protection.

Perspex housings are slightly less robust and need careful handling both in and out of the water. They are lightweight, which is convenient on land, but may be buoyant in water so you may have to weight them. They are far less costly and, if properly maintained, should give long service.

Flexible plastic housings are cheaper still. They have an optical quality glass port, which fits over the lens of the camera and built-in 'gloves' so that you can operate the controls directly. These are easier to use, but compress at depth so only give good results in reasonably shallow water.

Lenses and accessories
Whatever system you use, unless it is a very simple one, you will have a range of lenses from which to choose. Except for the new Sea and Sea system, all lenses must be changed topside. This means you'll have to choose a lens before you enter the water. If you are using a housing, the chances are that it will be designed for only one lens. The most useful choice in this case would be a wide angle (24mm), or a short zoom such as a 28–70mm, with macro facility.

For the Nikonos, the most versatile lens is a 35mm. This can be used on land or underwater, both as is and with either extension tubes or a close-up unit to facilitate macro photography.

A longer lens, such as the 80mm, practically a telephoto, is difficult to use and is almost useless in local conditions except with macro when it will enable you to photograph even (and only) the tiniest reef creatures.

Wider angle lenses, such as the 28mm, 20mm or 15mm, give excellent results underwater as they minimise backscatter and light loss by allowing you to get much closer to your subject. They are, unfortunately, not amphibious and so are useless on land. They are also very expensive, with the price increasing dramatically with decreasing focal length. The problem of composing photographs with the Nikonos can be somewhat simplified by the use of parallax viewfinders. These fit on top of the camera and compensate for the difference between what you see and what the lens 'sees'. These range in price significantly, with the more affordable option being a single viewfinder with different screens for different lenses.

As a general rule, you can use a longer lens in cleaner water, and macro photography, with extension tubes or a close-up unit, is the only possibility in very poor visibility. Extension tubes and close-up units have the same effect, they both allow you to get really close to your subject and fill your viewfinder with a small area. The close-up unit has one major advantage over extension tubes — it can be removed underwater, thus allowing non-macro photography on the same dive.

Lighting
The amount of available light underwater decreases with depth and different wavelengths of light are absorbed by water at different rates, or depths. The first to be absorbed is red, thus giving the underwater environment a bluish cast. If you have more skill and ingenuity than funds, this can be used to great advantage in natural light photography. Think of your photographs more as black and white than colour; concentrate on contrast, shadows and silhouettes and you will get superb shots, often capturing the atmosphere of the site.

In very clean, clear water with plenty of light, you can compensate for the colour imbalance by using a yellow filter, specially designed for underwater use. This will cut down the amount of available light so, if you are using a hand-held light meter, you will need to compensate about half a stop.

The most satisfactory system is to use artificial light, usually in the form of synchronised strobes. This solution is, like most aspects of underwater photography, not without its problems. The most obvious is that of backscatter; suspended particles in the water reflect the light of the strobe and show up as bright white spots in the photograph. This can be quite creative but is usually a nuisance. In order to minimise this, position your strobe as far from the camera as you can; most modern strobes are sold with brackets and arms to achieve this but you will still get some backscatter. The use of a slave strobe can help to solve this problem by adding another light source while at the same time evening out the lighting and eliminating shadows. The slave is programmed to flash in response to the flash of the primary strobe. The Nikonos V allows TTL flash exposure metering.

Film
You will obtain best results with colour positive (slide transparency) film of 50 or 100 ISO. If you are not too sure of your ability to obtain correct exposures, use a colour negative (print) film, as it is more forgiving. Regardless of the type of film you use, buy it from a reputable photographic store. Be sure to check the expiry date and store it in a cool, dark place (preferably a refrigerator). When travelling, keep it in a well-insulated camera or film bag. Try to get your films processed as soon as possible because they are at their least stable when they have been exposed but not yet processed, so be particularly careful to keep them cool after exposure.

On the Shoot
Take care in choosing a buddy as divers with cameras are often preoccupied with their subjects. Divers or underwater photographers should always be conscious of their dive plan and continuously monitor air consumption, depth, time and buddy position, as well as all environmental factors.

Subjects
What you photograph depends on your personal interests but there are a few generalisations which may help you decide where to start.

Macro photography is the easiest to get right, particularly with a TTL flash and a frame, as the lens-to-subject and flash-to-subject distances are fixed and the effects of silting in the water are minimised. Expose a test film at a variety of exposures; the best result will tell you the exposure to use in future for this particular setting and film.

Some fish are strongly territorial and therefore predictable; this is why, for example, there are so many excellent shots of clownfish. Manta Rays are curious and will keep coming back if you react quietly and do not chase them. Angelfish and Chaetodons (butterflyfish) swim off when you first enter their territory but, if you remain quiet, they will usually return.

Don't forget the wonderful potential of marine algae; some of the red seaweeds have the most exquisite textures.

Diver and wreck photography are the most difficult and require wide-angle lenses. You will need to instruct your model in the mechanics of photography so that he or she can best utilise the surrounding reef life and you will need to use a flash if you want the diver's face to be well exposed. You will get the best results on wrecks if you concentrate on small features — it is almost impossible to photograph a whole frigate underwater.

Underwater night photography can be very rewarding. Many interesting creatures, such as squid, cuttlefish and some sharks, are predominantly nocturnal, most invertebrates extend their feeding polyps at night and some fish are more approachable because they are half-asleep. However, focusing quickly in dim light is difficult and many subjects retreat into the darkness as soon as they are lit up, so it is important that you pre-set your controls.

Video

Some divers prefer to take videos rather than stills. It is, as a rule, easier to obtain good results and is considered by many to be a more interesting and dynamic medium through which to share the underwater environment with friends and family.

Choosing a camera

Besides the choice of video format, there are two basic choices to make: between a housed or a dedicated underwater camera. There are a few excellent dedicated cameras on the market and they have the advantage of being reasonably small and easy to manoeuvre, with the controls well laid out. If you already own a video camera, you may opt to acquire a housing. You may find one on the market or may have to have one made or modified. A disadvantage is that the controls are often difficult to handle. There are companies who specialise in this; you can find their addresses in dive magazines.

The choice of format depends, to a large extent, on what you plan to do with your footage. If you intend it only for domestic use, you could use a standard VHS camera. These are rather big, though, so a better choice would be 8mm or VHS compact. If you want to use your tapes for promotional, teaching or semi-public purposes, super VHS or Hi-8 would be a better but slightly more costly alternative as you will be able to make better quality copies. With any of these systems, you can edit directly onto your home VCR.

If you have higher aspirations or ambitions of being a professional underwater videographer, go straight to beta-cam and start building up a professional system. You'll spend a lot more money but you will have the capability of producing broadcast-quality footage.

Lighting

You can get away without artificial lighting, although only in very good conditions, as you can set the colour balance on your video camera to compensate, to a certain extent, for the blue cast. You will, of course, obtain much better results if you use artificial light.

Specially designed underwater lights are reasonably compact, neutrally buoyant and easy for a competent assistant to handle underwater.

Planning your shoot

Unlike still photography, it is usually not satisfying to get just one good shot or one good sequence on video; you will probably want to be able to produce a program of at least five or ten minutes, even if it is just for home use. To this end, you will need to do some basic scripting — at least in your head.

Work out a vague story line and ensure that you have footage which can support your script. Plan to film divers while they are kitting up, relaxing before and after the dive, and entering and exiting the water. Don't forget to get footage of the dive boat, scenic topside shots and close-ups of your companions. Before you enter the water, plan the direction of movement of all the shots in which the divers appear.

On the shoot

• Avoid diving with inexperienced divers as you will want a buddy who can hold equipment, such as lights, for you and who can keep track of the dive time and depth as you are bound to be preoccupied.

• Try to keep the direction of movement of divers constant (unless, of course, you are aiming for a special or humorous effect). Brief your models thoroughly, ensuring that they fully understand your requirements, and work out signals to communicate what you want them to do.

• Avoid the temptation to overuse the zoom — rather take the same shot twice, once on wide-angle and once on telephoto — you can do some creative editing later. If you don't switch the camera off between the shots, you can use the zoom section as well.

• As soon as you see something interesting, start the camera and then move into the shot as it is very difficult to edit in the first few seconds of any individual shot. For the same reason, leave the camera running a few seconds after you have taken the shot. This will make your life a lot easier at the editing stage.

• Take cutaway shots. These are sneaky little shots of arbitrary images, for example, divers' faces, small fish, fin strokes through the water.

Editing

This really is the fun part. You can be as serious or as frivolous as you like but a standard script would include pre-dive shots, entry, underwater footage including divers and marine life, exit and post-dive shots. This is where you will be grateful for those arbitrary little sequences you filmed. If you add two shots together and they tend to jump or otherwise not look quite right, experiment with adding a cutaway shot. You can even alternate short sequences of two long shots. This is your chance to have fun; if you don't like it, just wipe the tape and start again. What a medium!

Sound

Your underwater shots, if they have sound at all, will just have bubbles. You can add a voice-over; or commentary, or even music. If you are producing this masterpiece for purely domestic viewing, add whatever you like.

If, however, you plan to use the video for marketing or teaching purposes, check the copyright status of any music you plan to use. You can start your enquiries at a local video or music production company — they will tell you who to contact.

Bibliography

Byron, Tom (1987), *Scuba Divers Guide: Southern Great Barrier Reef; Northern Great Barrier Reef; Central Great Barrier Reef; Whitsunday Islands.* Aqua Sports Publications, New South Wales.

Coleman, Neville (1994), *Sea Stars of Australasia and their Relatives.* Neville Coleman's Underwater Geographic (Pty) Ltd, Brisbane.

Coleman, Neville (1993), *Hazardous Sea Creatures.* Neville Coleman's Sea Australia Resource Centre, Brisbane.

Coleman, Neville (1992), *Australian Marine Fish.* Neville Coleman's Underwater Geographic (Pty) Ltd, Brisbane.

Coleman, Neville (1993), *Australian Fish Behaviour.* Neville Coleman's Underwater Geographic (Pty) Ltd, Brisbane.

Coleman, Neville (1991), *Encyclopedia of Marine Animals.* Collins, Angus & Robertson, Sydney.

Coleman, Neville (1987), *The Underwater Australia Dive Guide.* Thomas Nelson, Melbourne.

Coleman, Neville (1994), *Australia's Great Barrier Reef.* National Book Distributors, Sydney.

Colfelt, David (1995), *The Whitsundays Book.* Windward Publications, New South Wales.

Commonwealth of Australia (1993), *Australian Fisheries Resources.* Department of Primary Industries and Energy, and the Fisheries Research and Development Corp., Canberra.

Index